IN CONFLICT
AND CUSTODY

IN CONFLICT
AND CUSTODY

Therapeutic Counselling for Women

Rani Dhavan Shankardass

www.sagepublications.com
Los Angeles • London • New Delhi • Singapore • Washington DC

First published in 2012 by

 SAGE Publications India Pvt Ltd
B1/I-1 Mohan Cooperative Industrial Area
Mathura Road, New Delhi 110 044, India
www.sagepub.in

SAGE Publications Inc
2455 Teller Road
Thousand Oaks, California 91320, USA

SAGE Publications Ltd
1 Oliver's Yard, 55 City Road
London EC1Y 1SP, United Kingdom

SAGE Publications Asia-Pacific Pte Ltd
33 Pekin Street
#02-01 Far East Square
Singapore 048763

Published by Vivek Mehra for SAGE Publications India Pvt Ltd, typeset in 10/13pt Palatino Linotype by Diligent Typesetter, Delhi and printed at Chaman Enterprises, New Delhi.

Library of Congress Cataloging-in-Publication Data

Shankardass, Rani Dhavan.
    In conflict and custody: therapeutic counselling for women/Rani Dhavan Shankardass.
        p. cm.
    Includes bibliographical references and index.
    1. Female offenders—Counselling of—India. 2. Female offenders—Mental health—India. 3. Women prisoners—Counselling of—India. 4. Women prisoners—Mental health—India. 5. Justice, Administration of India. I. Title.
HV6046.S45   362.83'860954—dc23   2012   2012003292

ISBN: 978-81-321-0889-4 (PB)

The SAGE Team: Prabha Zacharias, Puja Narula Nagpal, and Rajib Chatterjee

*Dedicated to the memory of my mother Shakuntala Dhavan,
the petit soft-tough woman from the North West Frontier who saw
the first draft but did not live to see the book in print and
to whom I owe more than I could ever repay.*

Thank you for choosing a SAGE product! If you have any comment, observation or feedback, I would like to personally hear from you. Please write to me at <u>contactceo@sagepub.in</u>

—Vivek Mehra, Managing Director and CEO,
SAGE Publications India Pvt Ltd, New Delhi

Bulk Sales

SAGE India offers special discounts for purchase of books in bulk. We also make available special imprints and excerpts from our books on demand.

For orders and enquiries, write to us at

Marketing Department
SAGE Publications India Pvt Ltd
B1/I-1, Mohan Cooperative Industrial Area
Mathura Road, Post Bag 7
New Delhi 110044, India
E-mail us at <u>marketing@sagepub.in</u>

Get to know more about SAGE, be invited to SAGE events, get on our mailing list. Write today to <u>marketing@sagepub.in</u>

This book is also available as an e-book.

Contents

List of Tables and Figures

TABLES

FIGURES

List of Photographs

1. Equations between prisoners—a comfort for the elderly. State Jail for Women, Hyderabad (Copyright: Rani D. Shankardass)
2. Children old enough to remember where they spent their formative years, Rajahmundry, 2000 (Copyright: Rani D. Shankardass)
3. Prisoners washing personal belongings at the common tank at Women's Jail, Warangal, 2002 (Copyright: Rani D. Shankardass)
4. Informal counselling styles to make the client feel at ease, Hyderabad, 2002 (Copyright: Rani D. Shankardass)
5. Another case of informal counselling, Hyderabad, 2002 (Copyright: Rani D. Shankardass)
6. Medical camp organized by PRAJA counsellors at State Jail for Women, Hyderabad, 2001 (Copyright: Rani D. Shankardass)
7. *Rangoli* competition organized by PRAJA counsellors at State Jail for Women, Hyderabad, 2001 (Copyright: Rani D. Shankardass)
8. Inner courtyard outside the barracks in Women's Jail, Jaipur (Copyright: Rani D. Shankardass)
9. The sewing room in Women's Jail at Jaipur, Rajasthan (Copyright: Angela Clay)
10. Prisoner's private prayer corner—the solace when all else fails, Rajahmundry, 2000 (Copyright: Angela Clay)
11. How old do they have to be to go home? Rajahmundry, 2000 (Copyright: Angela Clay)
12. Convicts assembled to be addressed by officers, Rajahmundry, 2000 (Copyright: Angela Clay)
13. Age no bar? Rajahmundry, 2000 (Copyright: Angela Clay)

List of Abbreviations

AMIMB	Association of Members of Independent Monitoring Boards
APA	American Psychiatric Association
BACP	British Association for Counselling and Psychotherapy
CCC	Complaints and Counselling Cell
C.O.	Commanding Officer
Cr.P.C.	Code of Criminal Procedure
DEVAW	Declaration on Elimination of Violence against Women
DIG	Deputy Inspector General of Police
DMSC	Durbar Mahila Samanwaya Committee
DSM	Diagnostic and Statistical Manual of Mental Disorders
ICD	International Classification of Diseases
IIPA	Indian Institute of Public Administration
IPC	Indian Penal Code
ITBP	Indo-Tibetan Border Police
KSLSA	Karnataka State Legal Services Authority
NALSA	National Legal Services Authority
NGO	Non-government Organization
NIMHANS	National Institute of Mental Health and Neuro Sciences
OCD	Obsessive Compulsive Disorder
PITA	Immoral Traffic (Prevention) Act
PO	Protection Officers
PRAJA	Penal Reform and Justice Association
PRI	Penal Reform International
PTSD	Post-traumatic Stress Disorder

PWDVA	Protection of Women from Domestic Violence Act
S.P.	Superintendent of Police
UP	Uttar Pradesh
WHO	World Health Organization

List of Annexures

Preface

The need for this book arose for two reasons: the first reason was that in the course of several projects run by us in Indian prisons for several years, my colleagues and I came across acutely troubled women, sent 'in custody' by the criminal justice system, many of whom were baffled and terrified by the system's complexities. Herded like sheep from one day to another, they soon lost their real lives and showed differing responses to the experience of being locked up, severed from all that gave any meaning to their existence. Simply saying 'don't worry' to them was not only misleading and inadequate as a response, but also failed to address some of the most dramatic changes in their lives and personalities that could cause visible and invisible damage that they would have to come to terms with for the rest of their lives. Depression (including clinical), tension, anxiety and aggression, personality disorders and even suicidal tendencies were not uncommon among the women whose age ranged from 17 to 70 and who had been brought there for major and minor offences. Something was missing in the way their needs were being met and the way they were being handled. For us the big lacuna was the neglect of their mental state. The idea of setting up counselling units seemed a first step towards addressing the women's plights and enabling them to express themselves and make their own statements about their lives. They needed to be enabled and empowered for the course of the rest of their journey in life. Counselling (*not* advice-giving) practised according to tried and tested standards and guidelines and structured by codes of practice seemed one method. There would of course be others.

The second reason for the book emerged out of a realization that related to the needs of the women and was also the reality that counselling, as it has been developed and practised in professional units in other areas of the world over the last 40 years or so, has not found a place in our part of the world. Sporadically it gets a mention when crises hit groups and/or individuals, and counselling is regarded by generalist do-gooders as a worthwhile thing to do. Having observed 'counselling shops' spring up everywhere and seen plain advice-giving pass for professional counselling without substantive knowledge or training relating to the subject, we believed we could fill a gap—both theoretical and practical—that could be developed upon by others who felt the need for such activity in their areas of engagement. We believed we could draw up a manual of sorts that would both define counselling and suggest how it could be structured and developed for different situations and circumstances to bring meaningful relief and assistance to distressed subjects.

At a basic level, this book would wish to suggest how to address constructively the acutely stressful circumstances leading to the agonizing experiences and emotional breakdowns of distressed women in two specific problematic situations in the Indian (and perhaps all of South Asian) society. It has discussed some professionally structured steps that can and should be taken to address this state of distress (and its origins and ramifications) by those called upon, equipped and prepared to do so. It is also about how these 'helpers' ('counsellors' once they are trained) need to and can improve their abilities to respond *effectively* to demands for help (at socio-personal levels) by those who seek or need it before their conditions and situations deteriorate beyond repair.

Helping persons in distress is not new—it has always had a prominent place in families, among friends and in communities. Problems, discord, disputes and conflicts, and any lack of harmony in social groups have been addressed/resolved down the ages by family and community members ('elders' in some societies). So what's new? Changing social patterns, individualized living and the increased pressures in day-to-day life leading to near explosions in personal relationships even within the family (particularly relationships with domination and power written all over them) have made the need for 'outside' assistance in coping and resolving conflict, critical. When family and community themselves became the source of conflict and discord and the individual needed assistance *as an individual,* the entry of an outside agent was a logical step in the search for harmony. As a team of activists whose help and assistance had been asked for in alleviating problem-ridden situations, we had been able to observe, participate in and actually try to supervise counselling and problem-solving activities for women in settings such as complaints cells and prisons where there was an urgent need to counsel and/or assist relatively ignorant, legally ill-informed, unaware, distressed, stressed, anxious and depressed women who had lost the capacity to cope with their lives in varying degrees. Supplemented with the utter neglect in the area of mental health generally and women's mental health particularly, the space for several interventions was unquestionable. We have tried to give some space to discussions related to the differences and/or overlaps between mental illness and mental disorder to acquaint readers with some of the background literature on formal classifications of mental disorders, most widely used as a reference point for practitioners.

The experiences that spearheaded the need for this book also presented evidence of the limitations of the law and the justice machinery in providing the relief that the vulnerable groups discussed here needed. While gender bias in society is sought to be resolved by the letter of the law, no amount of enactments and judicial pronouncements are able to address sufficiently all aspects of the social (masculine) milieu within which all manner of professional disciplines continue to function in the treatment and intervention zones for women. This includes medicine, psychiatry and psychology. One analyst has included media and advertising in the list of actors and agencies that are responsible for veiled gender biases and stereotyping in portrayals of women in our society (Ammu Joseph in Davar [2001]). These will be discussed later in the chapters on women and counselling in this book. In any event, counselling emerged as a dire necessity for addressing specific women's needs.

While we are on the subject of the 'why' of counselling for women in distress, it might be added that the failures of some formal mechanisms and disciplines (like those mentioned earlier) in addressing women's issues are related to their differing change-agendas. That the formal institutions came in conflict with women's movements advocating forward-looking change or feminist movements generally is not surprising. If one simplistically divided solutions for women's problems into those that need social solutions and those that need individual remedies, most interventions fell short of addressing one or the other, or indeed both. The experts (legal, medical and psychological) looked upon feminists as interlopers in areas that were a specialist's domain. Amidst the tussles and tensions on who is best equipped to address what is clearly a social *and* individual problem for women in terms of coping with their lives, a silent battleground seems to appear. We are advised that a more holistic approach brings us nearer the desired goals of assisting women in stressful times.

> Let us take depression for instance .... The feelings of powerlessness, frustration, inadequacy, guilt and loneliness that combine as depression cannot be understood if we look at it only in terms of the woman's psychological characteristics as a deficiency of inability to cope .... The social origins of depression, the impact of stressful life events and the complex relations between gender, social roles and mental health are well documented in sociological literature .... The presence of social support has been identified as a key variable in moderating the effects of threatening life events which push the individual towards mental distress. (Vindhya in Davar [2001])

Our own experience told us much the same. Many women told us in so many different ways how something inside them was cracking up: '*Roz roz chup chaap aasmaan ko dekh dekh kar dimaag kharaab ho rahaa hai*' (to keep gazing at the sky in silence each and every day is driving us mad). In this spirit and in environs where essential support systems have got marginalized, therapeutic interventions like counselling become germane to the survival of many who would otherwise perish in more ways than one.

Because distress can be constituted of subjective and objective features, the methods of addressing it do not have such characteristics of structure and formality as those required for ailments arising out of anatomical or physiological malfunction.

Psychotherapeutic methods are more than likely to be regarded as too fluid and rudderless to yield results of any consequence. Our experiences in the prison did, however, provide evidence of distressed prisoners (who may also have had medical problems) coming for counselling more readily and frequently than they visited the prison doctors for medical attention, even though they felt that having a fever was considered more serious all round than an anxiety disorder that bordered on the imaginative and hallucinatory. Doctors often called them 'shammers', dismissing them with remarks like 'kal to aai thee, ab phir se kyon aie ho?' (you came just yesterday with the same ailment, why have you come again). They turned to the counsellors as a fallback, and often got interventions that were able to address more than one kind of problem.

Even in its fallback or comfort-zone interpretation, prevalent views about counselling are unconstructive because of the generic meanings attributed to it, which in turn come from two contradictory directions. On the one hand, it is viewed dubiously, constantly needing to be justified, particularly when recommended in our (South Asian) region. Labelled variously as 'humbug', 'trite' and 'grandmotherly advice', counselling always seems to fall short of being granted 'professional' status and even when indulged it never finds the place that other interventions (medical, legal, etc.) do. On the other hand, counselling has caught on as a desirable add-on in several non-Western societies, primarily because of the (professional) status it has in other parts of the world. Hospitals, courts, educational institutions, police precincts, business houses, workplaces and other locales where stress-ridden situations are likely, room is being made for 'counselling' in the hope and expectation that the persona of the individual will be addressed. Faced with this new scenario, the South Asian response is: it must be useful if it is practised in advanced countries, so we should also do it. Many departments and institutions mechanically add it into the organizational structures without putting in place anything that remotely resembles what has been set out as the essentials of counselling. Britain, for example, has the British Association for Counselling and Psychotherapy (BACP) that gives recognition to institutes and provides guidelines and standards that have to be observed when counselling units provide a 'counselling service'. This point will be laboured, after we have set out the guidelines that we hope to, in the chapter on 'training'.

For the moment, in presenting this book we are taking the vitality and importance of counselling as a given in today's social scene in India. Since it is not any old counselling being recommended but the *counselling that needs to be carried out according to standards and structured guidelines,* there is an imperative for developing and improving the knowledge that accompanies counselling and the skills and understandings that are needed to carry it out. Nothing remotely resembling the fund of knowledge that is available in the West exists in any part of South Asia, so we shall not pretend to provide a guide or manual anywhere near the standards of sophistication that are found in the treatises on the subject by academics and practitioners in Western countries. Despite the existence of some scepticism about counselling in other parts of the world, the literature on the subject abounds and is used proficiently by those who have a professional interest in counselling. The endeavour here is to work towards a product that will fit the needs and particular contexts that we are addressing, which is a challenge, given the multidimensional variegated nature of the South Asian social fabric.

The nuanced context of the region presents us with women who have difficulty coping with the multifaceted and conflicting demands of and within such societies as ours—where tradition hallowed by custom and religion presents a strong resistance to the modern legal concepts of the rule of law and equality before the law. As a fundamental and vital component of everyday life in South Asia, tradition may not be regarded solely as a hurdle or obstacle when addressing women's predicaments: it does form the mainstay of their survival and the measure of their accomplishments. Far from wishing it away, it would need to be faced without prejudice and with a recognition that grants it as much value as that accorded to the so-called rational approach of the law. For example, notwithstanding all the prevalent scepticism about dowry, arranged marriages, religious codes and practices, taboos and bans, and all manner of ritualistic observances by women in the Indian subcontinent, addressing women's issues from a high moral and/or rational ground can be counterproductive: it might be tantamount to throwing the baby out with the bathwater. The counselling strategies that would need to be developed in such conflicting situations would need to be of a kind that prevent an already weakened woman client from viewing her situation as one where her abilities to surmount existing difficulties and problems are further diminished.

Rather than pretend to be a high-powered treatise on counselling, this book is intended to take counselling to some ordinary life situations for women who are enwrapped in layers of dos and don'ts that take them round and round in circles without providing any direction. Some of these situations are set out at the start before the theoretical foundations of counselling are analysed. In fact, we discovered that some of the real lives seemed so unreal that counselling too can be an inadequate intervention. Someone then has to urgently draw attention to the likely damage if medical assistance is not forthcoming immediately. The need for timely responses is as urgent in the area of mental disorders as it is in physical. While there is an emphasis on the theoretical foundations of counselling, the attempt is still to keep it rooted in the practical areas of usage.

While focusing on the methods and ways of counselling in situations and problems related to *dispute resolution and custodial environments*, the book does contain an introductory overview of counselling's purposes and processes whereby it is able to highlight simple fundamentals about counselling that can then be adapted to other areas of engagement than the ones we have focused on. As a process of communication between persons (counsellor and client) in which there is a relationship of giving and receiving help without judgement, prejudice and vested interest, counselling is painstakingly analysed here to reveal its composition at rudimentary and sophisticated levels of participation. The book hopes to provide guidelines that will enable wholesome and constructive counselling in particularly sensitive areas of engagement such as domestic or other dispute resolution and custodial environments by ensuring that there is a better understanding and more awareness of the highly ethical and professional nature of the activity.

The book is neither like a cookbook that offers recipes for best practices nor an attempt to provide the definitive off-the-shelf guide to solutions. It is a pointer to acquaint would-be counsellors with features of counselling that necessitate it to be seen, understood and undertaken as a special and specialist activity; and it is a reminder for those who wish to guide counsellors in counselling work about the nature of the activity, the stages, the skills and the depth of thinking that must accompany counselling if it is to achieve its worthwhile purposes. More specifically it relates to assisting the counselling of women in the two particular distress contexts mentioned earlier.

The structure of the book is simple:

- It provides historical and practical guidelines from several sources that are the most reputable in the area of counselling.
- It lays out the theoretical understandings that must accompany counselling in the most simple manner and style.
- It highlights the atmosphere and ambience, both physical and mental/emotional, that must accompany the activity of counselling.
- It elaborates the skills and methods that are a vital part of the process of helping particularly vulnerable people to sort out their lives in the best possible way.
- It demonstrates through living experiences the needs and requirements of distressed subjects that set in motion the demand for particular types of counselling.

Women's own experiences heard in their own voices are a vital ingredient of their life's realities that may not be ignored when interventions are being suggested. As a preliminary document, this book seeks to be located in the experiential without losing sight of the theoretical underpinnings of tried and tested approaches to counselling. The value of theory in practice is emphasized throughout the book. The assumption is that human relations being an area as vast and complex as it is, the theoretical underpinnings about human behaviour and motivations that have emerged out of the vast reservoir of knowledge about such behaviour in other regions and contexts should be used to steer the course of counselling at every stage of the process in our context as well. Caution is also suggested about the danger of losing the wood for the trees.

I would like to acknowledge the invaluable help of all the sources that have been consulted in the course of structuring and writing this book. While all of them have been duly referenced at the end of the book, I would still wish readers to appreciate that the studies of the theories and practices of counselling in other environs have provided the impetus that has facilitated this adaptation of the skills and techniques required for counselling in the South Asian context. Without those tried and tested templates this collection of accumulated observations and assessments may not have happened. The hope is that this effort will take the activity and practice of counselling to other areas of engagement where it is needed and produce more experience-related information that becomes a substantial body of literature on the subject in our own regional context.

The particularity about this treatise on counselling is its focus on two very specific situational boundaries or domains, and as such it is seeking to formulate such modifications and adaptations relating to the process as are seen to be relevant to those particular domains:

- In *mediation and problem-solving*, the suggestion is that while counselling is a vital component in the process of mediation for women in distress, many of its general features require adaptation and modification when women are seeking specific assistance to resolve specific problems relating to their personal or social lives. Counselling skills then need specific reinforcements to become 'mediation skills' even as the activity is called 'counselling'.

- In the specific area of *counselling women 'in custody'*, and more specifically prison, further specialization of the skills would be required. The assumption here is that the qualitative content of counselling incarcerated women would need to take full cognisance of the specificities of the women themselves, and of the penal system and all its ramifications. Acquiring the special 'knowledges' associated with these would be essential for wholesome counselling in this area.

It is hoped that the book will assist some organizations and groups that believe that counselling has value for those who want and need it, and who have not yet looked upon it as a discipline that needs in-depth knowledge and professionalism. As a book about counselling for women in *distress* and in *custody*, it is hoped that one treacherous feature of working with women will be avoided at all costs—that is, the construction of stereotypes of women and their problems built out of convenient 'knowledges' that are manipulative and controlling.

Last but not least, it is hoped that the book will go some way towards the introduction and formulation of courses in the theory and practice of 'Counselling and Psychotherapy' that can be introduced as part of a curriculum in such syllabi that relate to community and social work in its multifaceted manifestations. Providing a formal professional, recognized qualification in Counselling and Psychotherapy variously structured to address the differing needs of clients, in some of the areas where issues of mental health are at stake, would go a long way towards minimizing the ill effects of maladies that have been glossed over or neglected all this time.

Rani D. Shankardass

Acknowledgements

Deep gratitude and appreciation is owed to the colleagues and co-workers at Penal Reform and Justice Association (PRAJA) and to the bright and dedicated research associates who have worked with us for years in our prison projects. In several states in India, in central and district jails and in police *thanas* (police stations) and shelter homes, these bright young women have walked in and out of the locations with confidence and commitment, dispelling all doubts that people may have had about their ability to cope with the environments simply because they were young. The projects have had varying focuses—data collection, daily diaries of routines and procedures, human rights, health and hygiene, mental illnesses and disorders, organization of camps (eye, dental, etc.), staff training, legal aid and counselling—and the associates have acquitted themselves with exceptional skill and ingenuity in all of these. Some of our associates left midstream, 'unable' to put up with the seamy side of the work that had to be done. Others showed commendable resilience. Neelam Vishnoi, Jai Kirti Singh, Kanchan Sai Krishna, Vaidehi Reddy, Jyothishree and Deepali Verma deserve a special mention for their persistence in the face of difficulties related to the tough environment and sometimes tough persons they had to deal with.

I would like to acknowledge our appreciation for the prison departments of several Indian states that enabled the painstaking exercise, of which this is an outcome, by giving us the space (literal and figurative) to work our Counselling Cells as long as we wished in the prisons. In particular, the prisons departments of Andhra Pradesh and Rajasthan need a special mention for the cooperation and facilitation extended to the PRAJA teams as they moved from prison to prison and from barrack to barrack mingling unimpeded with the prisoners and staff. First-hand glimpses of the functioning of penal systems in other countries of the South Asian region have gone a long way towards helping us understand the equivalence of so much that is being addressed in almost all the region. As chairperson of Penal Reform International (PRI), an international organization that has worked incessantly for penal reform for more than 20 years, I was fortunate to have been part of the process of initiating reform projects and human rights programmes in several countries. To several colleagues at PRI, I would like to offer appreciation for their indefatigable energy in carrying on unparalleled work in far and away places. Glimpses of some of the horrors of punishments in the community in some of these regions has helped in understanding two features about punishment: (*a*) why particular groups in society are subjected to worse punishments than others and (*b*) why prison, an institution *we* view with disdain, is considered more civilized than other more horrific punishments. Our search for alternatives is still on.

There are some people in particular who have been a source of inspiration and encouragement at different stages of the work despite their demanding commitments and they need special mention. Apart from Justice Krishna Iyer, PRAJA's chairperson and patron saint of all human rights activists, we were fortunate to have Justices M. N. Venkatachaliah, J. S. Verma and A. S. Anand (all ex-Chief Justices of India) give unflinchingly of their time for our seminars and workshops in India, Nepal and Bangladesh. As chairpersons of the National Human Rights Commission of India, for over a decade, they continued to support our efforts in opening up issues of concern that came up as we peeped through the cracks in some parts of the criminal justice system that needed a hard second look.

Angela Clay, vice chair of Association of Members of Independent Monitoring Boards (AMIMB), UK, who accompanied us on our projects in some states, has provided some of the poignant photographs from her collection that tell many a story about the women we are addressing in our narratives. I am grateful to her for permitting me to use as many photographs as I wished.

Intruding into people's lives because we think it will help them is a liberty at the best of times. The prisoners who talked and listened were exemplary in their patience and tolerance. There were resentments and mood swings and sometimes harsh words but we knew the effects that being locked up and torn away from the family had on them and wondered how so many retained their sanity all through the prison experience. To all of them, a salutation for their forbearance!

Chapter 1

Introductory Insights

Historically women have functioned in the role of dominant carers of others in almost every society, a role that they have performed ungrudgingly and more often than not without due appreciation and recognition. Women have also received harsher penalties for non-performance of their roles and duties than have men in most societies. Portraying the role of women, most of our (Indian) ancient and hallowed texts (Hindu and Islamic) are careful to suggest that any exclusion of women from spheres of activity reserved for men is in their own protective interest. In the historiography, which makes of history what it will, what then emerges are images of ideal women from legendary epics that are heroic and inimitable, forming role models for women for evermore. Such exemplary models have no room for the erring woman and the prescriptive texts meticulously set out the punishments for all those sins of omission and commission that women might commit in their lives, mercy and clemency forming no part of the repertoire of treatment intended for them should they offend or violate social norms. Bearing in mind the fact that both the roles and duties and the penalties for non-performance have all been set and defined by men, and that women have been carefully excluded from many areas of activity, it is hardly surprising that women have also faced more physical, personal and social problems and hardships at every turn in their over-defined lives. The lack of understanding and interest about their problems and resulting (supposedly 'out of sync') behaviour is hardly surprising. In the ill-balanced relationships in which they are placed, each life situation has the potential to be conflict-ridden. This above all constitutes an urgent need to provide such 'enabling services' for women (counselling and awareness-raising for instance) that would result in more wholesome lives for them in the performance of their roles that might then be redefined to include a more fair recognition of the excessive demands made on them.

The search for these enabling services is accompanied by the realization that in addition to our bodies needing the attention of physicians to remain in good health, our minds too need the attention of 'therapists' when they are disturbed or distressed and produce behaviour that is 'objectionable' or 'unacceptable' for society but above all damaging for the actor herself. Some of the enabling services that would help vulnerable groups like women are education, better physical and mental health and increased general and specialized awareness programmes. The particular 'enabling service' of increasing vitality and value today if properly delivered and the focus of this book is that of *counselling and/ or psychotherapy*. A debate about theory and practice of counselling in India is still at a nascent stage; it seems appropriate, however, to embark upon a discourse that might take counselling in our social milieu along a road that is theoretically more rigorous and professionally more sophisticated even as we make it user-friendly and flexible enough for use in our own context.

To recap: The purpose of writing this book is to impart theoretical and practical guidance for trainers and would-be counsellors to enable them to equip themselves better for the purposes and processes of counselling, particularly counselling for anxious and distressed women with a range of social, legal and personal problems. The discussion in this book should also be of assistance to those who wish to understand the general purposes and principles of counselling and its fundamental skills, and take them to other areas of engagement where it may be modified and used. The wider objective of producing something substantive and usable for those who are, or wish to be, involved in training counsellors in other specific situations/circumstances is also to address the issue of women's mental health and their general ability to cope when faced with the rather more common problems of anxiety, tension, depression and stress. While not claming to be the definitive document on the theory and practice of counselling, the book does, however, seek to link evolved counselling theories to the skills and practices required within particular and different contexts. It hopes thereby to provide a base from which literature for formal professional counselling is generated in several institutional settings in South Asia that do acknowledge the need for counselling but have not managed to give it the professional status it deserves. For example, under the Protection of Women from Domestic Violence Act (PWDVA) 2005, there is provision for court-mandated counselling instigated by the magistrate when a matter of domestic violence comes before him:

> The Magistrate may, at any stage of the proceedings under this Act direct the respondent or the aggrieved person, either singly or jointly, to undergo counselling with any member of a service provider who possesses such qualifications and experience in counselling as may be prescribed.[1]

While the Act gives ample space to counselling conducted by professionals in an environment that would ensure the safeguarding of a woman's basic rights, the big question that is relevant for the situation and for our purpose for writing the book is the understanding of counselling that feeds the activity in such situations. In a manual for PWDVA protection officers (POs), prepared by the Lawyers' Collective in India, while the importance of counselling is highlighted, it is interesting to note that there is concern about how the counselling will be conducted and who would conduct it. Clearly the risks and dangers of faulty counselling are recognized whether it is carried out by 'lay people' or by POs themselves. In the case of both these groups, required training and acumen may be lacking and in the case of POs the conflict of interest poses a problem.[2]

This example is one of many that demonstrate that while some space is being created for counselling as an appropriate intervention for aggrieved persons, the accompanying steps and mechanisms to ensure that the counselling is indeed professional and appropriate have not yet been put in place. It is hoped that some parts of this book may provide assistance for the kind of usage suggested herein.

The specificity of the counselling highlighted is in two unusual and specific contextual situations—*women in conflict or dispute-related situations* and *women in custodial institutions*, referred hereinafter as counselling in 'conflict resolution' and counselling in 'confinement'. Nothing in the specificity of the mechanisms and guidelines precludes it from being adapted for related contexts (as the one in the case of the Act mentioned earlier).

In both these particular contexts we are concerned with most women having difficulties that relate to the following issues:

- Ignorance and fear of the nuances of the machinery that determines their status once they are caught in the web (whether it is 'conflict' or 'confinement').
- Inability to communicate effectively about the experience and its aftermath.
- Inability to cope with the wider ramifications (on self and family) of the situation in which they are trapped.
- Inability to come to grips with the acute stress resulting from the abnormal situation surrounding conflict and custody.

It must be emphasized that there are aspects of these difficulties that need to be understood with insights that require a study of the historical and social context in which women are located in this part of the world. Women's roles, generally defined and constructed for them by the power-wielders in society, often impinge on their most basic needs and requirements and need to be addressed at a level that yields more information about the limitations women function under and how damaging that may be for women to begin with. While the wider agendas and processes of restoring social and economic balances that are more just and equitable towards the vulnerable (women, children, elderly, the poor and powerless) are being worked out in society, any postponement of immediate remedial measures at various levels would spell disaster for those already damaged at the starting line. The 'trapped' cannot be expected to wait while society and its principal actor-agency—the State—sorts out any long-term agendas on these issues. Immediate steps that would enable these vulnerable groups to cope better with present difficulties and complications would be needed and counselling is one such immediate step being elaborated here in two especially delicate situations (conflict and confinement) in which women are at a total loss.

In between our recommendations for legal facilitation and therapeutic intervention designed in our view as empowerment or enabling tools for women, a third (alternative) category of intervention was often presented to us as we made our case for a thorough critical reappraisal of women in our society. Instead of trying to deconstruct so many existing images of women, we were told (at the many seminars and workshops organized by us in order to carry the administration with us) to try and find a more practical solution to helping women find their esteem and confidence: 'Let us gender sensitize the official machinery that deals with women whether it is at police stations or prisons. That will pave the way towards meeting women's needs more wholesomely.'[3] Clearly our explorations into the complexities of the problems women faced were awkward and threatening for the establishment. That the needs of vulnerable groups in society could and had to be renegotiated from a fundamentally different perspective from the ones that they were used to (that of talking *down* to rather than talking *with* the groups in question) was difficult for them to accept as a first step in avoiding the pitfalls of their much used path of controlled guidance.

Whether they *seek* Counselling Cells as 'free' women (if there were such cells that were professionally run) for resolving conflicts and disputes, or whether they *need* help in places of custody it is difficult to miss how so much of emotional turmoil and chaos runs like a common sore in so many women's lives. Caught in domestic violence or sexual molestation in the family, traded or lured into sex work by employers and relatives, harassed and then battered for dowry, compelled to sell contraband for survival, the stories are not so different. The differences arise when the long arm of the law is able to catch some women either by chance or because the women decided to strike out in retaliation if they believed they had had enough. There are Naxalite women in Indian prisons who are brazen in their attitudes and regarded as tough and bold by staff and fellow prisoners. Even they have a background that says something that would never get revealed if no one tried to scratch the surface of their lives. Labelling and stereotyping all of these women by being over-compassionate or too hard-hitting is the easy way out. It fails to address the 'why' of their lives. It also fails to deal with the most important feature in any human's life: the mental health of the person.

A mention would be made here of a belated but rising interest in the concept of mental health generally. That there needs to be a focus on the mental health of women specifically and still more urgently on those women who are in prison and other forms of custody is still absent. World Health Organization statistics suggest that one in nine of the total prison population of 9 million in the world suffers from some form of mental disorder or illness. Our work in prisons leads us to believe that at least 50 per cent of the women locked inside for more than six months show signs of some of the most common mental disorders of the accepted international list of disorders.

A study and seminar organized recently by the National Institute of Mental Health and Neuro Sciences (NIMHANS) in Bangalore (India) brought into focus the damaging effect of locking up on prisoners in general and women prisoners in particular. Addressing the seminar, the Chief Justice of the Karnataka High Court conceded that the combined action of losing personal relationships, belongings and normal life leads to mental illness and depression in the prison.

> The environment and culture inside the prison increases incidents of mental problems by three to five times more than in the normal population .... We hope to understand what changes the prison environment needs to reduce such problems in the future.[4]

There was a mention made at the seminar of the need for counselling in prisons. This is the point at which the lacuna in understandings about counselling needs to be addressed. Given what has usually passed for counselling thus far, it would be fair to say that the very concept needs to be studied and understood before it is placed as an item on an agenda.

It is the aim of this book to highlight the fact that among other things there is a pressing need to formulate specific and specialized forms of *counselling* for different contextual situations and here we are addressing the counselling that women need in two specific contexts (conflict/dispute resolution and custody). Moreover, even as the contexts would require differing expertise, there are certain features about these women's lives and about the counselling they need that run like a common thread; counselling in general and counselling for women in particular need to be stated at the outset. That is what the first three chapters of the book set out to do. Inevitably there is a special focus on the chosen subject 'women' in Chapter 2, which spells out some of the discrepancies surrounding our perceptions of women and how these have been adjusted and readjusted for the sake of convenience in being able to 'better' handle women—both to control and to 'help' them. Women seem to be offered a 'deal': if you want to be considered the same as men then here is what you get—the same treatment with no trappings for any difference no matter how fundamental it might be in your lives; and if you want to be considered different then you do not get that equal status (but you do not get something special for your difference either). The logic is fallacious and ends up as a 'no-win' situation. Specialized counselling would need to take these cultural and social inconsistencies into account. The predicaments faced as a result are presented in Chapter 2 to suggest the need for some reality checks.

In Chapter 3, the theoretical sources that have provided the bases for different approaches to counselling are spelt out: As an activity that addresses a person's psyche and behaviour, it is interesting to observe the changing emphasis on the relationship between the two at different periods of time in the history of counselling.

Chapter 4 spells out the structured process of counselling, at some length breaking it up for convenience into steps to be followed, not necessarily sequentially. The general principles and processes having been stated and set out, they are then situated in the two contexts (conflict resolution/mediation and custody) in Chapters 5 and 6 to see how they operate therein and where they need to be adjusted to meet the needs of each context. In both contexts, nothing sticks out more obtrusively than the fact that there is indeed a lot that is different for women (and this is not about biological, sexual and pathological aspects but social, economic and ideological aspects as well) and that this does indeed require *different* but not *differential and disparate* handling.

Each contextual setting uses exercises and case studies to demonstrate what direction counselling would take to meet specific objectives and purposes. Names have been withheld or changed for reasons of confidentiality in these all-too-real cases, some of which appear almost unreal and bizarre. Nowhere would the truism 'truth is stranger than fiction' have greater validity than in the lives of many women whose day-to-day living is uncanny to the point of being unreal. And nowhere is the need for interventions that address this reality (without being manipulative) more urgent than for women in distress.

NOTES

1. Section 14(1) Protection of Women from Domestic Violence Act 2005.
2. *Ending Domestic Violence through Non-violence: A Manual for PWDVA Protection Officers*, New Delhi: Lawyers Collective Women's Rights Initiative, 2010, p. 63.
3. Suggestions made by police and prison officers at Seminar on 'New Initiatives in Penal Reform and Access to Justice', Report of Conference organized by PRAJA and Prisons Department, Government of Andhra Pradesh, Hyderabad, in 2001 (PRAJA, 2001).
4. Seminar, National Institute of Mental Health and Neuro Sciences (NIMHANS), Bangalore, in January 2011 to discuss a study conducted by NIMHANS, National Legal Services Authority (NALSA), and Karnataka State Legal Services Authority (KSLSA).

Chapter 2

Theoretical and Experiential Fundamentals Relating to Women and Mental Health

Clearly, the underlying assumption of the book is that there are enough women in acute mental distress in our part of the world who could do with some alleviation of that distress to enable them to lead lives that are more gratifying than theirs have been. Before setting out some practical definitions and understandings of the 'Counselling' we would wish to advocate for the purposes we have in view, it seems appropriate to look at the real worlds of women within which we have located counselling and given it such a prominent role. There are some very simple basic points about women and their distress that most of us either underplay or overplay. Down the ages, in most societies, viewing women's mental disorders (from the simplest such as distress and anxiety to the most complex) as figments of the imagination, sexual/biological aberration, or diabolical possession, little was ever done to address the causes and symptoms of women's mental conditions. If our goal is to strive towards a social scenario where we enable rather than preclude one-half of our population from playing their fruitful part in society, any tainted portrayals of women would need to be almost completely deconstructed.

Despite the two principles that are supposedly the cornerstones of modern democracies and should affect women positively today—equality and freedom—in the South Asian context, older traditional perceptions of women have a strong presence and live side by side with modern ideas. They are still adhered to as practices in the personal and social lives of women and subconsciously internalized by women themselves when they perceive their roles in the family, community or society at large. Custom and tradition have given women extensive privileges on the domestic front alongside the burdens of the home and hearth that women have then made their exclusive (sham) power domains without realizing the extent to which they are really being excluded from other vital areas of decision-making. The lines they may not cross are supposedly always for their protection and safekeeping; stepping out of line and violating the rigid codes is inevitably immoral, sinful and punishable. There are always many reasons for being more ruthless if women violate the laws and codes set out for maintaining the social order. Most of the anxieties and misgivings about women's conduct emanate from factors that surround her sexuality. The 'mistress' of the 'secret of creation', women's and the earth's fecundities are considered one and for man this secret seems to pose a threat. Down the ages, even when women did have some rights, their image was always a bundle of contradictions: a woman could be a '*devi*' (goddess) or she could be a 'devil'. In ancient Hindu literature, there are mixed messages about women. 'One school is seen as declaring that the woman is the highest gift of God to man, while the other is seen as asserting that the best way to reach God is to avoid woman' (Altekar, 1959: 305).

Powerful goddesses are mentioned in Greek and Roman myths, but none to match the gods Zeus and Apollo; and goddesses are attributed less sexuality, suggesting by implication that in her sexuality lay the dangers surrounding the human female form. This suggestion comes through in most depictions of Greek and Roman forms of the most well-known goddesses: Hera (Juno), Aphrodite (Venus), Athena (Minerva), Artemis (Diana), Hestia (Vesta) and Demeter (Ceres). Women were accordingly encouraged not to step out of the parameters of the roles drawn up for them (both Odysseus and Telemachus in Homer's *Odyssey* urge the wife and mother Penelope, respectively, to confine herself to spinning and weaving).

Apprehensions about women spring from a deep fear that if not controlled, women may find a way to use their powers against man's supremacy. Barring her in as many ways as possible and as subtly as possible (making it sound like her own protection) was the easiest way, coupled with arguments that women did not possess the strength or skills of intellect for establishment work anyway. Any power women possessed was of malignant origin. Even Darwin's *The Origin of Species* (1859) influenced offending women adversely. Writers explaining female criminality just over a hundred years ago were arguing for atavism in offending women to build up a criminal type so that they could then be handled appropriately (Tarowsky, Lombroso and Ferrero). The dangers of these theories still lurk in our midst.

With women's own voices conspicuously absent in historical corridors, many of the reasons and causes of women's subordination have to be worked through from chronicled texts, oral traditions and collections of socio-legal and religious commentaries. It enables us to see how the status of women was constructed, how this defined their role and activities in society and how sacrosanct and hallowed customs developed to build around these constructions to form the gendered culture of that society. Social and legal codes of the lawmakers of most ancient civilized societies drew portraits of the 'ideal woman' and made special provisions for punishing the 'fallen woman' who transgressed the ideal.

The *Code of Hammurabi* (seventeenth century BC) suggested impaling women on sharpened stakes to punish the sin of abortion. In medieval England, a woman was burnt at the stake for killing a husband (it was the equivalent of petty treason because the monarch had been deprived of the services of a 'loyal subject'). Churchmen in medieval England and Europe devised lines of questioning for a woman confessant that usually related to her sex life and added several that pertained to sexual deviations that she must have indulged in. The most respectable women had to go to great lengths to prove their honour. Ordeals by fire and water are among the most well-known ways of proving innocence. Nearer home, Sita, the wife of the Hindu legendary hero and god Rama, went through fire to prove she was pure.

Contrasting images of women appear in most ancient texts depicting women as having equal (early Vedic period) and unequal status (from the later Vedic period to the Islamic invasions). The Quran also gives two views on the role of women: that men and women are equal before God in religious spheres—belief in God and the Prophet and performing religious rites: *namaaz* (prayer), *roza* (fasting), *haj* (pilgrimage) and *zakat* (giving charity); but women are also placed by God in the protection of men who are then totally responsible for them as carers and maintainers (Quran 4:34). For this reason there are social taboos for women and transgression is handled mercilessly.

In non-Western societies where ancient traditions are adhered to with uncompromising sanctity, the debate about tradition and modernity is not likely to get the simplistic treatment it does at the hands of some Western scholars. Roles defined by ancient customs have not always been seen as obstacles to social development, and reformers have emerged from within society to reshape the nature of customary roles to harmonize them with changing times and climes. The contributions of the Bhakti Movement, Sikhism or nineteenth-century reformers in British India (Ram Mohan Roy, Ishwar Chandra Vidyasagar, Jyotirao Phule, etc.) are cited as examples of people who believed in giving a status to women that had been denied earlier.

These historical pictures of women are being recounted with the object of suggesting that the package (it could equally well be called the 'baggage') that women are born with in many societies is a burden that is heavy, and any examples of women that break the barriers and attain what no man may have attained does not really change the general pattern of most women's second-class citizenship. The weight of the burden sometimes breaks a woman's back, but more often than not it is her mind that gives way and while the back may get attended to, the mind is the greatest casualty in her journey of life.

Unfortunately the images of the ideal woman outlined earlier are subsumed in our current legal enactments and remedies, even as the latter claim to guarantee women equality, freedom, opportunity and protection. This becomes clear when situations of domestic violence, rape and sexual harassment are addressed. (See pp. 41–52.) It also becomes clear at such sites that the archaic penal laws in most of South Asia relating to transgressions against or involving women are premised on *social* expectations where judgements about perpetrators and/or victims are based on guidelines of *social* mores. The remedial machinery of the law (police, courts, etc.) finds enough space to use the cultural aspects relating to women's status to mutate features of its professional delivery in handling violations. The legal charade further confuses the woman who is unable to juggle the two contesting frameworks—as victim or as victim/offender and often seeks a third option to make sense of her life.

The confusions are not as innocuous as they may appear. Suggesting recourse to the law and its implementing machinations to procure entitlements is a hard course for many women without the requisite awareness and assistance. Advocating instant brands of gender equality to those whose lives have been devoid of it does not help. How to enable them to strive for it in a graduated programme that is workable when the going gets tough may be one step in that direction.

Therapeutic intervention is not an alternative to justice for the injured, violated and betrayed; nor is it a recommended soft option for those who feel or are unable to contest or claim. It can be a method of equipping women (in South Asia) to envisage or start a journey that empowers them to take on the machinery, any machinery, whether familial, societal or State, to claim what is rightfully theirs. It is not enough for us to believe they have entitlements, *they* must believe it. A therapeutic intervention is that point in the continuum of redress where the state of mind of a woman is addressed with the object of restoring enough of her lost self-esteem and self-confidence for her to be able to exercise her own choices. It needs to be agenda-free even as it combats agenda that have been instilled into people's psyche from birth.

Highlighting the need for a process of restoration (of an undeveloped or eroded self-esteem and self-confidence) in women is not suggestive of any inherent drawback or limitation in their personalities. Social and other obstacles, notwithstanding women are able to show unmatched resilience in the face of adversity (see cases), and the stress and strain of proving themselves all the time takes a toll on their minds that can be damaging if left unattended. It is this damage that we believe compromises a woman's mental health.

In more recent times, while some (minimal) emphasis is being placed on women's mental health, the focus is more on mental *illness* (objectively and scientifically defined), and the graver the illness, the greater the emphasis on the recommended (*medical*) *intervention*. But clinical, medically defined illnesses are not what we are talking about here when we recommend alternative interventions such as counselling. Serious, listed mental illnesses need treatment and there is relatively less doubt or ambiguity in addressing these. Whether it is possible to draw clear objective lines between different and differing mental disorders (and there is an unending list of them), there are clearly some disorders that may be addressed through other simple (non-medical) interventions, and still be called 'disorders'. At no stage and in no way can it be suggested that a disorder needs less attention (for that person) than an illness that has been defined scientifically because it is in a list of medically treatable disorders. In real life both become intrinsic to the lives of the women that are afflicted by them and both need to be understood with informed competence and expertise.

In our present context (counselling as a therapeutic intervention), we are perhaps simplifying the differing interventions for 'illness' and 'disorder' fully aware that the international literature on this subject has other (differing) views. For some analysts, mental 'disorder' is a preferred term and for others 'mental illness' should be the overarching term that may also cover mental disorders. The debate is unresolved and should not be viewed as a hair-splitting exercise based on whether what afflicts the mind is an illness or not and whether it is called an 'illness' only because and when it may be addressed by medical intervention. There is always a possibility of some overlap of interventions and any rigidity in classifying disorders along the medical/non-medical model could deprive us of deeper understandings where there may be a danger of a common disorder becoming so serious that one does need medical intervention.

There are manuals that list categories of mental disorders and for the convenience of users worldwide reputed organizations have systemically classified their lists of distinct types of disorders to enable a reference point for all users. The two most widely used are the International Classification of Diseases (ICD-10) prepared by the World Health Organization (WHO) and the Diagnostic and Statistical Manual of Mental Disorders (DSM-IV) produced by the American Psychiatric Association (APA).[1] Without introducing an element of Foucauldian scepticism that would view such meticulous exercises of psychiatric regimentation as impositions of (bourgeois) morality on unsuspecting people, some queries do arise. One question that cannot be answered with precision is whether mental health then is the absence of all the listed mental disorders/illnesses, and does the list address all the indefinable in-between spaces that affect someone's mental health which we know is often socially constructed and socially defined and yet may have no name? In our time spent with the myriads of different women whom we would never have had the privilege to know given our lack of exposure to their worlds, we did feel the presence of disorientations and confusions writ large on their faces. There was no name or label for their anxieties but clearly they needed to be addressed.

While we have tried to steer clear of cultural relativity in determining the interventions and recommendations made for women in distress, addressing the problem of mental health among women in the South Asian region does inevitably throw up some issues relating to culture. We have had to take cognisance of the fact that women's mental health here is implicitly defined by socio-cultural features and any normative conceptualization of women's distress seems coloured by these features. In some locations where the motions of counselling were being observed and we had come in to professionalize it, cases were being handled by 'counsellors' whose cultural and religious backgrounds and experiences clearly had an impact on the methodology they were applying. The result was a mishmash of power and patronage that did little by way of help.

Apart from the debate about nomenclature relating to mental illness/mental disorder, the other confusion relates to the question: 'Is mental illness an illness?' While this may not be the place to set out the debate relating to this, it does impact on the importance we give to the symptoms that are generally attributed to particular mental conditions in order to enable us to define them and in the process determine whether mental illness or disorder can be objectively (scientifically) defined. The question assumes larger proportions when applied to women and their mental disorders. For our purposes we are interested first in how real a mental illness or disorder is and then with the remedial action which may or may not be medical.

> While there is debate over how to define mental illness, it is generally accepted that mental illnesses are real and involve disturbances of thought, experience, and emotion serious enough to cause functional impairment in people, making it more difficult for them to sustain interpersonal relationships and carry on their jobs, and sometimes leading to self-destructive behavior and even suicide. The most serious mental illnesses, such as schizophrenia, bipolar disorder, major depression, and schizoaffective disorder are often chronic and can cause serious disability. (Perring, 2010)

Inevitably the question that arises when mental disorders are made a focus of study or concern is whether and when can we call them 'illnesses', or are there only some disorders that would qualify as 'illnesses'. Is it the physical/physiological versus mental distinction or something else that determines what we call illness? In common parlance when someone gets the flu or even complains of severe headaches, we observe the symptoms and seek out the (physical) causes and promptly and unhesitatingly say she is ill. When someone has bipolar disorder, after some hesitation the label 'bipolar disorder' is used because of some familiarity with the symptoms and tried and tested interventions are set in motion. Is it an illness? Or would we prefer to call it a 'disorder' because it is a state of mind and not body? But if the state of mind has anything to do with the brain, then is the brain not a part of the body? Or are we going to call it an 'illness' because of the professionalism (psychiatric) that attaches to the intervention? A severe headache is sometimes a migraine or can be due to something else. That one will be called a 'physical' ailment and the other not so may not always be an accurate conclusion. It has certainly had an impact on our assessments of women's mental conditions in prisons.

Most of us would agree that the distinction between mental and physical illnesses cannot be drawn purely in terms of the simplistic causes attributed to the condition—that is, mental illnesses having psychological causes and physical illnesses having non-psychological causes. While we have not identified the causes of most mental disorders, it is possible that many may have physical causes and many are caused by other factors but may manifest physical symptoms, and yet others may only show mental/behavioural malfunction. The prospects of finding a principled way of drawing distinctions to match the way we are used to addressing and treating them may pose problems. (See Vimla's case in the following section—The Case of 'V'.)

Accompanying all these difficulties is also the fact that states of mind and the changes therein (caused variously) may result in behavioural changes that may be labelled 'abnormal', not always because of any objective assessment but due to value-ridden factors, and the 'treatment' may be equally value-ridden. A woman lost her speech because of continuous and intense badgering and maltreatment at the hands of her spouse and his family. She was not shamming—she really could not speak although initially the family said she was doing just that. Elders in the family then said that she was 'possessed', and she was taken to all kinds of charlatans to get her to talk. From sticking hot objects in her mouth to tying her up and subjecting her to physical pain so that she would shriek, to taking a snake close to her face for a verbal protest, the quacks tried everything. That there was a connection between the domestic violence and the physical affliction was not explored for obvious reasons: the vested interests of those in charge of her domestic situation. A similar case of abuse by a spouse resulted in a woman losing her eyesight intermittently. For days she was blind and then her vision would return only to disappear again. She said nothing about her husband beating her without provocation until her parental family saw the bruises on her body one day and decided to intervene. Over several sessions of psychotherapy she was able to reveal some details of her plight and while the problem was not addressed holistically, because she was afraid for her life thus leaving her with some permanent scars, she did recover her vision. And we saw her continuing to live unhappily ever after. It might be mentioned as an aside that the first woman was uneducated and from rural India and the second was an educated upper-middle-class woman from New Delhi. In the light of such situational problems, it is sometimes suggested that principled distinctions between physical and mental disorders should not be rigidly observed. In any event we find ourselves faced with different positions:

- A reductionist argument that mental disorders relate to the brain and therefore come within the purview of neuroscience (Guze, 1992).
- The biopsychosocial approach that disorders have features that are biological, psychological and social, and no illness would be exclusively psychological or biological (Engel, 1977).

While some of these positions are simplistic and state the obvious, we still need to see how an emphasis would impact our positions on counselling as a therapeutic intervention for women in distress? What should we be looking at to discover the nature of the disorder and how do we decide our approach to a remedial/alleviatory action?

Very broadly some focal points would need to be ascertained so that our theoretical and empirical knowledge about them can be developed towards practical ends:

- Understanding mental characteristics of women as persons, as assessed by both neurological and psychological studies, and then put in the context of the subjects in view.
- Surveying the psychosocial influences on women with particular emphasis on ordinary and extraordinary life-events and incidents, emotional attachments and relationships, and the strains and stresses related to all of these.
- Assessing the socio-economic backgrounds and the reinforcements or rejections associated with class, community, and culture that women are subjected to in their lives.

- Observing the effects of the overarching social, economic and cultural systems brought about by newer value systems in the new global order that promotes individualism, weakening social ties and creating ambivalence in the minds of women.

Mental illness and disorder can strike and affect anyone, but we are constantly reminded in relation particularly to the most 'common' disorders that the statistics for women suffering from them are far higher than for men. Women face problems and conflicts that come from larger areas of engagement than men. Even as we bear in mind all of the four different ways suggested earlier of looking at and for disorders that affect women, the biggest drawback in starting out is an existing cavalier approach to addressing these disorders in the first place. Ignoring, neglecting, avoiding, marginalizing, ostracizing, stigmatizing or simply trashing—these are the most common responses we came across in addressing what appeared an 'abnormal' woman. What is more disconcerting is the fact that many women almost expect to be treated the way they are when their circumstances bring them to the brink and they 'lose it'.

Equally disconcerting is the practitioner's threat of failure while working among and with women in hierarchical patriarchal societies no matter how one develops one's tools. While one assumes these interventions would help powerless women, one is acutely aware that the distress comes from conflicts that arise out of the very structuring of such societies. Unfortunately, most societies have managed to marginalize (and warehouse) their poor and powerless to an unimaginable degree and among them the greatest casualty is the woman. How one would access such women is a serious problem. Either we enter the warehouse or they leave the warehouse and come to us—it may sound simple but is the most problematic of all the obstacles one is faced with. The dividers in our society often make crossing the social boundaries difficult. One has to find a way.

Some of the women we encountered typified this reality of being warehoused to an extent that would make most of us ashamed. The belief that the (State) institutions we set up to restore balance in society would somehow be able to address the acute social and personal problems of women caused by existing imbalances remains an unrealized dream. Not all women are helpless and not all suffer 'the slings and arrows of outrageous fortune'. Many are even content with life in a man's world. But for those who have no negotiability and certainly no power to resist, if they should be abused, the road is arduous and steep. There were women in our journey that we could not help—they had missed the boat and consequently so had we.

In a prison, women are captive audience and one is always cautious about taking advantage of such a situation even if the objective is to provide assistance and succour. Where else would one find so many women in the throes of despair? But there too there are hurdles—both literal and figurative. We are lucky when institutions do not treat us as intruders in what they believe to be their territory. But each intervention is packed with difficulties that are sometimes insurmountable. There are cases that fall between psychotherapeutic and psychiatric intervention and a lack of cooperation from any end of the institutional framework is a recipe for disaster. Two such cases demonstrate the point. The descriptions are summaries of notes taken while carrying out case studies of women who either came voluntarily for counselling sessions or who were approached because they could not come.

THE CASE OF 'V'

Vimla (referred to 'V' from here onwards) looks 50, but her prison file tells us she is 36 years old. Medium height, thin, sloppy gait and fidgety, she looks unattractive and has dishevelled, and exceptionally dry, hair. Generally scruffy and grubby-looking, she is dressed in a *salwar-kurta* with a *duppatta* around her neck. She is always barefoot but that is not unusual in an Indian prison. Her blank look and expressionless face do make one wonder whether it is a good idea to go too close to her. The jailor has lined up the prisoners of 'Barrack 4' as if in a parade. V is now scratching her very dishevelled hair. I am already convinced she has lice in her hair, a not uncommon occurrence where women live together and hygiene is wanting, as in this part of the world, not to mention the acute shortage of water in this particular region. She then moves on to scratching other parts of her body indiscriminately and suddenly pulls up her shirtsleeve to do so. I notice the bruises: they are red and blue and the arm is swollen. I wince and the jailor promptly offers a lame explanation about her having fallen down the stairs (there are no stairs in this prison).

In the old days V would have been called a 'lunatic' and plain mad. Today that is not accepted parlance. Faced with the kind of person V is (or has become), it is clear she cannot be just be a *case* for us; she portrays one of the most important reasons for our work among women prisoners and epitomizes the most drastic effects that locking up can have on those who are on the verge of cracking up because of what they have done and what has been done to them.

V's case history is difficult to put together because unlike other prisoners there is little forthcoming directly from her. Bits and pieces gathered from records and conversations with other women reveal that when she first came she looked shell-shocked. Over time her behaviour deteriorated because she just could not cope with the 'do this', 'don't do that', 'sit here', 'finish your food', 'wash your plate', 'wake up', 'go to sleep' routine— the instructions were endless and no one assisted this traumatized being who had come with some rather sordid experiences as part of her baggage. When she went in for meals, people moved away from her because there was no telling what she might do with the food. Sometimes she just spat it out wherever she was, sometimes she would go and throw it in the toilet, often she would just not eat and if coaxed would run away from the kitchen throwing her *thali* (food plate) on the floor. Someone would then have to clean up the mess, and there was resentment among other prisoners.

There is no aggression but her whole demeanour, even when she is doing weird things only to herself, is something other women are unable to take in their stride and they just stay away from her. Most women know the penalties of not obeying staff (no matter what staff demands). V has no sense of any logic to draw upon to see her through her daily routine; no indicators that tell her that something is not a good idea and she should refrain from doing it. This is clearly a problem for her each day and a running sore for the establishment.

This paragraph is from Nina's notes (research assistant on the project):

> A cultural programme was organised in the prison by a group of women volunteers, and there was singing and dancing. We were all asked to participate so we also went along. Suddenly out of nowhere V emerged and lifted her dress right up and started dancing. She was not wearing underwear and it was really very embarrassing for everyone. She had no clue about what she was doing. Everyone was really upset and the staff was livid: a Convict Officer (C.O.) grabbed her forcefully, took her inside the barrack and gave her a thrashing and we could hear the screams and yells. As if that is an answer! Each day there is an incident relating to V that upsets people but in our perception damages V above all.

She has been put in the barrack at the end of the passage so that she is near the toilet and bathing area but she takes off all her clothes at any time and at any place, one of the women tells us. Each time she is reprimanded there is a moment when she is almost expecting to be told that she should take her clothes off; and then she waits to see what will happen next. Earlier people used to actually treat this as a 'tamasha' (spectacle; entertainment) and made fun of her and laughed at and mocked her as she did this. Some would even provoke her and say 'V kapre utaro' (V take off your clothes) and she would start doing just that and there would be jeers all around. Gradually the novelty wore off and they began treating it as a serious and disturbing problem, and a few of them would hurry across to tell her (gently) that that was not what she ought to be doing.

She seems to have lost track of the simplest things that she clearly must have known at some point in her adult life. She is at a loss when her monthly periods start. She just goes about as if nothing is amiss until someone notices her stained clothes and passes some rude comment. '*Arre pagli dekh to kitna khoon laga hai!*' (you mad-hatter, can't you see your clothes are all stained with blood). The taunts and locking up only make matters worse; she often just sits in the open courtyard and uses it as her toilet. Once she was actually seen handling her faeces and was prevented from putting it in her mouth by a fellow prisoner. That was when it was decided that there was a need for urgent and dramatic intervention.

The details of her case are coming through in bits and pieces: She was married to a drunkard who took a sadistic pleasure in thrashing her for the smallest thing. That wasn't all, he took a perverse delight in thrashing her naked. So each time he was drunk, he first ripped off her clothes and then beat her with any object that came his way. The staff had gathered this from her case records when she had had her hearing in court, and had shared these details with some of the 'old' hands at the prison. It took a while for us to gather this information, and a lot of things that V did then became clearer to us than they had been. She had none of the shyness relating to her body that other inmates were so particular about. Other women complained that there was no 'body privacy' in the prison: for dressing, for using the toilet, for a bath, for attending to other personal needs: everything was so public. But for V bodily exposure did not seem to be a problem. Some in the prison called her '*besharam*' (shameless), but it was evident that she had no sense of the 'shame' they were talking about and thanks to her husband's manipulations nakedness came with being ticked off. She had no awareness or comprehension about many of the things that others complained about and the behaviour she manifested as a result of this was punished as if she was being deliberately mischievous. No one bothered to go deep enough into her behaviour to see that V was mentally challenged and needed something different and special.

While it may be possible for us to go and look up the details of the 'case' in the District Court, we have decided that there is no time for all that if we are to get V on to the 'repair' programme. What we have pieced together is that one fateful day when her husband thrashed her (after stripping her of all her clothes), in the inebriated state he was in, she pushed him really hard as part of her resistance and he fell to the floor hitting his head against the stone floor. He was hurt but became more enraged because she had had the gall to retaliate, something that had never happened before, so he got up and pulled her by the hair and dragged her to the anteroom that was a store. She struggled and pulled herself away and picked up an axe that lay in the corner and struck him with it. There was blood everywhere and she was absolutely petrified. She has no recollection of the event—she blanked out and from what one gathered she stayed blanked out for a while. The day of the dramatic events that resulted in her husband's death is only sketchily available for us. But we have figured out that the minutiae of the 'event' was not really that important at the juncture we are at. The mission is different now.

Here was a case where the kind of counselling we envisaged was challenged; it was not the prevalent common disorder that more than half the women in any prison were experiencing. It was (or had become) a mental illness, and was also indicative of the fact that there were problems here that were beyond our expertise. So what was our role? In the first instance it was about alerting the prison management that there was a grave problem at hand. While the staff recognized there was something fundamentally wrong, here they were out of their depths and only saw V as a '*pagli*'. So the second step for us was to see that while the 'grave problem' was being diverted to the appropriate practitioners, V was being treated with some sensitivity and not being manhandled. This was important because it was not really clear just how aware she was of her own condition.

An interesting development in the case was the role of peers. What we in our capacity as counsellors could not address for reasons of security and logistics (we could only be there for an eight-hour day), fellow prisoners volunteered to do. Radha, a prisoner in the same barrack, had told us about several instances when V was subjected to private humiliations by prisoners and staff. She said she had seen the indignities that V was subjected to day after day and a point came when she felt enough was enough. Radha relates:

I intervened one morning and told the C.O. that by giving V a thrashing each time she 'misbehaved' she was being ridiculously uncaring. 'V is not normal and whereas she is a prisoner it does not mean she has stopped being a human being. How can you start beating her like that?' But the C.O. paid no attention. That day I decided I would do something about it. So I went to the Deputy Jailor and asked to be put in charge of V's care. I volunteered to help V so that we did not have the kind of distasteful scenes that were becoming frequent and were too damaging for V. Fortunately she agreed and from that day on I have been trying to assist V in whatever way I can. I try to make others see her less as an object of ridicule and more as a human being with problems that need urgent solutions. It has been absurd how we have all treated her as things got worse.

We noticed over time that Radha had decided to take charge of assisting V when things got out of hand for her. No more jeers and taunts for V and the restoration of some dignity in her quite dishevelled life.

We were reassured that the spirit of some form of counselling could be kindled within the prisoners themselves. Radha spontaneously offered to assist V to meet her needs and restore her self-respect as much as she could. Nina tried to assist Radha to address some of V's basic communication problems and to try and express herself if she could. That was not an easy task because by then she needed interventions that lay in the hands of medical practitioners.

The prison doctor prepared her case to be submitted to the hospital, suggesting that she needed psychiatric care and treatment. V was to be taken for tests and examination and if required be admitted so that the treatment was continuous and professional. But prison being prison, the administrative hurdles delayed her hospital visits considerably. It was a while before V was examined, tested and diagnosed with Post-traumatic Stress Disorder (PTSD) and related problems—symptoms of psychosis that we shall discuss in due course.

V was not getting better because the treatment was erratic, hospitalization of prisoners was a problem (security and other factors came in the way) and perhaps the prolonged neglect of the malady had exacerbated the whole issue. She was given drugs that were not monitored by the specialists because she was not taken to them regularly. She slept most of the time and was clearly becoming a lost cause: daily chores could not be performed because the drugs made her groggy all the time. She needed a safer environment. The prison department's answer was to send her back to her village without a thought about the fact that there was no one there who would and could care for her. She had a father-in-law in the village, and he was hardly likely to take back a 'mad' woman who had slain his son! As counsellors we were dismayed by the decision but had no say in the matter. Whether early intervention would have helped is difficult to say but certainly delayed reaction in this case proved a catastrophe for V.

There could be other Vs coming this way. Pre-empting future problems of a similar nature was part of our mission. There were some ways to begin—actively involving staff in some of the courses of action was one way.

V's diagnosis triggered several negative reactions from staff and management. They made a mockery of the seriousness with which we responded to the words 'stress disorder'. 'We all have stresses', they said, 'so why fuss when a prisoner has stress. We should all be taken to the hospital and treated.' V's deteriorating condition and the need for intervention had all been forgotten and our focus on V's 'stress' put them off enough to view our concerns with suspicion.

There was no denying that they had stress-ridden lives, and we assured them that that would also be addressed. V's condition we told them had gone beyond the realms of the stress we had been talking about; PTSD was something further down the line. Staff anxieties were understandable: they felt threatened and uneasy; working in a prison is not the easiest job. Locking up people each day, putting up with their idiosyncrasies and quirks, disciplining them, and still retaining some sanity to carry on with their own personal lives was consuming. Sometimes they felt it was difficult to say who the real prisoners were. They showed signs of 'burning out', and their personalities got affected in adverse ways.

> When we first came in [they often told us], we too had some good in us. We didn't come in to brutalize people. We started out believing that we would do jobs the best way we could and perhaps make a difference, a positive difference. But the institution took over: our ways and methods took shapes and turns that were determined by this wretched place. Yes it is a wretched place that makes many of us careless and sometimes ugly things happen.

Imperceptibly, and often unknowingly, a few of them turned into little monsters or big monsters; some retained a semblance of humanity that came to the fore at times of crisis. But they were swimming against the tide: the norm was a matter-of-fact approach according to rules without any deference to differences among persons or their needs.

Their reactions certainly made all of us pause to think about the environment we were working in. This was far from being an ideal institution; in fact it was deplorable that society had ever come up with such an abhorrent idea, locking up people in cages and believing that this treatment was going to make them better. It made everyone worse and that included staff—especially the staff that spent all of their time with these persons from all kinds of backgrounds that the system had condemned to this dumping ground—and the dumping ground was the staff's workplace, where they spent hours each day. Many told us they didn't even tell people outside they worked in a prison.

> Let's face it, the world outside looks at this place as the dustbin of society where criminals are sent as a punishment, and criminals are regarded as the scum of the earth are they not? Why would we go around saying we work in such a place?

Vimla and her PTSD brought this to the fore. Vimla's problem hasn't gone away, and we need to explain to the staff the relationship between prisoners' problems and their own. After all, it is the word 'stress' that got this discussion going and so it shall be: we shall address 'stress' and bring in staff issues as well. This is the opportunity perhaps to wrestle with some conceptual education for one and all—for us, for staff and for the outside world.

What came out of this was that the counselling we had planned for prisoners was now extended for staff as well, not only to stop them from trivializing V's PTSD, but also to educate them in all the mental disorders that were prevalent in the environment of the prison, such as anxiety, stress, depression, etc. Apart from consulting doctors (psychiatrists), we went as deep as we could into the two well-known documents (referred to above) that had information on mental illnesses/disorders: the APA's DSM IV and WHO's ICD-10 (referred to earlier and elaborated on in the Notes at the end of this chapter). We studied as best as we could the whole phenomenon of PTSD. PTSD we discovered is an anxiety disorder of serious magnitude. It can develop after someone has been exposed to one or more terrifying events in which someone was threatened, traumatized or a serious physical harm occurred. It is a severe and ongoing emotional reaction to an extreme and acute psychological trauma. This stress may involve someone's actual death or a threat to the patient's or someone else's life, serious physical injury or threat to physical and/or psychological integrity, to a degree that usual psychological defences are incapable of coping. In some cases it can also be from profound psychological and emotional trauma apart from any actual physical harm. Often the two are combined. The result is an extremely debilitating condition that is not only psychological but also physiological in nature. Above all, different people react differently to similar traumatic events. One person may experience a horrific event as traumatic, while another would not suffer trauma as a result of the same event. Such is the stuff that makes up a human being and his/her personality and psyche.

We had established that stress was known to contribute to and trigger psychotic states. Any history of psychologically traumatic events and any recent experience of a stressful nature could contribute to the development of psychosis. Short-lived psychosis triggered by stress, we gathered, was referred to as 'brief reactive psychosis' and patients could spontaneously recover normal functioning within two weeks. In some rare cases, individuals could remain in a state of full-blown psychosis for many years or perhaps have attenuated psychotic symptoms (such as low-intensity hallucinations) present at most times.

Our large poster 'The Human Body' in the counselling room that had formed an important part of the Health Education Programme was now needed to show the links between mind and body (in particular the brain) and difficult as it may be we felt the staff needed this instruction. We were not psychiatrists in the medical field but that had to be turned into an asset and it did since we were now required to use lay language to a lay audience. Explaining the anatomy and physiology of the brain (to the best of our ability), we moved on to disorders demonstrating with the help of the diagram that PTSD displays biochemical changes in the brain and that these were different in every mental disorder so that what happens in the brain when there is depression, for instance, differs from what happens when a person is going through PTSD. This was a lecture that we were reluctant to deliver but given the cynicism of the people around us (especially those who were going to be in charge of cases like V's), this needed to be done.

Moving on from PTSD, we explained that in a cluster of disorders in which the main component is distress and anxiety—assumed to be commonplace symptoms in every person's life—the kind of psychotherapeutic intervention that is most appropriate is counselling. It would not be alien and mystifying for women, they would relate to it comfortably and it would be a professional extension and development of a mode of support that they would have been familiar with in their lives—that of leaning on each other for solace and comfort (except that earlier 'support systems' would have come with power and authority written all over them). Modified and fine-tuned to address the lacunae in the earlier modes of assistance, counselling would concentrate on the client and his/her distress-causing experiences even if the solutions were not always at hand. The intervention would focus on the client and her experiences past and present with all the dos and don'ts that counselling requires and hopefully make some difference in the life of the client.

Those were the ramifications of the one (case) that slipped away. V was well past the kind of direct assistance we could have given as counsellors. She was a clear case of a disorder that reached an intensity that needed far more expertise than we had. But what we were able to do was point those in charge in the appropriate direction. It would be speculative to suggest that the turn of events would have been different had we been around when V first came to the prison, but the ripples her case caused were far-reaching. Everyone learnt from them: the staff, other prisoners, the management and certainly us. A general alert had been sounded relating to early interventions and the importance of mental health among persons the State had decided to lock up and keep in custody without deference to their minds. We needed to go deeper into the problem to position therapeutic interventions where they belonged.

Figure 2.1 provides a somewhat elaborate diagrammatic presentation that covers most of the disorders listed in DSM IV and ICD-11, classifying them into distress, disorder and disease and sets them out alongside the interventions that would help the client or patient. There are various distress-type disorders that could be addressed with 'Early Interventions', but if left unattended or for other reasons the affected person may need interventions that move into further grey areas of psychotherapy and finally pharmacotherapy. Anxiety disorders could be successfully tackled with counselling and support group therapy. PTSD further down in the 'Distress' column is a likely candidate for getting incrementally worse and needing first psychotherapeutic and then may be pharmacological intervention. V was a case in point; she slipped further and further along the grey area landing a little late in the deep-grey column where intervention was clumsily administered, leaving V worse than before.

The significance of these disorders and interventions cannot be overemphasized. They need to be analysed and addressed 'warts and all' and along with the focus on them from the viewpoint of mental health they also need to be placed in the context

FIGURE 2.1. Classification of Mental Disorders and Illnesses and Appropriate Interventions

	DISTRESS	DISORDER	DISEASE
	EARLY INTERVENTIONS: Mental Health Counselling, Support Groups, etc.	PSYCHOTHERAPY: Cognitive Behavioural Therapy, etc.	PHARMACOTHERAPY: Drugs
Psychological Distress	Stress, Grief, Suicidal Impulses		
Anxiety Disorders	Non-clinical Anxiety	Generalized Anxiety Disorder	
	Social Anxiety, Separation Anxiety	Social Anxiety Disorder, Separation Anxiety Disorder	
	Non-clinical Phobias	Social Phobias, Specific Phobias	
	Trauma	Post-traumatic Stress Disorder	
		Panic Attacks, Chronic Panic Disorder	
		Obsessive Compulsive Disorder	
Mood Disorders	Minor Depressive Disorder	Major Depressive Disorder	
		Bipolar Disorder	
Personality Disorders (PD)		Paranoid Personality Disorder, Anti Social Personality Disorder, Borderline Personality Disorder, Histrionic Personality Disorder, Narcissistic Personality Disorder, Avoidant Personality Disorder, Dependent Personality Disorder	

(Figure 2.1 contd.)

(Figure 2.1 contd.)

Psychotic Disorders	Brief Psychotic Disorder	Delusional Disorders	Schizophrenia
Eating Disorders	Mild Anorexia Nervosa / Mild Bulimia Nervosa	Severe Anorexia Nervosa / Severe Bulimia Nervosa	
Impulse Control Disorders	Addiction / Kleptomania		
Substance Use Disorders	Substance Dependence / Substance Abuse		
Adjustment Disorder	Adjustment Disorder		
Sleep Disorders	Insomnia		
Somatoform Disorders	Hysteria / Hypochondria		
Factitious Disorders	Münchausen syndrome		
Dissociative Disorders	Dissociative Identity Disorder / Dissociative Amnesia		
Developmental Disorders		Mental Retardation / Learning Disorders / Autism Spectrum Disorders / Attention Disorders	
Cognitive Disorders	Delirium		Dementia

Source: Author's own from various sources.

of women's experiences and their living realities. The history of comfort-providing, distress-alleviating activities among women seems innocuous enough on the face of it—that is, women come together, formally or informally, in the face of adversity, to solve physical and emotional problems. This history also reveals the areas and experiences that repeat themselves as major causal factors in complicating and convoluting the lives of women, suggesting that if all women go through these experiences models of solutions should be easy. The sheer frequency of particular sufferings has produced home-grown remedial therapies from within women's groups (in the family, community, and religious setting) that have brought temporary relief but sometimes permanent damage to many. Problem-solving and solution-seeking for women's problems is ridden with more complexities than it is for men and yet it is either neglected or dismissed all too easily as a temporary aberration that could be patched up by 'friends and family'. The reasons lie almost the world over in the way women and their roles have been perceived and regimented at each level of their existence and living realities and the way they themselves see themselves in their lives.

Some analysts have viewed the stresses and strains of 'modern' women who have a family *and* contribute to family earnings as if it were a new phenomenon, resulting from the demands of the industrial society and its effect on the lives of families and individuals. The fact is that women have always had to juggle their different roles in life (work and family life), and to put up with all the resulting tension of this juggling. But whereas in earlier equations prescriptive roles governed perceptions of women and made their 'handling' easier for those in charge, in the new scenario, with women functioning in uncharted territories and supposedly invading male bastions of activity, the 'handling' of women had taken ugly twists and turns. The need and requirement for strategically relevant interventions for coping effectively with new strains and tensions has emerged out of this history. The place of feminist agendas in these transformations cannot be ignored.

As just discussed, and contrary to what may be apparent, women's experiences are far more varied than those of men and their problems and conflicts come from many more areas of engagement than they do for men. And even here there is no uniformity; the multiplicity of situations and circumstances faced by women baffles those who would like to homogenize women's experiences. The task is that of addressing women's problems at several levels and bringing them within the ambit of counselling in order that they may be analysed more comprehensively and without stereotyping: this task has been affected by some factors associated with feminism as a movement. Some feminists (and others too who may not be feminists) are deeply suspicious of the value and role of counselling because it is seen as part and parcel of a world that is steeped in patriarchal and hierarchical attitudes. Far from being an empowering activity, the counsellor–client relationship is seen by some feminists as yet another form of hierarchy where solutions are sought within accepted traditional forms of patriarchal functioning that brings marginal changes without rocking the boat. This has a great impact on how counselling is viewed and planned for 'traditional' societies where images of womanhood might still be wrapped up in appealing metaphors to conceal the interest-oriented chains of command.

Two specific areas of engagement have thus affected the way that counselling as an activity has been shaped to make it less nebulous and more productive: (*a*) feminist thinking about counselling and (*b*) the (success and failure) of the legal machinery as a provider of succour and relief for those (in this case women) in need.

(a) The value of feminist counselling may not be dismissed. It brings a dimension to counselling as an activity without which counselling for women would be both deficient and dishonest. The many resulting attempts made by concerned persons to break the implication in women's lives of rigid biological determinism that injects concepts of 'inferior' and 'superior' into relationships surrounding women's lives are still looked at with mixed feelings by the protagonists of the status quo. Without compromising the goal of strengthening women, feminist counselling would also need to not throw the 'baby with the bathwater' and perform a role in which for instance the 'typical values' associated with men and women (*assertiveness* for men and *caring* for women) are not dismissed as humbug qualities in themselves by society; and that there would be an attempt to work towards a society in which caring and assertiveness are regarded as *equally* valuable, one not being considered inferior to the other.

(b) Just as feminism has shaped the parameters of counselling for women both in suggesting what feminism offered and where it went too far, the role (or lack of it) of law and justice as sites for seeking help in case of trouble and distress has also affected the enhancement and fine-tuning of counselling for particular groups that are referred to here as vulnerable (see pp. 41–52 on domestic violence). The theoretical claim of the law to be homogeneous, and universal across class, caste, gender, race, religion or region has in practice proved problematic for the upholders of the law; they are constantly faced in their line of duty for instance with images of women's real lives that are rife with experiences of gender inequality, and the efforts to fit these into the gender-neutral images of the law they uphold is one of the most challenging tasks they face, and which they discharge not always equitably.

In the Indian or indeed the South Asian context, the traditional images of women have been a neat fit in social functioning, and many women have been able to accommodate features of modernity alongside their customary roles and functions as carers. Many women assert clearly that they do not feel the kind of clashes in their day-to-day lives that their feminist advisers believe they do. Unfortunately there are clashes and they appear when their coping abilities are challenged by the adversities and oppressions that inevitably arise from the patriarchal structures that define their lives. A controlling husband who sets the mood and temper of the household returns home drunk and becomes violent. A demanding mother-in-law decides to taunt her about not having brought enough by way of dowry. A flirtatious brother-in-law molests her whenever he finds her alone. All these become the way of life for her before she knows it and the same coping abilities that she relied on for mundane living begin to give way. Life is then full of contradictions and upheavals and the question of where to turn becomes primary. The community only helps the way they know best: grin and bear it. But the point at which the hurt and pain becomes unbearable is the moment when neutral intervention becomes an imperative. There is the law and its machinery (to be treated separately as we will show later) that provides remedies that the woman must gear herself for, and there is professional counselling that provides the strength to seek recourse in the law and to the remedies that the law may or may not recommend. To avail of the law's remedies the women would need to be apprised of the consequences of the steps the law recommends. Separation from a violent husband may be a good legal remedy, but for a woman whose awareness of the law and its procedures is as scant as the results of the legal action, there would be an urgent need to be counselled about how she would have to alter the tenor of her life completely. Professional counselling would be the enabling motor that would give her the confidence to make the choices and decisions that would show her the way, some way.

What has posed problems for those who claim and have the power to give women the deal they deserve and need (traditional and official actors) is their inability to perceive in depth the multiple realities of the roles of women in society. Women operate at levels that are both more numerous than, and different from, the levels that men do, despite the widely held belief that men as income-generators are exposed to far greater risks and perils than women. Women's arenas are both extensive and intensive and the performance demands on them can have greater adverse affects on them than is acknowledged. Women are full-time players in the many social groups of which they are a part (family, caste, community, geographic area—district, village, etc.), the economic structures in which they have prescribed roles, the regional activity in areas where they live, on issues—such as health, religion, child-bearing and rearing, and so on. Their positive feelings are, however, eroded by society's discounting and invalidating of the crucial roles they play.

The specific failure of existing formal mechanisms to give due place to these multiple arenas and roles in the first instance when addressing women's distress is the moment at which the space is created for the development of those appropriate mechanisms and instruments for intervention that would address the ruptures and fissures that develop when women (indeed anyone) cannot cope. One such instrument is counselling, as a properly constructed agenda-free, non-manipulative activity that takes full cognisance of all aspects of the lives of women. Although it did not develop as a response to women's needs, its constructive role in the lives of women increased in intensity as women's areas of engagement increased.

The structure and process of the counselling model that any organization would design and build would be influenced by many factors. A fuller idea about the problems women experience and wish/need to be counselled for might be obtained from the following features relating to women and the society they belong to:

- The general perception of women in a particular society;
- The self-perception of women in that society; and
- A straightforward list of the experiences gathered in counselling forums and complaints cells about the problems and complaints that women bring.

The amount of flexibility and creativity required to respond effectively to the needs of women needs to be taken on board when the conceptual content and techniques and skills for counselling women are placed in an organizational model. Women's counselling organizations can be broadly classified and structured according to the kind of needs and demands they are able to address.

The different ways in which the counselling function is expressed in the case of women defines *the nature of the service* that a particular organizational model offers.

1. Some organizational models have the provision of a therapy and counselling service for distressed and anxious women as a primary function. They could work individually or in groups, and the service they offer could be called counselling, psychotherapy or therapy groups. The subjects they address range from depression to acute anxiety disorders, including event-related problems such as abortion, rape, etc.

2. There are also organizations where counselling accompanies other assistance that is offered as a response to specific demands related sometimes to a particular crisis or predicament. Counselling is offered side by side with the service of suggesting legal options, or offering mediation and alternative dispute resolution.

3. Then there are organized groups that make use of counselling skills clarifying at the same time that the volunteers and workers who are using these skills are not (technically) 'counsellors', although they do undergo some training in suitable and appropriate skills to be a listening and supporting service. They are thus equipped to work in one-to-one situations and also in groups. In such settings, suitable training can be designed and incorporated to assist the nature of this (para)counselling service.

An important feature of services that offer counselling and/or other responses to women's problems is the realization that comes with developed understandings of how most issues in women's lives are inevitably interlinked. Women's problems have shown the necessity of responding to women as 'whole people' (Perry, 1993). A woman with a marital problem, for instance, would need to be viewed beyond her role as a wife. In the South Asian context, her location in a joint family, in her religious group and the caste/ community of which she is an intrinsic part would colour any account of a marital crisis. The sociocultural scene and its impact on women and their potential in that society, perceptions about their strengths and weaknesses both general and within particular relationships, views about the importance of their health and education would all be brought within the ambit of the counselling programme as features to be studied and trained in. The interlinking of issues will become increasingly apparent as details about areas such as depression, abuse of women, etc. are revealed.

Related to this is the fact that counselling and/or any intervention in women's problems cannot proceed without adequate observation of the criss-crossing of the different oppressions experienced by women: class, caste, race and gender intersect in complex ways and in a manner that would need to be thoroughly analysed with would-be counsellors to understand just how these oppressions affect the modalities of women's lives, making them respond the way they do under pressure. This is not superfluous to the mediation/counselling process given the fact that the counsellor and client may come from different positions and locations and any slurring over nuances here would lead to imperfect counselling or counselling-in-mediation.

A brief word about 'feminist therapy' which has been discussed in detail in Chapter 3: While we have placed the feminist approach alongside the repertoire of theoretical approaches to counselling and suggested that it would influence the actual activity of counselling by designing its substance and content and determining the skills that would be used, its more important function is that it plays a vital role in the process of building a society that does not yet exist. One writer rightly states that it is not possible to go beyond a certain point in the changes we advocate for women and their development. 'It is difficult to be healthy in an unhealthy society. ... There are so many contradictory messages being conveyed to women today ... no wonder so many of us are neurotic' (Chaplin, 1988: 16).

Feminist counselling would need to be carefully worked through in the general counselling processes and techniques and supplement the other approaches. There is no one 'feminist approach': feminist counselling can be radical, humanistic, socialistic, or spiritual: it can be many things that would need to be worked out by the counsellor. Some features would, however, be common to all situations (like the implications of hierarchical thinking) and some would need to be worked through in the particular context in which it is required (women in custody). Some writers refer to the tendency to incorporate different varieties of feminism as part of the 'second-wave feminism' which, simply stated, suggests the central importance of women's experiences in formulating any theory (see Perry [1993: 101] and Humm [1992]).

A few words here about the status of counselling in general for women. Despite changes that have made counselling an acceptable and expanding activity/profession over the last decade, especially for women whom the formal justice machinery fails miserably as a result of archaic attitudes and expectations, scepticism still surrounds the activity of counselling. This scepticism stems from several factors that are political in nature. Often both in independent counselling projects and counselling forums within larger (women's) organizations when funds need to be reconsidered or cuts made, the axe falls on counselling services. The arguments are rationalized for economic reasons including the argument that counselling serves no purpose in the general uplifting of all of society. It is seen as an ineffective and inconsequential palliative and not worth the resources it takes up.

As part of the political belief that finds it difficult to rethink its attitudes about the value of nearly 50 per cent of its population, constituting women, such arguments are unable to recognize or acknowledge the extent of women's real sufferings and the extent to which they are discriminated against. The ability to justify for instance that spending money on counselling for women who suffer violence in the home is out of order because it is a domestic matter is only one of the absurdities of the aforementioned position.

As later discussions will demonstrate, counselling when viewed simplistically as advising or guiding inevitably produces cynical reactions, born out of a general ignorance about counselling as psychotherapy. This is accompanied by an ignorance of and indifference to the gravity of the problems that counselling is intended to address in ordinary women's lives. The mind of a woman, it is often said, is not a priority anywhere and more so in cultures where traditional mores have a role to play in society.

A few things need to be underlined to highlight the problems of adequate emphasis being placed on oppressions in women's lives, which are as follows:

- That many of the problematic situations that women are exposed and subjected to neither could nor do occur in the lives of men.
- That differentials in the oppressions that different women face in the same society can produce problematic categories that are as dissimilar from each other as chalk and cheese.

While there are shared understandings and common strategies for resistance and/or confrontation that need to be drawn up when women seek assistance in oppression-ridden situations, the nuances of situations and circumstances that make each case dissimilar would also need to be worked through in structuring counselling strategies and preparing mediators and counsellors for their work as interveners.

This is probably an appropriate juncture at which to make a few cautionary observations that pertain to women as victims. In this area (handling of women as victims), the approaches logically range from interventions by the law and justice machinery to counselling and healing therapy. As stated earlier, myriads of women are petrified of the legal system's ramifications—both procedural and consequential. Victims of rape, sexual molestation and domestic violence have grave reservations of reliving their experiences publicly in courts of law. They need forums that give them some privacy and serenity to talk about what they went through and what they might do to heal their wounds and move forward. Counselling steps in to offer just that, although that too can pose problems if approached with single or multiple agendas. If the aim and purpose of the exercise is ideological or political and it is carried out with the superficial skills that do not take the complexities of particular situations and the heterogeneity of particular disorders into account, not much good would come out of the exercise.

This might be best demonstrated through the example of domestic violence—a widely experienced phenomenon among a majority of the women we encountered both in conflict resolution situations and in custody. Dichotomized positions based on ideological stances are often worked into the framework within which domestic violence cases are placed. On the one side is the pathological view that views cases of domestic violence as instances of individual/family abnormality or deviation that needs interventions that address a perpetrator's deviance and a victim's vulnerability. On the other side is the patriarchal viewpoint increasingly activated in all such cases that sees the whole issue of domestic violence as rooted in patriarchal social structures that presumably support and encourage individual men to maintain their status, control and privilege in the home through various forms of dominance including emotional and physical abuse. The nature of the remedial intervention that follows has the potential to be distorted and made ineffective if the problem is placed exclusively in the one or the other domain. It could be a mix of both and much more.

Unfortunately, while domestic violence (also known as 'intimate partner abuse' in the literature on the subject in the West) has been recognized as a problematic in most societies, the problems of handling set out earlier have not found easy solutions. Law enforcement responses are usually 'top of the list' as remedial measures—policy changes, laws and courts, social service organizations and professional mental health interventions. The distinctions and categorizations in this approach are somewhat simplistic in these responses—looking at perpetrators and victims in which the one needs incarceration or punitive handling and the other refuge, shelter or related therapy.

While the volume of research and the debate on the subject of domestic violence is phenomenal in the West, there is a paucity of evidence-based material in the South Asian context. It has been suggested that the pervasiveness of feminist ideology has thwarted the efforts of practitioner-therapists in arriving at appropriate models for suitable intervention in domestic violence cases: the 'one-size-fits-all' model with patriarchy as its prime mover often proves to be counterproductive in the quest for the appropriate therapeutic model. (See Hamel and Nicholls [2007] for some interesting analyses and perspectives albeit from a Western perspective.)

Domestic violence in the context and region we are discussing (South Asia) is a category of oppression that women are subjected to with a frequency and intensity that varies according to class, caste, religion, sub-region, and from situation to situation. Women are often prone to dividing themselves into (undeclared) groups depending both on the intensity, degree and circumstances of the oppression that they are subjected to on the domestic front. The realisation that regardless of its intensity, magnitude and so-called reasons and circumstances domestic violence is a violation of the dignity and respect of a human being that flouts every principle of human dignity and of the right to be human gets underplayed in this classification. Unfortunately, domestic violence is an area of inquiry and exploration that is more often than not relegated to a back burner in many societies and more so in ours where custom and legality conflict to produce results that are obviously more than damaging for women and for the society we live in. The reasons are as distressing as the act itself: The International Institute for Population Studies figures show that almost 56 per cent of Indian women believe wife beating is justified in certain circumstances. A wife looks upon certain aspects of housekeeping as her primary role and duty (sham powers referred to earlier at the beginning of this chapter) and believes non-performance would merit punitive measures. Neglecting household chores or children, failing to provide a proper meal or now in urban environs watching television are regarded as adequate reasons for instigating the husband's fury. Add to that the fact that the woman's own parental family members never encourage her to leave the marital family. Victims invariably deny abuse and are able to do so easily since it is usually in the privacy of their homes.

The following conversation with 'S' demonstrates the victim's own perception in cases of some quite common cases of domestic violence.

Q. Your lip is swollen and bruised and there is a blue and black scar around your waist. What happened? Would you like to talk about it?

A. What is there to talk about? There was a quarrel yesterday and my husband hit me.

Q. And you don't consider that a violation of your respect or dignity apart from the fact that it is against the law.

A. This is a common feature where I come from. All my *sahelis* [friends] have similar experiences. With some it gets out of hand when the man is drunk, otherwise it is part of life. Some of my friends have broken bones because their husbands beat them in a drunken state.

Q. What triggers the violence in your case?

A. Well, if his dinner is not ready on time or it is cold or not to his satisfaction he first throws it away and if I make the slightest comment about why he did that he strikes me saying '*Tumhari ye majaal ki tum jawaab deti ho*' ['You have the nerve to answer back']. And if I should give one more reply he goes into my entire history with rude comments about my parents and upbringing and what a lousy deal he got with hardly any dowry.

Q. Are you aware that he is committing an offence if he treats you with violence or any kind of brutality? There is a law about these things now.

A. What will the law do? We have lived like this for generations. Where was the law all these years when everyone said that this was part of a woman's *kismet* [destiny] and that a woman is a man's property to do with her as he wished?

Q. Yes, that was then, but now the law is in place and you can report this kind of violence to the police and they will take action.

A. Police will help a woman! You are joking of course. And then where will I go? Tell me. To my *maika ghar* [parental home]? We all know that does not happen and once a woman marries she never returns to her parental home. '*Izzat ke khilaaf hai*' [It is against everyone's respect].

The conversation goes on but the underlying sentiment is the same: that this is part of being married and it could be worse.

The question and answer session above could be analysed within a framework set out by Geldard and Geldard (2003) to illustrate the way a helpful conversation evolves and thereby ascertain the quality of the skills that have been used and how they might be improved. (See Annexure A on helping a person to identify the central problem.) Focusing on the central problem needs delicate skills to clear the person's confused state of mind and get them to state the quandary that they constantly find themselves in when faced with a situation like domestic violence. Usually asking too many questions may not be a good idea, but if it leads to the person focusing on the central problem and aquainting them with the inner conflicts they are facing then some question and answer sessions are useful. In this case, it would be the tussle between the custom of staying in a marital home despite abuse and the law that provides a remedy. A counselling session can be the route through which the person is apprised of what she may not have known vis-à-vis the law on domestic violence.

Most of the countries of the South Asian region have now enacted laws on domestic violence and their legislations have been influenced considerably by the United Nations Declaration on Elimination of Violence against Women (DEVAW, validated in 1993). The definition of domestic violence in DEVAW covers physical, sexual and psychological or emotional violence within the family and includes beating, battering, sexual abuse of women and children in the family, marital rape, genital mutilation and other practices harmful to women, dowry-related violence and violence related to other exploitations.

Legislation in the different countries of South Asia differs. In the Indian legislation (2005), the focus of protection is women and does not include other vulnerable groups such as elderly and disabled persons, or domestic servants, such as the legislatures in

Sri Lanka and Bangladesh. Pakistan's Prevention of Domestic Violence Act 2008 covers some features that are present in the Indian legislation and in DEVAW and like the Sri Lankan enactment also includes in the Act some parts of the Penal Code that may relate to domestic violence.[2]

Domestic violence received some recognition as a criminal offence in India before the specific domestic violence legislation of 2005, when Section 498A was introduced into the Indian Penal Code (IPC) through Act 46 of 1983. It was the first time that subjecting a woman to cruelty (by her husband or relative of the husband) was given such importance and above all mental cruelty got the significance it deserved.[3] There were many reasons why this would be insufficient to protect women from the kind of violence they suffered within the confines of their homes: It provided for some punitive measures against the perpetrator but hardly gave a woman the security she needed to continue with her life. Much more was needed. Women have been enduring domestic violence out of a sense of insecurity, shame and lack of choices. Often the rearing of children is a reason that prevents them from even thinking of leaving the marital home, no matter how degrading the treatment meted out may be. And there were no rights that she could assert to stay in the marital home. It took more than 20 years of active agitation by well-meaning lawyers and activists to get for women what they had needed all along in their own homes: protection all round.

The Protection of Women from Domestic Violence Act 2005 became an Act of parliament from 26 October 2006. Its primary purpose was to provide protection to a wife or live-in partner from domestic violence at the hands of the husband or male live-in partner or his relatives. Domestic violence includes actual abuse or the threat of abuse whether *physical, sexual, verbal, emotional or economic* (emphasis added). Harassment for dowry was also covered under the definition.[4]

For our present discussion two features are significant, one general and the other specific. Generally the fact that so prevalent and odious a practice was now getting legal attention may be considered laudable even if long overdue. However, the same prevalence and invisibility of the practice made sure it was not going to disappear just because an Act had been passed by parliament. Women still needed to be otherwise encouraged to come forward to talk about their personal experiences, something the women of this region in particular were not likely to be persuaded to do easily. The 'blue bruises' syndrome referred to earlier in the case of 'S' is a common feature, particularly of married women's lives in more than 60 per cent of South Asian homes.

More specifically, the inclusion of *verbal and emotional abuse* in the definition of domestic violence was significant. As with 'mental cruelty' referred to earlier (Section 498A), emotional abuse has never been a focus in any list of abuses that needed to be addressed at any level in our society, least of all at the domestic level. Unfortunately, the degree to which women are subjected to emotional abuse and the damage it inflicts on their psyche cannot be measured in any conclusive visible way. It does, however, manifest itself in one-to-one counselling sessions when women decide to come forward to share and lessen their grief. That is the site where encouragement can be given to enable women to come forward to avail themselves of the protection offered by laws and statutes where possible. The women who suffer these atrocities are not the ones who would come forward to fight in law courts for their rights.[5]

Domestic violence may or may not overlap with sexual violence. The collection (also referred to as a 'continuum') of sexual crimes that women are subjected to range from rape, sexual molestation, sexual harassment, sexual assault and other forms of sexual violence. There is much statistical, descriptive and analytical literature on the many forms of sexual crimes and it is not within the scope of our study to discuss each at length. Some references are given in the Notes of this chapter and at the end of the book. Sections 375 and 376 of the IPC set out what constitutes rape (with exceptions) and what are the punishments. Sexual harassment does not have any recognition as an offence in the IPC. It has usually been addressed through legal sections that are concerned either with how the harassment affects the public domain or how it violates images of the ideal woman rather than with the woman as person. Implicit in Sections 294 (relating to obscenity), 354 (outraging a woman's modesty) and 509 (insulting the modesty of a woman) are all the moral overtones of behavioural norms to be observed by a woman. If a woman's modesty is 'insulted' or 'outraged', she obviously failed to safeguard it adequately.[6]

Without elaborating on all the forms of crimes in the continuum of sexual violence, two—rape and sexual harassment—are being discussed as the most common and universal occurrences everywhere in the world regardless of class, age, race, religion or region. Attitudes to both have a trajectory that is more similar than different in most societies although the intervention of the law is slower in some contexts than others and non-existent because not used in still others (South Asia).

THE CASE OF 'P'

'P', a personal acquaintance of counsellors, is a case in point. No legal remedy and no counselling left this victim of rape by a relative scarred for life. (Counsellors' analysis can be referred to in the Notes of this chapter.[7])

'P' was 17 when the incident occurred. She is the youngest of four sisters. 'K', the eldest, was 30 and had been married to 'M' at the age of 20. The families live in the same neighbourhood, and visits by K's sisters to her home were a frequent occurrence. M was a flirt and K's parents were very careful not to expose the other daughters to his indiscretions. On one occasion, when the parents were out, M went across to P's house and took her out for a treat. She foolishly consented (he was after all a 'relative'), and before she knew it he took her to a secluded home and raped her.

P said nothing to the family out of shock and shame and before long she became visibly pregnant, much to the horror of her parents. Her parents were traumatized by it all and out of their depth about what to do. An uncle was taken into confidence and he escorted the mother and daughter to another town, where P gave birth to a stillborn and when the 'mess' was cleared up they returned to their hometown. The involved family members were sworn to secrecy and in due course a spouse was found for P and she was married. For the entire world things were normal and life moved on.

The reality was that P never actually recovered from the rape incident. She cultivated an overtly gregarious personality to assure herself she was popular because she was attractive and could talk incessantly with everyone she met. She visited the sister's home frequently and brazenly faced her rapist (without speaking with him) and considered herself normal as she did this. But every now and then she would have an occurrence that was referred to as a 'breakdown' and she would go under and no one in her nuclear family knew why. Others who knew kept mum—it was not a subject that ever surfaced. But P became a highly strung paranoid who could never take criticism of any kind from anyone and she clearly needed help. Years passed and while the incident had been brushed under the carpet there was no way it had been wiped clean on P's slate. She prided herself in being pretty and cultivated that feature of herself above all else. It never struck anyone that she needed counselling and therapeutic help (professional and confidential) probably because there was nothing of that kind available and known about in the Indian environment then. And this was the kind of thing that was never exposed to the world anyway. It was a source of shame.

She is a grandmother now and will carry all her baggage to her grave. The 'rapist' is dead and no one talks about him. His deeds have been obliterated with his death. But P has a personality disorder and is unable to cope with adversity or unforeseen events in life and takes the option of having a 'nervous breakdown' every now and then. She is then fussed over and comes out of it in a few days but she clearly still has problems.

Just as domestic violence, once granted the sanctity of being a 'private matter' (*'ghar ka mamla'*), was relocated in penal law as violence against the person of the woman, sexual harassment and rape are being subjected to the same scrutiny to make them an offence per se rather than an instrument for gendered norms. The male perception that hitherto (mis)defined the shape of the laws that related to crimes against women has been subjected to rigorous interrogation by women's movements. Making the modesty of a woman the main object of protection *in public* (354 and 509) only perpetuates the gendered logic of control and regulation that has a profound effect on women's self-perceptions. Apart from demanding conformity and orthodoxy for women's behaviour for purposes of management and control, such laws have an in-built obstructionist feature in them that blocks any chance of empowering women to see themselves as more than the roles they have been assigned in each society. *Izzat, sharam* and *aabroo* (variants of the words 'shame' and 'honour') are words that all women in the region are familiar with for they define the compliance that is expected of 'decent' women and willy-nilly enters their handling at the hands of the implementing machinery of justice.

In addition to the law then there is the implementing machinery of the law that should have a significant part to play in empowering women. Police, courts and prisons have all sprinkled their implementational rules and techniques with features of gender equality that do not really alter the status-ridden perceptions of women in any substantive way. Police stations have gender sensitized themselves by having enough women police officers to handle women complainants/victims physically and emotionally (through 'counselling') and offering opportunities for mediation and reconciliation for victims supposedly to save them further trauma. Such services by the same personnel that have powers of arrest, detention and custody seem a sham and fail to address the imbalances that lead to the victimization in the first place. Such a façade may address allegations relating to women being turned away from lodging complaints and receiving some attention at police stations; but more than that it helps to keep the station's crimes-against-women figures down, thereby enhancing the station's performance record. New laws without meaningful corresponding modes of implementation bring women back to square one.

Rape is defined in Section 375 of the IPC and placed in the category of sexual offences by Act 43 of 1983. Though definitions vary in different jurisdictions, fundamentally rape is sexual intercourse or other forms of sexual penetration of one person by another person without the consent of the victim. In some jurisdictions, rape covers only acts involving penile penetration of the vagina and all other types of non-consensual sexual activity are sexual assault. Section 375 does not include acts of forced oral sex, sodomy or penetration by foreign objects: such acts are criminalized by Section 354 ('criminal assault on a woman with intent to outrage her modesty') and Section 377 ('carnal intercourse against the order of nature'). The exception in the Act provides that 'sexual intercourse by a man with his wife, the wife not being under fifteen years of age, is not rape'. Section 376 that sets out the punishments for rape ('not less than seven years but which may be for life or for a term which may extend to ten years') also makes the exception: 'unless the woman raped is his own wife and is not under the age of twelve years of age, in which case he shall be punished with imprisonment for a term which may extend to two years or with fine or with both'.

The two sections set out interpretations that can be misleading: (*a*) that if the wife is not underage (below 15), *the intercourse is not rape* (Section 375) and (*b*) that *if the woman 'raped' is his wife* and not below 12, the punishment will be imprisonment, or fine or both (Section 376) (emphasis added). The operative terminology in 376 is 'if the woman raped is his wife' and it may be assumed that the act fits the six descriptions of rape in Section 375 and is therefore punishable, but with a lesser punishment.

The law's inadequacy relating to the definition of rape and especially to marital rape is the subject of debate at several levels in South Asia. Changes that may have come have not, however, addressed squarely the issues of (*a*) marital rape and (*b*) all other forms of penetration.[8] Historically the concept of 'conjugal rights' within marriage underlay all discussions related to rape in marriage. In course of time the accelerated pace of a human rights and feminist discourses shook the belief in the marital right to sexual relations and more importantly in the exemption of marital rape from rape laws. The UN DEWAV (1993) established marital rape as a human rights violation.

In countries where the Islamic law coexists with secular laws, the dilemmas become more serious. The sections of the IPC (discussed earlier) were the framework for legal positions on the subject for most of the South Asian region. In Pakistan, the Women's Protection Bill was passed in 2006 to move the prosecution of rape cases from the *Hudood* Ordinance to Pakistan's secular penal code, to enable judges to try rape cases in criminal courts instead of Islamic Courts. The need for multiple male witnesses to a rape to prosecute was done away with as also the sentence of death for consensual premarital sex, for which the penalty was to be five-year imprisonment. Marital rape remains excluded from the category called 'rape'.

A new law on sexual abuse, 'The Sexual Offences Special Courts Bill', is proposed in India that proposes to treat sexual abuse on par with rape, which means that punishment for both will be equally stringent (the present punishment for sexual abuse is a maximum of two years). Sexual abuse will be defined to include not just physical abuse but also mental harassment, and the onus to prove that a suicide was not due to sexual harassment lies with the accused. All cases of sexual abuse are to be dealt with by special courts and cleared within a period from six months to a year.

The remedial power of the relatively new and still developing legal measures enumerated in the earlier pages must not be overrated in the context we have been discussing. To avail themselves of what the law offers, the women in question would need to have every set of consequences of an action set out for them in unequivocal terms. If the legal remedy is separation from a violent husband, the ramifications to the personal life of the particular woman would need to be spelt out and her own views on her strength and capabilities determined.

The most important facet of this is the demonstration by mediators and counsellors that modes of intervention that bring some empowerment and negotiability (two features that are absent from the lives of women from birth) are crucial for *all* such cases. Similarly, it is now recognized in some cases that the disempowerment of the perpetrators is not the solution, even as empowerment is being sought for victimized women.

In the aforementioned case of 'P', legal help was not an option. It was an act of shame all round, and the family could not take recourse to anything that would have exposed the incident and then come under public scrutiny. Therapeutic counselling confidentially carried out might have made some difference to 'P' and her family, but one would never know—professional counselling of the kind we are studying now was not there as part of any remedial system. The blot may not have been wiped clean, but the persons may have coped better.

It would be an incomplete discourse that does not place, particularly for the informed and initiated, the potential limitations of counselling regardless of the worth that is attributed to it. Counselling women in distress is not intended to be a general or specific panacea for what are repeatedly and correctly referred to as the 'social stressors' that act on women's lives from very early ages. The social deprivations and discriminations that are characteristic of bringing up girl children in India (and all of South Asia), and of Indian women's lives generally, leave them in a strange moral predicament that can hardly be resolved through counselling. Davar's excellent exposé lucidly sets out the paradoxes surrounding the philosophy of *care* (a *non-contractual* aspect of the human experience), a quality lauded among women for its 'other-affirming role', but containing within it a politics of allocation that leaves women devoid of negotiability even within the settings in which they exercise their caring functions.

> High caring + low negotiability, that is adherence to a philosophy of Care at the cost of a 'rights' orientation, can be psychologically taxing, even though the philosophy of Care may arguably be an experientially and morally superior alternative. (Davar, 1999: 209)

There are, says Davar, moral affects associated with the perspective of care (shame and guilt when accused of non-performance, for instance) that could well be termed the 'psychological cost' of caring (they are predominant in depression). In the case of women, they are associated with blameworthiness, and the whole process imperceptibly points to 'control'—in the case of women towards conformity within the patriarchal set-up.

So what kind of intervention does counselling offer to women who need to be addressed as 'individuals', but also as the women who come with all the difficulties of their social baggage, and above all with the depression that accompanies the guilt and shame that haunts their every act when they do not fully toe the line (including the commission of a legal offence)? This is a question that should arise at each point in the somewhat clinical layout of the counselling process that follows. Should and can counselling in the Indian (and South Asian) context really be carried out and promoted the way it is universally defined: should and can the moral and political questions be sidelined? Is it really client-centred counselling if, while we supposedly seek to empower the women who come to be enabled to 'cope' or 'handle' the difficult situations they face all through their lives and not just in crises, we are not able to provide the one feature they have never learnt—negotiability.

So while subscribing to some universal principles of counselling, a greater emphasis has been placed on the context that requires the addressing of some common distress situations surrounding women by facing and handling them not only as the individuals they have the potential to be, but as the social beings that they are, where they are. The social circumstances (deprived social experiences) of most women cannot be shied away from and perhaps the interventions we are seeking would therefore need to have a general reformative component in addition to the elements that are event/incident based.

No discussion about women and counselling would be complete without a mention of the ethical factor in counselling. We have suggested in the sections on the definitions and process of counselling that judgement, prejudice, bias, interest, subjectivity, partisanship and ideological political leanings have to be consciously set aside in counselling. In the case of women, there is a danger that all of these features do somehow get subsumed in the *approach* and then affect the *process*. However, it is also being suggested that counselling therapy devoid of ethics (read 'principles' rather than 'morals') would be too clinical, soulless and therefore pointless.

NOTES

1. The two established and most frequently referred to systems that classify mental disorders are:

    (i) International Classification of Diseases (ICD-10, Chapter V) produced by the World Health Organization (WHO)
    (ii) Diagnostic and Statistical Manual of Mental Disorders (DSM IV) by the American Psychiatric Association (APA)

    The ICD-10, as it is widely known, is an international standard diagnostic classification for a wide variety of health conditions. Chapter V of the document on mental and behavioural disorders covers 10 main groups, with each group having subcategories:

    - F0: Organic, including symptomatic, mental disorders
    - F1: Mental and behavioural disorders due to use of psychoactive substances
    - F2: Schizophrenia, schizotypal and delusional disorders
    - F3: Mood [affective] disorders
    - F4: Neurotic, stress-related and somatoform disorders
    - F5: Behavioural syndromes associated with physiological disturbances and physical factors
    - F6: Disorders of personality and behaviour in adult persons
    - F7: Mental retardation
    - F8: Disorders of psychological development
    - F9: Behavioural and emotional disorders with onset usually occurring in childhood and adolescence
    - In addition, a group of 'unspecified mental disorders'

    It is currently being revised for an ICD-11 to address some sections, for example, F6 on personality disorders which are problematic for some analysts who question their placement alongside other mental disorders. The ICD-10 does not look at mental disorders with the exactitude that the DSM does and implies 'the existence of a clinically recognisable set of symptoms or behaviours associated in most cases with distress and with interference with personal functions' (WHO, 1992).

    The DSM IV attempts to address the 'whole' individual by using a multi-axial or multidimensional approach to diagnosis. It tries to account for the fact that in order to intervene in a mental disorder, the affected individual needs to be considered from a variety of perspectives. Thus, the individual is assessed across five axes:

(i) *Clinical Disorders*: Axis I describes the principal disorder that requires immediate clinical attention (e.g. a major depressive episode or an exacerbation of schizophrenia).

(ii) *Personality Disorders and Mental Retardation*: Axis II indicates any personality disorders that may not require immediate care but should be taken into account as it may be complicating individual's response to the Axis I problem. Axis II also indicates any developmental disorders such as mental retardation that may be predisposing the individual to the Axis I problem (e.g. an individual with paranoid personality disorder or severe mental retardation may be more likely to succumb to a major depressive episode).

(iii) *General Medical Conditions*: Axis III lists any medical or neurological conditions (e.g. diabetes, hyperthyroidism, brain injury, HIV/AIDS) that should be taken into account because they may play a role in the development, persistence or exacerbation of Axis I and II disorders or have symptoms or side effects that may be similar to and mistaken for Axis I and II disorders.

(iv) *Psychosocial and Environmental Stressors*: Axis IV specifies the major psychosocial stressors the individual has experienced (e.g. death of loved one, divorce, dysfunctional family, poverty), which can impact the Axis I and II disorders.

(v) *Global Assessment of Functioning*: Axis V rates the individual's level of function across various categories (e.g. social, occupational, academic and interpersonal) at the time of assessment, and their highest level of function within in the past year. This rating provides insight into how Axes I–IV are affecting the individual and what changes can be expected in the future (e.g. score of 10 indicates 'persistent danger of severely hurting self or others' and score of 100 indicates 'superior functioning in a wide range of activities').

With these axes for assessment, the main categories of disorder listed are as follows:

• Disorders first diagnosed in infancy, childhood or adolescence such as mental retardation and attention deficit hyperactivity disorder (ADHD).

• Delirium, dementia and amnesia and other cognitive disorders such as Alzheimer's disease.

• Mental disorders due to a general medical condition such as AIDS-related psychosis.

- Substance-related disorders such as alcohol abuse.
- Schizophrenia and other psychotic disorders, for example, delusional disorders.
- Mood disorders such as major depressive disorder and bipolar disorder.
- Anxiety disorders which are usually disorders caused by anxiety.
- Somatoform disorders that are disorders caused by somatization.
- Factitious disorders such as Munchausen disorder.
- Dissociative disorders, for example, dissociative identity disorder.
- Sexual and gender identity disorders such as dyspareunia, and gender identity disorder.
- Eating disorders, for example, anorexia nervosa and bulimia nervosa.
- Sleep disorders such as insomnia.
- Impulse control disorders such as kleptomania.
- Adjustment disorders.
- Personality disorders, for example, narcissistic personality disorder.

Other conditions are mentioned that are considered a focus of clinical attention such as tardive dyskinesia and child abuse.

2. Bangladesh's Prevention of Oppression against Women and Children Act, 2000, does not contain any specific definition of domestic violence. However, the *Law Commission of Bangladesh Report*, 2005, proposing a Domestic Violence Act in the country gives a definition to domestic violence as the commission of any or more than one of the acts that constitute: (*a*) physical abuse, (*b*) sexual abuse and (*c*) psychological abuse by any member of the family, excluding a child or handicapped adult, against any other member of the family.

What constitutes these abuses is spelt out in each section. Domestic servants form part of the legally recognized persons within the domestic sphere. Although it is a gender-neutral legislation, yet there are certain acts which are thought to be gender-specific, for example character blemish in case of a female member or, in case of a male member, torturing parents by a husband at the instigation of a wife.

Sri Lanka passed the Prevention of Domestic Violence Act in 2005. Chapter XVI of the Sri Lankan Penal Code is included in the Act as a part of what constitutes domestic violence which is a chapter on offences against the human body. A significant part of this Act is the emphasis on emotional abuse suggestive of concern for the individual woman.

Pakistan passed the Prevention of Domestic Violence Act 2008 in August 2009. This legislation resembles the Sri Lankan in that parts of the Pakistan Penal Code are included within the definition of domestic violence, besides adding the three other abuses that are a part of the Indian legislation. The Act covers (*a*) economic abuse, (*b*) emotional–psychological and verbal abuse and (*c*) sexual abuse and harassment. There is an attempt to define harassment in this legislation and that combines traditional and modern methods of harassing—telephone calls and emails. It is a different issue that to trace perpetrators of technologically advanced harassment is legally much more difficult.

Marital rape is not included in any of these legislations.

3. Cruelty was defined as

   (a) any wilful conduct which is of such a nature as is likely to drive a woman to commit suicide or to cause grave injury or danger to life, limb or health (whether mental or physical) of the woman; or

   (b) harassment of the woman where such harassment is with a view to coercing her or any person related to her to meet any unlawful demand for any property or valuable security or is on account of failure by her or any person related to her to meet such demand.

4. (1) For the purposes of this Act, any conduct of the respondent shall constitute domestic violence if he—(a) habitually assaults or makes the life of the aggrieved person miserable by cruelty of conduct even if such conduct does not amount to physical ill-treatment; or (b) forces the aggrieved person to lead an immoral life; or (c) otherwise injures or harms the aggrieved person. (2) Nothing contained in clause (c) of sub-section (1) shall amount to domestic violence if the pursuit of course of conduct by the respondent was reasonable for his own protection or for the protection of his or another's property.

5. The National Crime Records Bureau 2007 survey suggests an increase in crimes against women by 12.5 per cent over 2006 and 31.8 per cent over 2003. This is a section entitled 'Myths and Facts about Domestic Violence', clarifying that domestic violence is common the world over, including India; that the assailant is likely to be a family member; and that circumstances compel women to remain in violent domestic situations. Being economically dependent, women feel theirs is a life without options and they stay on in abusive relationships.

6. Section 294 of the IPC holds that 'Whoever, to the annoyance of others, (a) does any obscene act in any public place, or (b) sings, recites and utters any obscene songs, ballads or words, in or near any public

space, shall be punished with imprisonment of either description for a term that may extend to three months, or with fine, or with both.' This provision is included in Chapter XVI entitled 'Of Offences Affecting Public Health, Safety, Convenience and Morals' and is cognisable, bailable and triable by any magistrate.

Section 354 IPC: 'Whoever assaults or uses criminal force on any woman, intending to outrage her modesty or knowing it likely that he will thereby outrage her modesty, shall be punished with imprisonment for a term which may extend to two years, or with fine, or with both.'

Section 509: 'Whoever, intending to insult the modesty of a woman, utters any word, makes any sound or gesture, or exhibits any object, intending that such word or sound shall be heard, or that such gesture is seen by such woman, or intrudes upon the privacy of such woman, shall be punished with simple imprisonment for a term which may extend to one year, or with fine, or with both.'

Word, sound, gesture, insult to modesty and intrusion on privacy with intent to insult a woman's modesty are the keywords in the Section, in Chapter 22 of the Code entitled 'Of Criminal Intimidation, Insult and Annoyance'. Regulation of behaviour in the public domain in the interests of decency in society seems to have been the objective rather like laws of public nuisance in nineteenth-century England, implying once again that in a woman's modesty (defined by her own sexual behaviour and the behaviour towards her) lies the well-being of the society.

7. Counsellors' analysis of the case of 'P', who was raped within the family:

Four counsellors commented on the incidents and outcome of this case as it had happened. The events took place 50 years ago, and the case was brought to the fore by Counsellor 'A' who had a family link with 'P' and had always been perturbed by the case once she heard about it from the 'grownups'.

Counsellor 'A': I recoil at the idea of such an occurrence because I wonder where one is safe. In our society, young girls are never sent alone with strangers but relatives (such as uncles, brothers-in-law, brothers and nephews) are regarded as 'family' and thereby allowed to escort and accompany girls to school or college, friends' homes, travel in cabs, etc. How did this brother-in-law have the chance and audacity to abuse this privilege? And what was 'P' thinking when this was happening? No screams? No protests? No hysteria when she came home? Why? I am 27 today and married, and if my brother-in-law did this to me when I was 17 I would have kicked him in the private parts and run or screamed or come home and shouted my lungs out. But 'P' kept mum till she was well and truly pregnant. And then there are the parents and uncle? How did they all conspire to hush it all up? Why did they allow the pregnancy to continue to such a late stage and then have an abortion? Was there no one to counsel and advise? Why did the uncle not think differently?

Counsellor 'B': I think most of the reactions of the persons in this incident are real and natural, given the society we live in. This is a complex scenario with no black-and-white responses. Imagine if 'P' had shouted and screamed and protested and kicked—there are two possibilities at both ends ('Rapist' and 'P') and neither includes the 'rapist' brother-in-law having a second thought. (*a*) The brother-in-law had clearly taken a fancy to 'P' fairly early on and was just waiting for the opportunity to have intimate contact with her. If she had protested, no matter how violently, he would have probably done worse with her. (*b*) The brother-in-law relied on the fact that neither 'P' nor her family would have the nerve to expose the incident beyond 'the four walls'. The stigma would ruin them, not him. He also had a sense of how gutless 'P' really was and took full advantage of that. There is no way that the family would have done anything other than what they did whether they knew the details earlier or not. The fact that it was within the 'family' makes it worse because innuendos about 'willing to go with him' and 'consenting' are thrown around and there is no way 'P' would be able to answer the question of all questions: 'What were you thinking?'

Counsellor 'C': Indian families have a strange way of playing out their relationship equations. It is assumed that when we have labelled people with titles like '*bhaisaheb*' (brother), '*chachaji*' or '*mamaji*' (paternal and maternal uncle, respectively), etc., they acquire halos that place them beyond the pale of indecency and reproach. In the details of the case it is said that when the two families would sit down to a meal, he would say: 'I will only begin eating when "P" does.' Was someone listening? Also, was 'P' flattered or embarrassed? There is a convoluted tension at both ends, and the 'elders' of the family sometimes deliberately wear blinkers believing that strong reactions may wreck the elder daughter's marriage. Finally, between an indecent brother-in-law, a rather simple (almost unwise) 'P' and a meek helpless family this was bound to happen.

Counsellor 'D': This is any Indian parent's nightmare: It isn't for nothing the phrase 'lock up your daughters' comes into play. All this business of the law helping out and suchlike is rubbish. What can the law do? It is the fate of one daughter against another. Going in and out of homes in families is a common thing in India: So much works on trust. But you know sexual attraction is sexual attraction, and no amount of declarations about the high moral ground have any place in such a scenario. But the fact that the incident had a long-term effect on 'P' and indeed on the parents is the regrettable part of the story, and if there had been a confidential intervention by a specialist to address that, maybe it would have helped.

8. See *Sakshi v. Union of India*, 1997, and Report 172 of the Law Commission of India on Review of Rape Laws, 2000.

   The Criminal Law (Amendment) Bill, 2010, contains amendments to the IPC and Code of Criminal Procedure (Cr.P.C.). that would affect definitions of rape and of sexual abuse of minors in Section 375.

Chapter 3

Definitions, Aims and Approaches

Counselling has been referred to as an 'overused word and a misunderstood activity' on which everyone has a view: the 'less the knowledge, the more strident the claim' to an opinion on counselling (Hingdon, 2004). In reports of unforeseen and unusual events and experiences the media talks of people 'receiving counselling' as if it were a religious ritual like communion or *'prasad'* from a priest. There are no simple answers to the question *'What is counselling?'* Nor is there a crisp answer to *'How does it differ from other forms of helping?'* In fact a good starting point in any training programme directed towards teaching and training in counselling techniques might be to elicit responses from would-be counsellors to these two questions about 'counselling'.

In the first simple exercise conducted with a few of our counsellors before their formal training in counselling in the specific contexts we were engaged, their answers revealed some not unexpected responses. 'What is counselling?' was answered with the words 'guiding', 'advising', 'sympathizing', 'comforting' and 'problem-solving'. The second question fetched longer answers like 'Counselling is different because it is done in private' or 'counselling is for specific problems as opposed to general help' or 'counselling addresses the client's ignorance' or 'counselling is done by educated people unlike the help given by simple family and friends'. Results from the discussion revolved around the two questions and their answers revealed just how difficult it could be to define counselling in a way that precisely, unambiguously and accurately places it beyond misunderstanding and that also clearly demarcates the boundary that makes counselling entirely different from other similar (help-giving) activities. It must be reiterated that counselling as it is being discussed here is an activity of recent origin and most of its theoretical underpinnings can be located in ideas that have evolved in the twentieth century, particularly in the industrialized world. It would be unwise to be too rigid about its definitions, the theories that underlie these definitions and the processes and techniques that need to be employed for making it effective. The contexts in which it is used and is required to be used are expanding, and each context may need differing approaches that need to be spelt out again and again for would-be practitioners. Equally it would not be appropriate to attribute nebulous qualities to what is in fact a near-precise set of ideas and principles that links together the very different uses to which counselling may be put; nor would it be accurate to suggest that it is a rudderless activity still evolving and therefore without principles and firm guidelines.

Even as the word 'psychotherapy' is often used interchangeably with counselling, strictly speaking and historically, psychotherapy has its origins in response to specific or non-specific manifestations of clinically diagnosable or existential crises. Some psychotherapeutic interventions are designed to treat the patient employing the medical model. Many psychotherapeutic approaches do not adhere to the symptom-based model of 'illness/cure'. Some practitioners, such as *humanistic* therapists, see themselves more in a facilitating/helping role. As sensitive and deeply personal topics are often discussed during psychotherapy, therapists are expected, and usually legally bound, to respect client or patient confidentiality. The critical importance of confidentiality is enshrined in the regulatory psychotherapeutic organizations' codes of ethical practice.

Whether used interchangeably or with determined distinctions, there are clearly difficulties when it comes to trying to drawing distinctions between counselling and psychotherapy. The distinctions are often seen as ranging from the degree of disturbance in the client to the setting, length of process, the type of problem, the techniques used, and the type and duration of the counsellor/therapist's training. Some writers suggest counselling for normal grief reactions and therapy for abnormal reactions, therapy thereby taking on the role of a medical term for more serious and deep-rooted difficulties (Worden, 1991). Over time and expressly as a result of usage in different contexts, addressing and handling anxiety, fear and distress situations arising in day-to-day life is referred to as counselling—a distinction originally adopted by Carl Rogers. Even before the publication of his well-known treatise *Client-centered Therapy* in 1951, he had used the phrase *non-directed therapy*, which was later developed further in keeping with the principles he was describing and using to apply to a variety of contexts and not just strictly in a therapy situation. Drawn from his own experience, he introduced the term *person-centered approach* later in his life to describe his overall theory. Person-centred therapy is the application of the person-centred approach to the therapy situation. It is in this manifestation that it is used interchangeably with counselling.

It might be mentioned here that the parallel usage and consequent confusion about the distinction between *counselling* and *psychotherapy* also stems from early innate prejudices of medical practitioners (particularly in the United States) who saw the 'professional' help they were rendering as exclusive to their medical qualifications and not as the business of 'lay' experts. Interestingly, whereas all psychological therapies trace their origins to Freud, who was indeed a medical practitioner (neurologist) himself, Freud as the founder of psychoanalysis strongly supported the idea of lay analysts without medical training being therapists as long as they had the requisite training and adhered to the guidelines emanating out of the theories of the mind and resulting knowledge about behaviour that he had spent much of his life on. His own daughter Anna Freud was one such 'lay specialist' who worked with him and went on to become a leading psychoanalyst.

The tradition of lay involvement in psychotherapy encouraged by Freud developed sporadically in the UK through the efforts of Ernest Jones, a Welsh medical practitioner (often referred to as Freud's apostle in the English-speaking world). A vocal promoter of what was then called the 'psychoanalytical movement', Jones was like Freud a neurologist and ardently promoted Freud's postulates of psychoanalysis, attempting to strip it of pessimism and its 'dark side'. The recognition of psychoanalysis and psychotherapy in the UK in fits and starts did result in producing institutional recognition for practitioners—psychoanalysts, psychotherapists and counsellors—with a lay background. The US prejudices towards lay practitioners' involvement in psychotherapy was addressed by developing high standards of 'professionalism' and specialized qualifications and criteria for psychotherapy more widely referred to as *counselling*.

All this background and history is aimed at revealing the involvement of well-known high-level players in the area of psychoanalysis in making a concerted effort towards addressing the human mind directly, or indirectly (through behaviour), to reveal its functioning (and malfunctioning) with a view eventually to offer methods of treatment that did not always have to be medical. The search for definitions and meanings of the terms that emerged in the field of psychotherapy reflects the historical meanderings of the movement that believed that 'states of mind' needed to be taken seriously if the health of individuals in society was important.

Definitions and boundaries emerged as the debate continued and the core components of the activity were not difficult to establish. The British Association of Counselling and Psychotherapy[1] offers the following definition of counselling:

> Counselling takes place when a counsellor sees a client in a private and confidential setting to explore a difficulty the client is having, distress they may be experiencing or perhaps their dissatisfaction with life, or loss of a sense of direction and purpose. It is always at the request of the client as no one can properly be 'sent' for counselling.

Some typical and quite general responses that have been collected by those who have researched and practised counselling as a professional activity along the evolutionary lines of the activity described earlier are listed below (see Hough, 1998; Sutton and Stewart, 1997; Manthei, 1997; O'Farrell, 1999):

- It revolves around persons, problems and prospects.
- It is essentially determined by the client's needs.
- It is a relationship with boundaries.
- It is a special kind of communication.
- It requires patient (trained) listening.
- Its premise is that someone is to be helped according to his/ her circumstances.
- It is confidential and non-hierarchical.
- It seeks to build the capacity and strength for problem-solving in the client.
- It is an activity carried out by trained persons.
- It is guided by theories about causes of problems, some understanding about personality and society.

Counselling thus emerges as essentially a therapeutic process. Very simply it could be described as (*a*) a process usually but not always conducted face to face, (*b*) between two or more people and (*c*) involving an intentional use of particular skills: the aim is to help others identify and implement solutions to their problems (conflicts/disputes) including the ability to cope with them through purposeful communication. It is guided by theoretical and practical rules strongly rooted in principles that have their bases in different disciplines such as philosophy, including ethics, morality, psychology, law and jurisprudence, and sociology and anthropology.

In one way we all 'counsel' at some point or another in our lives. As parents, teachers, doctors, lawyers, priests, group leaders, political leaders and social workers, we counsel people all the time, if by counselling we mean giving advice or guidance. Counselling has, however, been developed as a special and different form of help because it seeks to achieve what advice and guidance may or may not achieve:

- Empowering the 'client' to equip herself to help herself
- Being non-judgemental and free from agendas and interests through the entire process

- Understanding the person and the problem without innate or acquired prejudices
- Negotiating and cooperating with rather than manipulating and compelling the client to arrive at the best possible way he/she can cope with the problem
- Relying on specific definable skills at each stage of the helping process

Any definition of counselling as an activity would therefore need to come as close to the aims, objectives and purposes for which the activity has been developed and 'professionalized'. There could be several equally valid definitions of counselling with varying emphases. The emphasis in turn would be determined by the context from which it has emerged (prison, acute traumatic experience, domestic dissonance, social exclusion and/or oppression).

Most people in difficult life-situations need counselling at some time or another and the more vulnerable groups in society need it more than others do. We have chosen women as one such group and suggested counselling for women as an area of expertise that might be gainfully developed particularly in regions where the literacy and awareness rate among women is poor. There are other groups that might benefit just as much from counselling being developed as a worthwhile skill and expertise. The young, the old, the (physically and mentally) sick and those socially or economically marginalized in any society face a multitude of problems that fail to get addressed in the normal course of things. The term *counselling* as our colleagues demonstrated in their first opening exercise is frequently confused with advice giving, and dictionaries still define counselling in terms of advice and guidance. Table 3.1 clarifies the differences between advice, guidance and counselling.

There are other distinctions that also need to be made. Feltham (1997) suggests that counselling is 'a relationship which is experienced as healing.... It is markedly different from friendship or psychiatry.' There may be similarities between friendship

TABLE 3.1. THE DIFFERENCES BETWEEN ADVICE, GUIDANCE AND COUNSELLING

Advice	Guidance	Counselling
Mainly a one-way exchange	*Mainly a one-way exchange*	*A two-way collaborative exchange*
Giving an opinion	Showing a way	A supportive relationship that is voluntary
Making a judgement	Educating	Enables clients to explore their problems freely
Making a recommendation	Influencing	Enables clients to understand the need for action
Persuasive	Instructing	Enables clients to take appropriate action
	Encouraging	Provides hope and comfort

Source: Adapted from Sutton and Stewart (1997).

and counselling; but in counselling some features are evident to a greater degree:

- The relationship between a counsellor and client is voluntary.
- It is aimed at finding solutions.
- It is based on the use of interpersonal skills.
- It relies on the maintenance of confidentiality.
- It may not compromised by any other relationship between counsellor and client (such as a friendship, filial relationship, or a professional authority).

Another variation between the different types of interventions that are help-providing but not always 'empowering' in the manner that counselling tries to be is demonstrated in Figure 3.1.

As stated earlier, the difficulties surrounding definitions and distinctions between counselling and psychotherapy should not deter those engaged and committed to developing counselling as a therapy for those in need, and Table 3.1 and Figure 3.1 are only intended to give some substance to each activity as it is intended to be practised for the goals in view. Theorists and practitioners do use the words interchangeably, and others make

FIGURE 3.1. Types of Interventions and Their Impacts

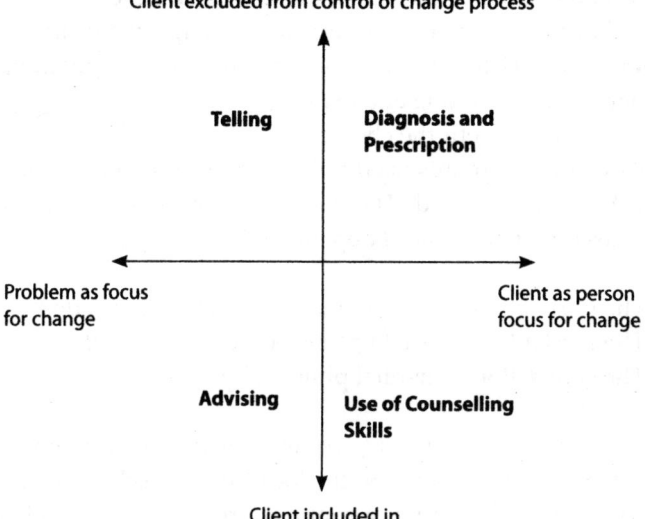

Client excluded from control of change process

Telling   **Diagnosis and Prescription**

Problem as focus for change   Client as person focus for change

Advising   **Use of Counselling Skills**

Client included in change process

Source: Author's adaptation from relevant sources.

determined distinctions. It may not always be about splitting hairs: it is suggestive of differing emphases that in turn determine the approach and methodology of the activity. These differing emphases may range from the degree of disturbance in the client to the setting, length of process, the type of problem, the techniques used and the type and duration of the counsellor/ therapist's training.

Whatever words we choose to define the activity of 'counselling', a few things seem to be clear:

- The goal of counselling is some kind of *change*: change in the way the client thinks and change in the way he/she is disposed towards future action in a problem or in a conflict situation.
- And before change can actually become a part of any visible agenda, there is a first step that needs to be taken: that of *understanding*, which is a goal in itself.

These constitute the more general goals of counselling and are based on two assumptions: (*a*) that the client believes or hopes at least that life will somehow improve through the counselling experience and (*b*) that the counsellor is not doing something *to* the client but is facilitating and exploring *with* the client a range of choices that will benefit the client.

Three further points need to be made here about the means by which this is achieved. The means that are used or the form that counselling takes would depend on

- The particular context in which counselling is needed
- The model for counselling chosen by the counsellor
- The counsellor's personal philosophy

All of these would need to be integrated with each other because whatever the situation or the locale of counselling, many of the underlying goals and assumptions are universal. It is being suggested therefore that some parameters and principles need to be set out at the start. Many of these have been collected and arranged from sources that have looked hard at counselling in various contexts and we have picked those that have relevance for our particular purposes.

The three constituents of a counselling-situation or setting are:

- A *client* in need of counselling
- The client's *problem* (including its sources)
- A chosen *counsellor*

These constituents or ingredients need to be placed within a structure that is defined and developed according to the nature of the ingredients themselves, that is, the client's needs, the nature of the problem and the counsellor's methods and skills. This 'approach' could itself be given a name—a problem-solving, skills-based model geared towards solutions rather than analysis of difficulties. In any event a framework or model needs to be developed that is 'neither too loose nor too restrictive' and 'flexible and robust enough for counsellors to incorporate aspects of other approaches' (see Manthei [1997]).

The broad framework for all counselling gets structured something like this (Foggo-Pays, 1983):

- A Process
- Objectives
- The Relationship

Whatever the particularities of the ingredients which constitute the counselling situation, and whatever the theories, processes, structures and methods that are put in place to work these in specific contexts, one thing is clear—that *techniques and skills are required and necessary for every model.* These skills are in turn of course dependent upon both the ingredients of the situation and the processes of counselling. Years of work by those who have written about experiences in counselling suggests that no one theory or approach emerges as superior to another. In fact it seems apparent that often a multifaceted approach yields better results.

However, it is also clear that with increased information available, and with the increasing ability to transmit ideas about the subject through written and spoken words across the world, counselling today is both in better shape and fast developing as a skill that could be sharpened through training and exchanges from it used in differing contexts. From what was considered a wishy-washy nebulous area of work, for which almost anyone with time on his/her hands volunteered, counselling is now given serious consideration as an *art* with a professional code of ethics and as an *activity* that needs to be pursued within professional parameters and rules.

All these realizations make the task of defining, describing, clarifying, discussing and restructuring the theory and practice of counselling even more desirable and necessary so that it is made universally intelligible and understandable and capable of being interchangeably used for similar situations anywhere. This means clarifying both what counselling is not and what it is. Counselling is *not* simply the use of some techniques of advising people in a spirit of warmth and sympathy. Counselling has wisely been called an 'ethical task'—its purpose being to serve the client's best interests. As one analyst has said, it is based on the principle of empowerment.

Clearly what we are suggesting is that even as the specific situations that form the setting of particular counselling processes differ, there are underlying features about the (*a*) *aims of counselling* and (*b*) *the activity of counselling* that run through every type or model. These underlying common features have to be juxtaposed with the three constituents of counselling mentioned earlier, that is, a client in need of counselling, the client's problem and a chosen counsellor. This has been set out in Figure 3.2 to show how and where all the aspects—theoretical approaches, aims and objectives, and the activity of counselling—actually *connect*.

FIGURE 3.2. The Holistic Approach to Counselling

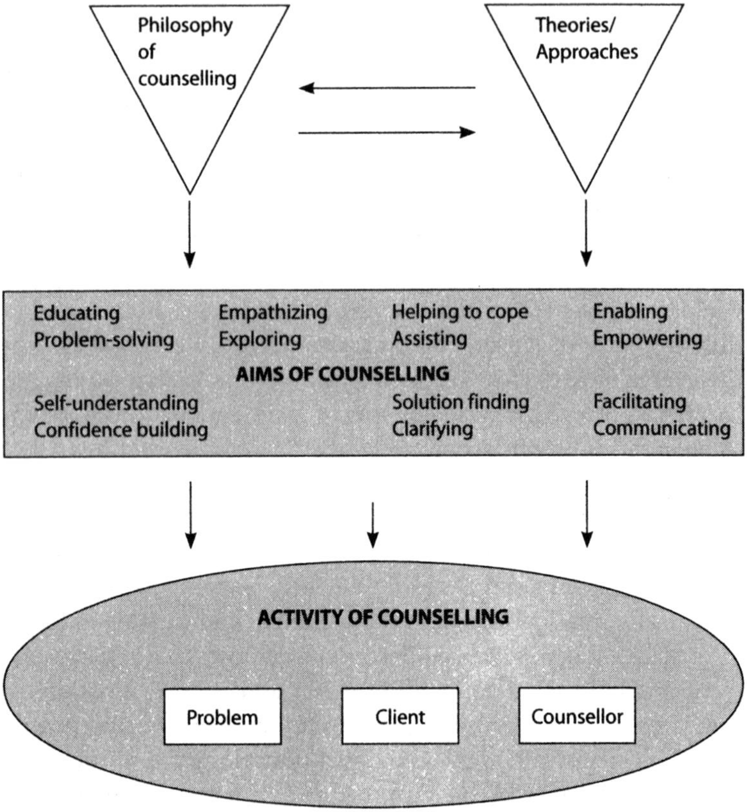

Source: Author's adaptation from relevant sources.

Simple as this diagrammatic representation seems, it really covers more than it suggests at a glance. The words seem simple; but if we are talking for instance of *enabling, educating* or *assisting* in either of our two counselling contexts (mediation and custody), which we will be discussing later, it would be difficult for a counsellor to *educate* or *enable* her client to reflect and express herself on issues if she herself is not equipped in as many aspects that pertain to these women's lives as possible: these would be knowledge and understanding of the functioning of the mind; its relationship with behaviour (psychological aspects); the laws on all such issues that women come face to face with at every turn, such as the prison; social institutions such as dowry, traditional marriage practices, features of religious practices (sociological aspects); the formal rules and regulations in a society/State that govern the individual's functioning (legal aspects); etc. Therefore, easy as the exercise may seem, it ends up being a demanding activity and not one that should be regarded either by the client or counsellor as simple and easily handled.

It becomes clear that the aims (general and specific) of counselling cannot be found in a definitive list. They emerge out of the theories of counselling that have developed and formed the several approaches to counselling that have been tried in different situations. We are told there are over 400 different theories and approaches to counselling or psychotherapies (see Karasu, 1986; Manthei, 1997). Counsellors do need to acquaint themselves with some of the theories of counselling so that they can draw fruitfully upon some useful features that these theories highlight. Theories offer new perspectives on problems and methods for exploring newer ways of help that can be assimilated into a counsellor's existing methodology.

While Freud's *psychoanalysis* and the contributions made by his followers form the source of most psychological therapies, developments into areas that are regarded as more realistic and practical as usable techniques in therapy have produced more modern approaches to counselling and psychotherapy that are now much more firmly grounded in other bodies of thought. The immediate descendants of Freud's approach are characterized by a focus on the dynamics of the relationships between different parts of the psyche and the external world; hence the term 'psychodynamics'.

A separate strand of psychological therapies developed later under the influence of psychology and learning theory and leading thinkers such as B. F. Skinner. Rejecting the notion of 'hidden' aspects of the psyche which cannot be examined empirically (such as Freud's rendition of the 'unconscious'), practitioners in the *behavioural* tradition began to focus on what could actually be observed in the outside world.

It is in this category that we find Carl Rogers who, though influenced by Adler and Rank, pioneered the third way stated earlier—the 'client-centred' and later 'person-centred' approach—focusing on the experience of the person, neither adopting elaborate and empirically untestable theoretical constructs of the type common in psychodynamic traditions nor neglecting the internal world of the person.

While avoiding a blind advocacy of 'brand name' theories and an overreliance on single theory approaches, it might still be useful to focus on some of the different theoretical approaches to counselling, starting with the three that Margaret Hough has highlighted (see Figure 3.3):

- The psychodynamic approach
- The behavioural approach
- The humanistic approach

There are other approaches that are worth looking at and some are subtypes within each branch that have evolved into approaches in their own right. But these three main theoretical underpinnings of most approaches to counselling methods and skills are being briefly described to understand some fundamental differences of approach:

1. *The psychoanalytical (psychodynamic) approach*: There are three main thrusts to this approach: (*a*) the acknowledgement of the influence of the past on the present; (*b*) an awareness

FIGURE 3.3. Theoretical Approaches

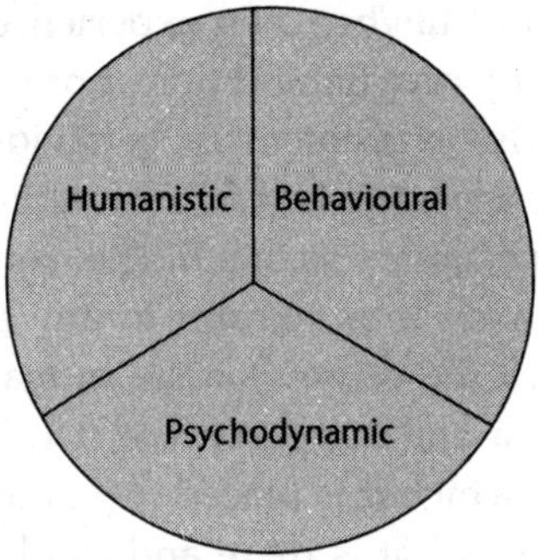

Source: Author's adaptation from relevant sources.

that there are many and differing ways in which people seek to defend themselves against unpleasant experiences and (c) resulting from these, the attempt towards identifying the not-so-apparent (or unconscious) factors that influence the thought and behaviour of an individual. Central to psycho-dynamic theory are ideas that relate to unconscious moti-vation, psychosexual stages of development, innate sexual and aggressive drives, links between childhood and present behaviour, and the nature of defence mechanisms and their use (Hough, 1998: 25).

2. *The behavioural approach*: This approach views the human personality as a collection of learned behaviours. It focuses on the actual behaviour of people, on how people learn to behave the way they do, and how they perpetuate this be-haviour pattern through 'reinforcement', that is, if particular behaviour gets a desired result it is repeated, if it fails then it is dropped. The behaviour may well be problem behav-iour for others and it is here that this approach to behaviour change is of value for counselling. The difference between this and the psychodynamic approach is that the behaviour that is addressed is observable behaviour.

3. *The humanistic approach*: The emphasis here is on the innate potential of a person rather than on objectively observed behaviour patterns or on the influence of the unconscious

underlying reasons for behaviour. Each person is viewed in the context of his/her own experiences and expressions and the driving force behind this approach is that the focus is not primarily on problematic behaviour or on a person's neurosis. The message is that a more holistic approach to the person is necessary so that his/her constructive potential can also be taken into account in any attempt at change. Higdon places the origins of the humanistic approach in North America and suggests that it reflects the values of the society in which it is placed (e.g., the American dream) and it relies on what is there and available, which in turn then affect the individual's striving for his/her potential. This differs from the psychodynamic approach in which 'the truth is layered and not immediately exposed to the surface' (Higdon, 2004: 3).

Having said that, there are a few things that need to be clarified for all counsellors and psychotherapists. There is a growing consensus that with a realization about the complexity of psychological problems and their causes and effects, the limitations of pet theories have become apparent. Disillusionment with single therapy systems has led to what has been referred to as a 'metamorphosis' in mental health: *the integration of the psychotherapies* (see Norcross and Grencavage in Dryden and Norcross [1990]). Three broad areas are identified in the contemporary movement to integrate the psychotherapies: (*a*) technical eclecticism, (*b*) theoretical integration and (*c*) common factors. Of these the debate over the first two is of importance for clarifying the importance of choices in the process of counselling and psychotherapy. There is also a need to spell out just what integration means before it is taken to be a simple 'melting pot' technique in which approaches can be mixed and matched at will.

There have been serious attempts to explain integration so that it is properly understood. Common clarifications are (*a*) that integration would miss out the alternative visions of life that different therapies embody and (*b*) that a 'common factors approach' is a way of thinking, it does not tell us how to conduct

TABLE 3.2. Eclecticism versus Integration

Eclecticism	Integration
Technical	Theoretical
Divergent (differences)	Convergent (commonalities)
Choosing from many	Combining many
Applying what is	Creating something new
Collection	Blend
Selection	Synthesis
Applying the parts	Unifying the parts
Atheoretical but empirical	More theoretical than empirical
Sum of parts	More than sum of parts
Realistic	Idealistic

Source: Higdon (2004).

therapy. Apples and oranges might both be 'fruit', but the difference between them is as fundamental as are the similarities. Writers have therefore warned against excessive simplifications (Messer). To help understand this, a distinction has been made between eclecticism and integration (see Table 3.2).

Lazarus has been described as the most eloquent proponent of technical eclecticism and it is suggested that in this scheme of things no necessary connection exists between 'metabeliefs' and techniques. One can, it is suggested, utilize the technical procedures of different theories and conceptions without attempting a new composite theory or a 'theoretical rapprochement'. 'To ignore technique specificity is a serious breach of professional responsibility' (Lazarus in Dryden and Norcross, 1990: 34).

The typical proponent of (theoretical) integration seems to be Bietman (in Dryden and Norcross [1990: 51]). The distinguishing feature of his approach is his total view of counselling: A relationship that exists as a process that is intended towards the psychological change of the one called 'client' and that must be moved along and nurtured to achieve that purpose. To that end, Bietman wishes to discover a few general principles that may be applied to a large number of situations rather than primarily gathering many bits of data that apply to limited situations. Building theories of personality and psychopathology can become a focus on their own: 'the ability to alleviate a mental problem must be distinguished from the ability to define the manner in which the problem originated'.

Bietman (in Dryden and Norcross [1990]) suggests that it is important to differentiate between theories and models so that both are used appropriately where they belong.

A model is an abstraction from observables; it condenses the multiple manifestations of a general phenomenon into a comprehensible configuration.

A theory is primarily an attempt to explain causation; it seeks to answer the question why. Its value comes from the well-established belief that knowing the why of a phenomenon helps to change it.

A 'collection of techniques' approach, therefore, is something Bietman is unsatisfied with; his aim is to conceptualize psychotherapy, to develop a model of it that is firmly rooted in undeniable general principles closely tied to the real-world behaviour of clients and counsellors. The need is for recognition of what integrative principles really are. While there have been clearly defined schools, there is a move towards increasing convergence and a recognition of common factors. Commonalities may be obscured by different terms (Norcross and Grencavage, in Dryden and Norcross [1990: 10]).

The above-mentioned analysis of different approaches, trends and moves towards better models and methods has been discussed to highlight the vitality of familiarizing the counsellor with the central issues involved in the activity and making him/ her fully competent to make informed choices. A significant way of determining what is the best approach in counselling or psychotherapy for the particular problems at hand is to keep assessing and analysing by means of measures and gauges arrived at through direct feedback from client–counsellor locations. These could be ascertained through narrations of personal experiences, interviews and questionnaires. Added to one's own experiences, and to the existing literature on counselling, the activity would become both more professional and real.

What we are looking at and for when we counsel and how we look at it is determined by the theoretical approach we adopt. Whether the counsellor is mediating, solving a problem, building confidence or whatever, it is necessary to see how much of the client's past we go into, how much of the behaviour do we observe, how positive we are, how critical we decide to be and how subjective we end up being; all this in turn depends very much on the manner in which we structure our theoretical approach and build the model we want. The importance of counselling in modern society and its development and growth to meet the different specificities of social life are evident everywhere. But as with any new area of activity, counselling has the potential of taking shape according to the interests of those who have the power and ability to mould it. It is therefore even more necessary to approach counselling with all honesty, professionalism and ethical integrity that it deserves and needs.

So while we have highlighted counselling and the reliance on the three main approaches to effective counselling (reduced to 3 from about 400 we are told) and an attempt is made to draw upon all of these as wholesomely a possible, there is a fourth emphasis or approach that has been mentioned by some experts—that of cross-cultural considerations. This is not intended to offer a specific single model of multicultural counselling but is intended to pose to counsellors the significance and value of diversity among people. The meaning of culture is here often expanded to go beyond the usual definition (language, customs, religion, art and folklore of particular ethnic groups) to differences in age, culture, race, education, gender, economic status, etc.

The fourth dimension—*the cross-cultural*—in approaches to counselling opens up a fresh debate that might be mentioned here before we move on to the actual process and activity of counselling, its beginnings, its progress and its near conclusions. This is a debate about the degree to which counselling is a universal generic activity that transcends specific cultures, and how far it is culture specific, requiring different skills and emphases that fit the characteristics of different groups. Perhaps the answer has been provided by those who suggest a middle approach, that of 'an essential balance that acknowledges both similarities and differences' (Pedersen, 1993).

Related to this is yet another (fifth) framework for counselling (theory and practice)—the *'pluralistic'* approach (Cooper and Macleod, 2011). This approach seeks to meet the view often made, even as traditional ways of looking at counselling continue, that there is no right way of providing therapy and different clients need different things and have changing needs. There can be a selection of therapeutic methods that can be used with a flexibility that would be determined by a client's needs and also the therapist's knowledge, wisdom, experience and skills.

And last but far from least is an emphasis that must enter the counsellor's repertoire of theoretical understandings and approaches, that is the *feminist approach or emphasis*, which will be discussed later. The main approaches to counselling configuration are being amalgamated by us and presented diagrammatically in Figure 3.4.

FIGURE 3.4. Fundamental Approaches and Influences in Counselling

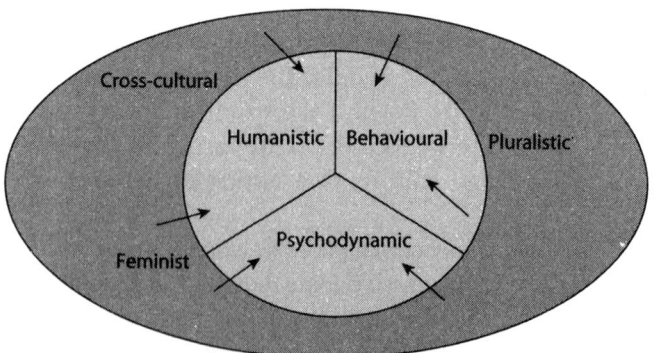

Source: Author's adaptation from relevant sources.

Against all of these approaches, differing emphases and the search for the best it is now befitting that we actually go into the activity called 'counselling'.

The activity or process of learning to counsel it has been suggested involves three elements (Sutton and Stewart, 1997):

- Knowledge of counselling theory
- Skills development
- Personal development or the enhancement of self-awareness

The specific components of each element and its use by the counsellor would be shaped by the context and content of the needed counselling. Acquiring knowledge about theoretical approaches, developing nuances of particular skills and developing one's self as one moves forward are all intimately related to what the counsellor is faced with. It is also related to what is learnt out of each experience as one moves on the road to counselling. The assumption that attention to the three elements would make for a smooth ride would be erroneous. There are jolts and hiccups that are often unforeseen, and predicaments that were not factored into the process could arise. Counselling is about some kind of alliance between two persons even if it is not a balanced alliance. Clients do not always meet the counsellor's expectations (known in the jargon as 'resistance' or 'non-compliance') and as a therapist the counsellor would be required to enhance her skills for reengaging with the client for taking the activity forward.

With these facts as given, we need to give shape and form to the ideas about counselling that we have highlighted as crucial for counsellors who are engaged in the activity so that it can be conducted in the most informed and accountable manner. This means understanding that there is a goal somewhere that has to be achieved even if it seems vague and ill-defined at the beginning of the process. This goal relates to some form of problem-solving, and even if not all counselling is simply and specifically about problem-solving much of it is—if by problem-solving we mean the resolution of a discrepancy and about changing something and bringing it close to what is desired by the person and the circumstances.

A crucial question that is best given some thought here, even though it may be interspersed at different points in discussions after sessions between counsellors, is that of 'change' as a goal of counselling. How is change to be brought about if the counsellor must maintain a conflict-free environment in which he/she must not assert his/her views and only *enable* the clients to find their own feet in the sticky situations they face? This is a difficult one that needs to be treated with care. Windy Dryden (in Dryden and Reeves [2008: 5]) has an interesting observation on this issue that can be extended discreetly to differing environs by enlightened counsellors:

> While the distinguishing feature of the bond in its early stages is one where there is a comfortable fit between counsellor and client, productive change is more often predicated upon the resolution of manageable conflict in the bind than it is on the perpetuation of early feelings of comfort in that relationship.

We will return to this point again and again when discussing specific counselling in some specific contexts; suffice it to say here that a total agreement of views is not what is advocated when different stages of the counselling process are being followed. Subtly but surely some 'productive change' needs to be achieved.

Before moving on to how the actual process of counselling should be conducted, a simple point needs to be made to emphasize the status we wish to give to 'counsellors'. Using counselling skills may be a laudable activity in everyday life, but it would not make someone a counsellor. It has been succinctly noted that 'counselling is significantly different from using counselling skills in everyday life' (Geldard and Geldard, 2005). The two activities may be placed at different locations on a continuum, but they are different and some of the highlights of 'counselling' described earlier (training, understanding of psychology, knowledge of counselling theories, working within theoretical frameworks, etc.) have been spelt out to suggest that counselling essentially requires a 'set of standards and guidelines', 'codes of practice' and 'ethical standards' generally determined and acknowledged by professionals and forming the goals of counselling. The counsellor would have to be recognized for his/her expertise in the personal/ social domain just as a lawyer would in the legal field or a medical practitioner in the field of health and medical care.

NOTE

1. BACP has its origins in the Standing Council for the Advancement of Counselling formed in 1971. It became the British Association for Counselling in 1976 and was renamed the British Association for Counselling and Psychotherapy in 2001.

Chapter 4

Structuring and Getting Started

Having clarified and put in place what might be called the 'theoretical' and 'experiential' fundamentals of counselling and placed them against the perceived problems of counselling women in the South Asian cultural environ, we need to move into the area of structuring and setting out some details of *how the actual activity or process of counselling would be conducted* generally and for particular clients. Much of the designing of the process has emerged out of the real-life attempts at transplanting as constructively as possible what we gleaned of the process from our research of the literature and of the backgrounds and personalities of the clients in question.

Before moving forward, there is a small clarification that needs to be inserted here. Having emphasized the professionalism of counselling and suggested that 'cowboy counselling' is unacceptable, the category called 'unprofessional counsellors' needs to be explained. Kennedy and Charles have given the subtitle *Basic Guide for Non-professional Counsellors* to their book *On Becoming a Counsellor*. This is NOT suggestive of any casual treatment of counselling. In explaining the significance of the work performed by this category of persons, the authors suggest that there is enough room in the help-providing world for these 'paraprofessional counsellors' who are in fact carrying out most of the counselling done in the world—far more than the highly trained therapists who are the experts but not always there when trouble strikes the sufferer.

> [They] work in life as it is, with people as they are, at the blood smeared accident site rather than in the sterile surgical suite. They resemble medics more than specialists and as such they cannot be

selective about those they are called upon to help. (Kennedy and Charles, 2001)

Given the absence of professionalized expertise in counselling at specially designated centres in our own regional contexts, it is our endeavour in this book to give professional counselling a user-friendly face that makes it available and appropriate for those who are designated counsellors by the needs of others and by their abilities to enter the world of others. The process we set out is therefore jargon-free and simple, and the psychological-minded will know just how to draw on the information and guidelines provided here with ease.

In designing a process for the kind of counselling that is professional or paraprofessional, we are suggesting frameworks and boundaries to avoid amorphous or nebulous activity that would defeat the purpose of the activity of counselling. The counsellor would need a structure that should be adhered to unselfconsciously. At no point should there be a panic like 'Oh I think I overlooked Step 12' or 'Did I determine my theoretical approach properly?' Throughout this exercise in form- and content-building we have tried to maintain a balanced awareness of the following:

- Theoretical positions
- Approaches to counselling
- The background and persona of the client
- The many apparent and subtle practical needs of client
- The specificity of the problems at hand
- The range of possibilities gleaned from the client's requirements

The earlier chapter on 'definitions' should be of value in communicating these positions. If there is a particular emphasis that becomes apparent, here it is on Rogers' person-centred approach to counselling which some analysts believe to be a philosophy more than a technique. As indicated earlier, the significant feature of this approach (unlike Freud's pure analysis approach) is its optimistic view of the individual and of her capacity to change her own life with some help. Person-centred counselling takes the client through the process of understanding herself, of identifying the nature of her conflicts/problems, of her limitations and potentialities, and through self-awareness and acceptance empowering the person to make her own choices and have a say in her own life.

This sounds easier than it is in the contexts we are focusing on (conflict resolution/mediation and custody) and becomes more difficult against the social background of the women we are likely to encounter in these contexts. The person-centred approach is tempered moderately with some of the messages from the feminist approach although we have been cautious enough not to overstate the patriarchal agenda (see Chapter 2, p. 42). Staying clear of dichotomous analysis the underlying effort is still to address the woman client in all her manifestations, not all of which are clearly visible. Unlike the visible symptoms of physical illnesses that can be diagnosed and treated by physicians, here we are talking essentially about invisible hurts and emotional bleeding all wrapped around unhappy life histories that first have to become visible for counsellors to heal and restore the person as the individual and social being that she is.

In the two contexts we are talking about, the need for 'homework' on the part of the counsellor is vital to the process and the result. In a custodial environment, the chances of the counsellor being thoroughly informed about the intricacies of the site, venue and functioning of the system are slim. There would be a need for the counsellor to apprise herself of as many details of the circumstances as possible to make the exercise fruitful and meaningful. The nuances of the location and the client's positioning within it, whether police custody or prison, take on shapes that are significant in an understanding of the problem and the client's perceptions of herself. In custodial environments, the atmosphere is charged with an unreality that would unnerve the most capable of persons. Unfortunately those who are caught in the web and have problems both past and present to deal with at either location are from socio-economic backgrounds that have given them raw deals all round. Getting to the root of the multifaceted and multilayered problems being faced at either location would need bringing a lot to the surface that lies beneath—at both ends. Making the client feel confident enough to unravel the mind's fears and anxieties both about what may have happened and what she fears is likely to happen is a difficult task.

To make some of the invisible undercurrents visible, the entire process from start to finish would need to be meticulously developed. What happens at the place of custody, why it happens the way it does, what and who causes tensions and why, and how secure the client feels about being where she is are all matters that an informed counsellor would need to know. The custodial environment being the 'domain' of the practitioners who are in charge of it, the counsellor needs to tread carefully lest she step on people's toes inadvertently. It is a tightrope walk that needs to be covered delicately and without tension and anxiety. When the location is one where conflict resolution or mediation has to be carried out between parties, the counsellor's sense of preparedness would need to be more about different sets of persons and their backgrounds than the site and physical location and its functional features. We have tried to consolidate the general features and components of the counselling activity for both situations and then arranged them in some kind of pattern for smoother functionality. This does not imply rigidity and inflexibility in the procedure—the spirit underlying the process is central to the activity. The methods and style would be adapted to the need at hand. Above all it needs to be accomplished without tension and stress.

Basic information gathering, planning, and then embarking on the road to actual engagement is being set out as

1. Structuring of the Process
2. Getting Started

Each of these has elaborate ramifications and subdivisions that we will develop as we go along. It needs to be reiterated, however, that the earlier reference (in Chapter 3, p. 79) to the three main elements of the counselling process or activity that counsellors must carry with them throughout the process need to be recounted. These *three main elements* were spelt out as:

- Knowledge of counselling theory
- Skills development
- Personal development or the enhancement of self-awareness

The division of counselling into *Structuring of the Process* and *Getting Started* does not imply a sequential list that has to be followed in a particular order. Nor does it mean that each part of the process has to be ticked as a checklist as one goes along. Such a division simply suggests that the components in counselling that are conceptual and based on certain principles have been clubbed under 'Structuring of the Process' (*the thought*), and others covering the mechanics and procedural aspects of the process have been clustered under 'Getting Started' (*the action*).

STRUCTURING OF THE PROCESS

The 'structuring of the process' involves the thought processes and conceptual preparation suggested earlier that must be deliberated and reflected upon given the specificities of each context that one is working within but fully cognisant of the principles of counselling discussed earlier. It is a marrying of the principles with the context at the level of thought and deliberation, leading to action planning. Before developing the first part—the structure of the process of counselling, there are a few steps that would need to be taken that could be called 'pre-counselling steps or moves'. In any given setting requiring the development of counselling skills, there would be a need for some preliminary classification. This would be in the first instance of the following:

1. The nature and types of persons coming for conflict resolution and/or mediation as a part of counselling
2. The general trend of the problems/complaints they bring

This is not as simple as it sounds: The philosophies of counselling and the approaches of counselling (discussed in Chapter 3, pp. 71–81) have a bearing on this part of the process. By 'nature and type' is meant both descriptive and qualitative (age, social including educational background, family circumstances, communicative ability, body language if apparent, personality traits such as shyness, sullenness, etc.). Included in 'general trends of problems/complaints' are the broad categories of anxieties, worries and concerns that have prompted them to come for counselling in the first instance; for example, in the case of a custodial environment, it would be both their past before custody and the present at the place of custody. Each would need to be noted and addressed separately and with precision without blurring the needs of either. In the case of conflict resolution and/or mediation, the issues could be an abusive spouse or in-laws; loneliness and neglect in a marital home; losing a family member and not knowing how to cope with the loss; old-age problems; widowhood and so on. Familiarity with such situational circumstances and the attainment of some expertise (psychological and other) to be prepared to direct clients further would be an asset. The initial encounters would suggest what areas of engagement need a 'brushing up' for better management of the counselling session.

Whatever the context and whoever the client, the conceptual preparation is important to avoid blundering through things like wrong opening lines in conversation, rubbing someone the wrong way, failing to observe how far the client will go in sharing experiences and thoughts and suggesting of 'next steps'. Some very simple and basic guidelines would have to be set out and followed to make the sessions effective and productive. To facilitate this attention would need to be given to some preparatory steps:

- Choosing appropriate counsellors (if there is a team) in accordance with some methods and reasons.
- Setting up a congenial and warm scene for the activity of counselling.
- Ensuring and providing the right skills for different situations.
- Putting in place some mechanisms for supervision and evaluation.

These preparatory steps have a special significance in the light of the varied nature of the clientele in the South Asian region. Class, caste, religion, region, tradition and custom, language, education and several other features that determine the identities of the women who come for assistance and help would all need to be addressed when the approach and style of counselling is being formulated. Would-be counsellors whose ideological leanings would interfere with understandings of the social backgrounds from where women clients come would need to be appropriately trained in the principles that form the core of counselling. Too far out on any continuum of beliefs and views would be detrimental to the client. Counsellors steeped in customs and traditions and living their own lives according to beliefs that may be the source of problems for particular clients would need to rethink their ability to deal with these clients.

Similarly, there may be a problem in placing a counsellor with strong feminist predilections who may be tempted to humbug all that constitutes the social identity of a client in order to empower her. Undeniably there is an intrinsic tension in respecting the group identities (with customary and ritualistic baggage) that put women in their problematic situations in the first place and empowering women so that they can stand up to the deprivation of their bargaining power so neatly enmeshed into rituals and practices of which they are made sole custodians. It would lie in the skill and sensitivity of a counsellor to take the client on the journey of realization that her preoccupation with one identity (cultural) is to her own detriment. And all this would need to be done without any moral or other pressure from the counsellor (Coomaraswamy, 2005).[1]

The need for a congenial and warm setting is not about any special or fanciful arrangements. It is about making the place of counselling of a nature that is welcoming for all manner of clients regardless of their class and status. Even the humblest of persons needs to be put at ease and not intimidated by the setting and atmosphere. Simplicity should be the guiding principle of the arrangement and tidiness and order should be apparent to the observer. Clients often come from the simplest of homes and need to feel 'at home' with the counsellor. Some of the visual images provided in the book to demonstrate the manner in which counselling in Indian prisons was actually carried out are suggestive of the need to turn around some of the suggestions of Eurocentric counselling books in order to meet the comfort and ease of clients in South Asia.

Even if particular counsellors have special expertise in specific fields, they would need to have skills suited for handling the particular situations that present themselves. A growing familiarity with the kind of clients and nature of problems that the unit is faced with can point the counsellors in the direction of the areas where there might be room for increasing their knowledge and skills.

If there are sensitive and complex issues that have to be handled, it is a good idea to have some supervision of counselling sessions at hand. When there is more than one client in a mediation situation, a counsellor would be well advised to have a senior colleague present to avoid any misunderstanding or misinterpretation of proceedings of the session. Also some kind of evaluative templates can be prepared in advance to have records for comparison purposes.

With these preparatory steps, the actual underlying precepts for *structuring the process* of counselling need to be set out to ensure thoroughly professional sessions. These are set out in *11 simple, 'mini' steps* and are not sequential. They are the features that ensure the conscious adherence to proficiency:

1. Matching of counsellor and client
2. Reflection on theoretical orientations/approaches
3. Self-reflection and self-examination of values/attitudes by counsellor
4. Thinking through the problem-solving model
5. Reviewing the (albeit limited) information
6. Working out the ground rules for all: flexibility/sacredness
7. Setting a time frame and timetable
8. Determining type of counselling, e.g. facilitative or directive
9. Goal setting (intermediate and final)
10. Patterns of record-keeping and note-making
11. Evaluation and stocktaking—tools and methods

All of these are really the consolidation of the propositions and discussions set out in Chapters 2 and 3 and are quickly internalized by the counsellor after a few sessions. Rather than serve as a quantitative checklist, they are best served as qualitative pointers towards wholesome counselling.

GETTING STARTED

Deliberations and planning having been accomplished in the case of each setting (differently for conflict resolution and custody), the actual act of the face-to-face encounter is the flesh and blood of the activity. It centres on the substance, manner and style of communication (both silent and vocal) between counsellor and client and is the most crucial part of counselling from the client's perspective. The *(six) further steps* that move the sessions towards the actual activity or interaction between counsellor and client constitute the second part of the process that is specific to the locale. It involves the mechanics and procedure of the engagement, and we are calling it 'getting started' to suggest just that. It covers the actual physical arrangements and activity-oriented preparations required to enable the activity to begin in full earnest. These would be features like:

12. The physical setting
13. Introductions and greeting between counsellor and client
14. Exploring the problem of the client (specific reason for coming)
15. Information-gathering about the client and problem
16. Attitude-developing (shedding one's conditioning)
17. Communication techniques and skills (language—verbal and body, etc.)

Each of these features is related to the purpose and context within which either mediation, counselling or mediation-cum-counselling is located. It could be victim oriented, where counselling is aimed at coping with situations that are causing grave harm to the client (mental or physical abuse, domestic violence, isolation, bereavement, harassment—at home or at the workplace, oppression at home, sickness, disability or confinement of various sorts). It could also be a general depressive state that is developing in a custodial environment and leaving the client unable to cope with routine activity and passing the hours. Each counselling site that seeks to address one or more of these would need to have a content and methodology that takes full cognisance of the particular purpose for which the Counselling Cell or unit has been set up. The kind of counselling skills that would need to be developed would vary with the context in which they are placed. It would be erroneous to think that counselling could be embarked upon without due regard and attention to the specificities of the requirements of the context and of the skills that such a context demands.

All of these *17 steps* are vital and essential even as they do not need to follow a sequence or rigid pattern of observance. The emphasis would depend on the context and the requirements of the particular case and the steps would need to get arranged according to the need of the case at hand. Anxiety to start the activity of counselling often results in the counsellor believing that the action must begin straightaway, whereas what may be needed is often clarity in vision for the counsellor so that the dos and don'ts are properly followed.

The two specific areas (of counselling for women in distress) that are the subject of our analysis and assessment here (as stated at the beginning) are (*a*) counselling as it accompanies conflict in the lives of women and (*b*) counselling as it relates to women in prison or custody. The 'steps' suggested above are common and basic to both these types even as the need of the women in the contexts differs. In both contexts there may be additions and subtractions to the steps—but that in no way minimizes the necessity of the observing the steps as a basic minimum requirement for the process. For instance, there may be a need in some cases for the client to be 'led' towards being empowered (even as it is being suggested that strict neutrality is a requirement for counselling). Such a feature would depend on the nuances of the case at hand. There may also be a reason to take a stand on some rigid customs and traditions within the society that may be sacrosanct but affect women adversely and have the potential to be used manipulatively by one party against another. Advising caution to the client in such cases would constitute a further 'step' in the process that might be entitled 'empowerment'. While we have suggested caution in over-enthusiasm with the gender-based approach, 'empowerment' does underscore most of the counselling process when women in particular social contexts are being addressed.

This brings us face to face with counselling and change—a feature that springs up again and again both in the theoretical underpinnings of counselling and in the practical applications of the activity. Decisions about the best theoretical approach and most suitable working steps would need to be predicated on some change as an objective, without which there would be sterile counselling sessions mechanically carried out even when all the steps and moves are in place. Working towards change is the essence of counselling and does not conflict with the prerequisite of neutral agenda-free counselling. The art of counselling would lie in the counsellor's ability to juxtapose the need for qualitative change with the precondition of interest-free therapy.

NOTE

1. Coomaraswamy's comment about the extent to which identity politics have conditioned many of the modern debates about rights and justice is worth noting for those constantly engaged in battling with this dilemma. Rooting it out of the human personality or from the constructions of a region's social order become academic questions against the facts of the real world. There is an understanding of identity that might help:

   > Identity is not an essential immutable permanent status. It has many constituent elements, and future experiences will transform the nature and direction of personal identity. This leads to a sense that identity is often composite, made up of multiple selves, often contesting, contradicting and transforming the other. Identity is therefore constantly reconstituting itself reacting to and negotiating ideology and lived experience. (Coomaraswamy, 2005)

Chapter 5

Conflict Resolution and Mediation

We now need to see how the two parts of the processes described in Chapter 4 (of 'Structuring the Process' and 'Getting Started') can be actually situated and worked through in the two specific contextual settings: conflict resolution/mediation and custodial counselling. This may seem a tedious exercise at first but the nature of problems in the two contexts and the responses that would follow would be different enough to merit different kinds of focus and attention. In one context, women would be coming for counselling and/or mediation in an ordinary simple unit set up for addressing the problems and situations arising out of their 'normal' living realities. The other context, a setting where women would seek help in the unnatural confines of a prison or in police custody, is an abnormal environment where there are layers of constraints and restraints to start with. This would be a far cry from anything that can be labelled 'normal' even for a crisis. The confinement itself is often the source of the problem.

The *first context*, which we have called 'Counselling Context 1', is one of situations where women bring their complaints/ problems to a forum either for solution or for mediation in dispute-resolution—and the interventions we are discussing are *mediation* and *counselling* as supplementing activities. Another way of describing it would be that 'mediation' as an activity requires a *specific* application of counselling skills. This merging of the activities of mediation and counselling relates to the essential nature of the disputes and conflicts that occur in women's lives in the particular societies (South Asian) that we are concerned with. The kinds of interventions required by the women are defined and decided by their living realities and the way they are placed and positioned in their social environments. Information and details about these realities are obtained generally through social sources but above all from the client herself whose own personal perceptions are gleaned through her narratives.

The twinning of mediation and counselling at locations where provisions are made for women to come and get help in redress of grievances is important. These are the locations where appropriate intervention can prevent situations in homes and other familiar places from turning violent and criminal. The significance of this intervention is being highlighted given the paucity of locations where women might receive professional guidance on how they should react to violent oppressive behaviour by 'others'. Most of these women would rather not go to the police in the first instance even when situations take an ugly turn.

It might be mentioned here that locations where mediation or conflict resolution is offered and counselling accompanies this service, it is often ensured that the 'service' has some links with a formal machinery (e.g. police or courts) that can be reverted to should all else fail. Police or courts should be aware that there is a conflict-resolution service available and that there might be referrals from that service to them. In some areas, police stations have themselves welcomed the setting up of mediation/counselling services to prevent persons with disputes entering the 'legal conveyor belt'. This may or may not work given the likelihood of the service being provided by the same persons whose goals as police personnel may conflict with the goals of a neutral, impartial and agenda-free counselling service. It was also discovered by some of our counsellors that in cases of domestic violence, policewomen had difficulty in believing that there were gross violations of dignity and rights of the women who came for redress of grievances. The reasons given were that since domestic violence occurred in so many homes and was a normal thing, why were the women making such a fuss. The location of an independent counselling unit becomes a matter of some importance if corrupted ideas are to be kept out of the exercise.

What is discussed here are not so much the entire processes of mediation (for that would require a treatise on its own), but *the nature and style of counselling methods that need to accompany the process of mediation.* When mediation-cum-counselling is put in place in contexts/situations where women come for help, there is a need to ensure that all the fundamentals of counselling discussed earlier are translated into features such as recruitment of suitable counsellors, venue development, training of counsellors for the purpose at hand, constant skills improvement and evaluation alluded to earlier. At each moment of the process of training and inculcation of skills, the provision for feedback needs to be put in place through the conduct of *'Exercises'* so that understandings are developed and the horizons of would-be mediators and counsellors is widened. Also, as we list out and elaborate the process of counselling, some facets that are specific to counselling for women need to be highlighted. This brings home the point that women's needs and circumstances may require something more than the generalities in which the process of counselling and its methods have been structured in most of the literature on the subject.

We know from our working in the field, for instance, that women's experiences in the formal justice machinery in societies like ours are unfair and unsatisfactory. This is also our experience with women in other developing countries in Africa and South America. Between the formidable formal justice machinery, beyond the reach and comprehension of many women, and the oppressive arbitrary informal (community based) justice machinery, real justice continues to elude most women. Efforts are therefore needed and made to suggest the best ways to fight for justice. However, we also know that for women in societies like ours there is a tremendous pressure to adopt caring and giving roles. Any woman who seeks to define her own personal boundaries and place her choices and wishes within personal boundaries (even as she seeks justice) is likely to be viewed as an aberration of the ideal image of a woman.

The justice that women have got in society is the justice that has been agreed by society's norms and rules more often than not made by (male) lawgivers. This justice has been unequal and discriminating and the principles of that inequality and discrimination have been agreed within the society. Women's capacities to struggle or fight for anything outside of agreed norms have always been limited and constrained by the roles that determine their very existence. Any stepping outside these roles (both literally and otherwise) has landed them in deeper trouble. This would apply for most women in the context of South Asia and indeed much of the 'developing' world.

Exercise: Would-be counsellors and mediators are asked to reflect on how and why justice becomes out of reach for women in our society, and to give their views on how this affects women in distress in homes and outside. Some of their answers should be noted to see if the ideas undergo any change as they proceed. Such an exercise would be useful for the counsellor's own purposes and serve as a reminder of her own earlier perceptions of the realities of the women's lives and the limits to which they would be prepared to go.

Counsellor's Analysis:

- Our society accepts that gender inequality is inevitable and all our beliefs tell us that the man is the superior of the species. So women accept their place despite all adverse circumstances.
- Marriage and the family are the most important institutions for a woman and they have to be respected and revered at any cost. Justice is something that lies 'outside' and is unrelated to their lives.
- Domestic abuse—physical and verbal—become acceptable in a woman's life because society has suggested that this is part of her package and is not a crime as any law may wish to suggest.
- Silence is the women's answer to domestic abuse because in her view revelation of her private life reflects her own inadequacy— she would not even turn to a neighbour if she could, leave aside a formal institutional mechanism for redress.

This subject—of the place of justice in women's lives—seems to be ridden with contradictions and complexities. What constitutes dispute or conflict in a woman's life for a start is itself a matter of much speculation and disagreement. This is because areas of 'dispute' or 'conflict' are not seen in some societies as disputes worthy of needing resolution; they are considered part and parcel of the relational realities of any woman's life. Anything that looks like a conflict where the woman appears 'hurt' or 'injured' is regarded as nothing but the equations within the society where inequality is an acknowledged reality, and any friction caused as a result has to be surmounted through acceptance and not resisted or fought against. These frictions are required to be overcome in a manner that is in the interests of a larger whole rather than the interest of the individual/person (a concept not quite defined in the region under discussion). Even if a conflict involves violence there is a reluctance to expose it: Violence is an accepted part of life and fear is second nature because patriarchal values are so intensely ingrained that challenging what has not been challenged by other generations is a risk to the victim. Above all, the question is one of alternatives—another place to go to and other persons to be with. Both are dead-end roads.

This means that women in some societies who live their lives under two regimes—of customary and traditional rules, and of legalistic modern rules—are constantly in a quandary or dilemma. Positioned as they are in the midst of contesting mandates—of social norms and state laws—they are hardly in a position to determine when they are really in dispute- or conflict-ridden situations. Distress by itself is not enough as a reason for seeking help either in the form of mediation or counselling. More often than not women in such predicaments are encouraged by friends and neighbours to seek help: On their own they would rather live the rest of their lives suffering the discomfiture and humiliation that they have done for most of their lives.

Exercise: Mediators/counsellors are asked to suggest in training and orientation courses such situations as might constitute 'grey areas' where it is open to discussion whether the problem is a conflict situation in need of resolution and/or mediation, or other form of address, for example, harassment or mental cruelty.

Counsellor's Analysis:

- When women's needs and requirements are not top priority as in most ordinary South Asian households, continued denial or neglect of a woman's wants causes her acute demoralization turning soon to a depressive state. She wants help but has nothing specific in mind. She dare not say for instance 'I have never been given a new *saree* since I was married'.

- A nagging mother-in-law and an uncaring husband constantly taunt her about how little she brought by way of dowry but do not actual physically assault her. How shall I survive is her question.
- Her husband is an alcoholic and squanders all the family money on drink. He comes home in an inebriated state everyday and although there is no violence there is likely to be once the money runs out. She can see it coming and is in fear. She also feels the children being affected by the problem and by her helplessness.

Within the process of recognizing and determining such situations as conflict situations (or distress-causing situations that have the potential of becoming conflicts) lies the beginning of the process of a help-seeking or relief-providing service. This recognition needs adequate sensitivity and training to identify and perceive the problem areas of a relationship or situation that are the distress signals that may lead to violence. The presence of a forum where timely assistance to cope can be provided by measuring and assessing the problem areas with the client's cooperation has the potential of going a long way towards restoring balances in domestic situations. These 'problem areas' would show the presence of some of the following identifiable features in a measure considerable enough to cause a lack of equilibrium in relationships or day-to-day living:

- Bitterness
- Distress
- Discord
- Disharmony
- Disunity
- Dissension
- Friction
- Hostility
- Rancour
- Resentment

Unless these are methodically identified and then seen as needing remedial action, no step is likely to be taken by any party (either in a relationship or in a situational circumstance) that would be a step in the direction of counselling, mediation or settlement, or indeed any form of therapeutic intervention that might be a combination of any of these.

Exercise: Counsellors could have a discussion on each of the emotional states listed above and suggest how acceleration in each would lead to worsening living realities for women. This could be an exercise that produces variegated responses suggestive both of the social and individual features of different women.

The appearance and (conscious) experiencing of any of the aforementioned 10 'feelings' in the life of a woman is likely to constitute the beginning of a felt need and/or possibility/likelihood of relief providing intervention. It would also constitute the beginning of the process of *defining the need and determining whether the service on offer (here mediation/counselling) responds to the specific need suggested by the client herself.* This latter feature is of supreme significance in therapeutic interventions. It is also the point of entry for the assimilation within our formulation of the activity of counselling, mediation, or understandings of the principles of counselling (discussed earlier) and of the subjects of the counselling process (women as they are positioned in our society and their realization of how they are positioned).

What we need to do now is to *structure the use of counselling skills in mediation and dispute resolution* by bringing in the parts and steps of the process discussed earlier (see Process of Counselling in Chapter 4, pp. 87–94. While we begin the positioning of the steps of the process in one context, some of the details would be common to the other context as well. In addition, there is the specificity of the other context—of women in custody—that would need additional factors to be considered for counselling, which we shall do in the next section.

STRUCTURING OF THE PROCESS

We begin then with *the first part* of the process of counselling women who come for mediation in dispute resolutions—that of *Structuring of the Process* (in Chapter 4, pp. 88–92 that has been laid out in 11 steps: At the cost of repetition it may be stated that these

11 steps are those that need to be worked through by the counsellor almost in her mind and all through the process preferably, but not always in the order suggested.

Step 1: Matching the Client and the Counsellor

If we are talking of 'situations with special needs', then while it is assumed that with a modicum of learning and training in the objectives, principles and skills associated with mediation and counselling each member of a team will be able to 'deliver the goods', it is likely that a particular problem/situation might need particular counsellors to deal with particular clients. A counsellor with more experience in specific areas (of dispute and conflict) or with some legal experience, or other skills (in psychology or other background) might be better suited for particular clients/cases and would need to be assigned to that client by someone who has the authority to make that decision. The point made earlier (in Chapter 4, pp. 87–89) about a simple use of counselling skills being quite inadequate must be kept in mind at all times. The most well-intentioned counsellor might fail to achieve any change if some expertise and knowledge of the issues at hand are absent.

Exercise 1: A client comes to seek assistance on the subject of dowry harassment. *She is faced with a counsellor who knows no law and advises her from a common-sense perspective. How might the situation be improved if a counsellor who is better informed about the subject were assigned the case?*

Counsellor's Analysis:

> As an uninformed counsellor, my own personal experiences will colour my interaction. I may have had relatives who went through dowry harassment and the intervention of other relatives may have resulted in a reconciliation that suggested a return to harmonious living. In my client's case, the harassment may be unbearable and verging on the abusive, making the client's life a living hell. If there are violations of the client's human rights entitlements and legal boundaries are being crossed without adequate information about these entitlements, I would not be able to assist the client in looking at appropriate alternatives and then make up her mind about how

far she is prepared to go and how much she is able to forego in the interests of 'harmony'.

Exercise 2: Some of the complaints brought by a client in a matrimonial dispute clearly violate human rights agreed upon in most 'civilized' societies. A counsellor seems unaware of these specific rights: how does it affect the activity of counselling and mediation?
Counsellor's Analysis:

> Domestic violence is one of the most prevalent of these violations. Wife beating and vile verbal abuse has an acceptance rate that is mind-boggling. An ignorance of statutes and rules that relate to the most common causes of complaints would be a shortcoming that would affect the client adversely and nullify all the courage and effort she may have mustered up for coming to the Counselling Unit. I believe I would need to study the rights that relate to the issues that come before our Unit: the counselling I undertake would suffer if I did not.

Step 2: Reflection on Theoretical Orientations/ Approaches

The next 'step' would be to remind one's self of *the theoretical approaches that underlie counselling* so that it is not regarded as a random ad hoc activity carried out according to the mood of the moment and without the understandings that must accompany the activity (see Chapter 3).

Here again the fact that the counselling is for women in the social context specified becomes important. There is every chance that the women in question have never actually been in situations where their own individual and personal needs are being addressed. The problem therefore spills in all directions at first and several ways of addressing it need to be considered. Psychoanalytical, behavioural, humanistic, cross-cultural and feminist (see Chapter 3)—each of these approaches has a place in the activity and the importance of each in specific cases would have to be worked through by each counsellor according to the case and client. While looking at the person and the problem, the emphasis and the narrative would both need to be viewed from influences of the past, subconscious influences and behaviour patterns that are described as appropriate by the clients and why, objections by either party of the others' behaviour(s) to the point of total unacceptability and why—all these would enter the encounter between mediator and client.

Exercise 1: A woman makes a complaint about her husband's family and their attitudes to her. She wishes to be guided about how she can get her husband to live with her without his other family members (parents, brothers, their spouses, etc.) in the interests of a congenial conflict-free life. How does a counsellor intervene?

Counsellor's Analysis:

> Acutely conscious of the cultural pattern in South Asian society, where living in the joint family is prevalent and acceptable, as a counsellor I feel there may be a need to assess just what toll this is having on the woman's personality and behaviour. I believe there may be some gain from asking the client to elaborate her views on the gains and losses in her life as a result of sharing everything with everyone. I would like to take the client through the steps of envisaging a life where she is free from the 'other family members' and ask just how she feels. 'Guilt', 'blameworthiness', 'selfishness', 'self-interest', and 'shame' have been some of the responses to this exercise. I would like to ask the client whether she would like to bring her husband to the next session and see how he feels about any new arrangement.

Step 3: Self-reflection and Self-examination of Values/Attitudes by Counsellor

The third 'mini' step amongst those relating to the structuring of the process is of vital importance: it is that of self-reflection, self-examination or self-awareness. Almost as important as knowing the client and her problems is knowledge and awareness of one's self. A lack of awareness of one's self can damage the relationship between client and counsellor as well as the activity of counselling itself.

This part or step of the process would need to be followed almost consciously a few times at each assignment so that it gradually becomes an intrinsic part of the routine. There may be a need to actually formulate a sample or model of questions that each counsellor would need to put in place for herself. It can be done through discussion and consultation or it can be through a systematic writing out of issues and guidelines that are perceived by the counsellor as likely points to ponder over and consider so that there is untainted analysis of what she is faced with.

Designing a specific training module (which this is not) or writing a book to enable help-giving or mediation or counselling as an activity to become more professional (which this is) must begin by suggesting that the would-be counsellor or mediator would need in the first instance to ask questions of herself. If both counselling and mediation are activities in which there is a relationship between counsellor and client(s), they must begin with bringing challenges and snags at both ends of the equation to the surface. Not all the difficulties lie at the client's end of the equation: Many difficulties revolve around the would-be counsellor and/or mediator and his/her perceptions and/or inbuilt prejudices and biases. Coming to terms with these snags is possible only if the counsellor and/or mediator reflects on two related aspects about herself that are vital ingredients in the process or activity of helping:

1. *Awareness of one's self:* Why is this so important in developing skills for sustaining the counselling/mediation process? If counselling others and mediating is about resolving their disputes or conflict-ridden situations, and relates to the other person, why is the first set of questions addressed to one's self?

Exercise: A worthwhile exercise would be to ask counsellors/mediators the questions mentioned above—a discussion around their answers would lead to further elaboration and explanation. A specific line of inquiry can be should a counsellor be affected by her own experiences in life or consciously steer clear of them?
Counsellor's Analysis:

Being aware of how I am constituted and what identifies me as me seems relevant to the activity. I am my physical self, what defines me are my physical background, my parental guidance, my community's beliefs, my religious leanings, the nature of my education, my marital home and relations, and more. Which part of these features is important for me differs with time and circumstances, which in turn are part of my life's baggage. Sometimes if I want to do something my way, and differently from how I have done it before I find myself stopping in my tracks for reasons that lie outside of me: I am dictated to do something else out of fear of someone ('what will people say') or out of habit. Unless I analyse all these I will be leading someone seeking my help along my path and it may not be her journey at all.

The issue of self-awareness has been much written about in counselling and therapeutic treatises. One of the most common diagrammatic representations about just how much we really know about ourselves is popularly called the 'Johari window'[1] (see Table 5.1).

TABLE 5.1 The Self in Johari's Window

1. Known to All	2. Blind
3. Hidden	4. Unknown to All

Source: Adapted from Luft and Ingham (1955).

The Johari window divides our representation of ourselves into four parts. The first part is a view that is open and visible to all—we freely express this part of ourselves to all through what we say and through our behaviour and attitudes. The second part is a blind area for us that we cannot see but others can through our behaviour and body language. Our self-awareness can be enhanced from feedback from others about this area. The third area is personal to us and consists of our secrets (including guilt) that we choose not to share with others. It can only come to the surface through our own self-disclosure. The fourth part is unknown to all including ourselves and consists of our impulses, needs and anxieties. This is the part that can be accessed in the counselling process.

This is a way to assess one's self and may challenge our self-awareness, that is, how far we share ourselves with others and how far we are willing to explore the unknown. Awareness of one's self is important because the 'self' will be engaged in the process of making decisions with 'another' about *them*. There will be a partnership in which the partners will sit as equals and strive towards a goal that will enable one person (counsellor/mediator) to help another. It seems fit that we should be looking at ourselves and enhancing our self-awareness to see the obvious features about ourselves and also the not-so-obvious facets that manifest themselves now and then. Knowing our *knowns* and *unknowns* would help in the ways we strive to assist others by reminding us to think about our limitations and our facilitative strengths. In order that this is done in a manner that brings maximum benefit and advantage to the 'seeker' of help, the helper must be able to strip herself of particular attitudes that relate both to her position as helper and particular personality traits that would come in the way of the best way of reaching the goal of dispassionate help.

2. *A look at one's self*: The helper/counsellor needs to look at herself for a variety of reasons. The exercise is not unrelated to that of a person looking at her physical self in a mirror.

Exercise: An exercise might be conducted among participants to see the range of answers that are obtained to the question: Why do we look at a mirror each day?

The list of answers from counsellors suggests the degree to which some would emphasize the positive features of looking in a mirror and some the negative.

- I like to look presentable.
- I want to be accepted and looking good is one way.
- My mother always taught me to look neat and clean and so I make sure I do.

- I look at my face and see spots and try to find ways to remove them.
- My face is dark and dull and I apply some make up to look good.
- Sometimes I look at myself in the mirror and lament the fact that I am not as pretty as my sister.

It might be suggested here that physical appearance and acceptance is important both for the counsellor herself (feel-good factor) and for creating some impression on the client who would feel assured of her own worthiness. The mediator/counsellor must make an impression—in appearance, words, ideas, style and mannerisms. We are moving here into the realm of *personality*.

And this is where we come to the importance *of looking at one's non-physical self*. Like the look in the mirror this too has specific objectives. The look at one's person goes beyond the look at the mirror—into looking at one's personality and personality traits. The questions that emerge are likely to be:

- Am I patient?
- Am I polite?
- Do I inspire the other?
- Do I have an attitude problem?
- Do I prejudge a person? Do I have biases in life?
- Do I consider myself 'superior' to others by virtue of being the helper/counsellor/mediator?

Clearly this look is essential to assess whether there are traits or signs of being:

- Overbearing
- Dogmatic
- Opinionated
- Headstrong
- Self-willed
- Bigoted
- Narrow-minded

The objective behind using counselling skills for mediation is not likely to be achieved if the process is begun with a self-righteous attitude.

Apart from individual positions that a counsellor might adopt out of individual personality traits (being aggressive, impatient, etc.) there are social attitudes that she might have from her position in the social milieu to which she belongs. She may

- have religious leanings that might affect her thinking on a particular issue;
- be conservative about her views on age, gender, class or caste; or
- believe in particular customs practised in the society even when they are damaging for the self-esteem of the client.

Exercise: Would-be mediators/counsellors are asked what they would say about particular customary practices and their violations:

1. *inter-caste/religious marriages and*
2. *the idea of 'suffering in silence' to make for greater matrimonial stability. How far should the suffering go?*

Counsellors expressed themselves with conviction on both issues. On (*i*) they had some reservations that clearly sprang from their upbringing and family attitudes. Some expressed themselves against the idea of interreligious marriages based primarily on experiences of failed marriages in their own families. At the suggestion that perhaps the marriages failed because of the lack of support of the family they were silent and then added that that may be true. The idea of suffering in silence, in (*ii*), was unambiguously addressed in the negative. They did not believe that any human being should suffer in silence and that it was too painful because it only brought on more suffering by others to whom the first suffering was not conveyed.

Such personal expressions of attitudes of would-be counsellors/mediators need to be analysed and subtly exposed in a discussion without causing any cantankerous or belligerent emotions to arise in the discussion.

Step 4: Thinking through the Problem-solving Model

The next step is on how one thinks through the (*mediation–counselling*) model. It must be kept in mind that counselling as it accompanies mediation or assistance in dispute resolution must begin with the following:

1. two sets of '*knowns*' and
2. one set of '*unknowns*'

The 'knowns' are the counsellor's awareness about herself (albeit developed consciously) and the developed knowledge and training required for effective counselling and help-providing. The 'unknown' is the client and the client's problem(s).

The first 'known' has been discussed and its importance highlighted. Without a focus on one's self as a subject of analysis, mediation-cum-counselling cannot be productive. It will be tainted and judgemental. The other 'known' is the content and process of mediation-cum-counselling that constitutes the subject matter of this treatise. It is the tried-and-tested theories, approaches, styles, techniques and methods that are used, monitored and then evaluated to reach standards that conform to those principles of justice and equity that we are striving for in society.

The unknown for the mediator is the client and her problem. This needs special care in handling and understanding and each step of the counselling process has to be designed to bring the unknown slowly but surely into the realm of the known. It has being suggested here that the model we shall advocate is the problem-solving model. There is nothing complex in this model and it is as simple as it sounds. A few things about it need to be simply laid out for better understanding: Problem-solving is an activity with a desired result—that of reducing the distress and disharmony that has come about for a variety of reasons in a particular social setting. It needs to be planned and the moves and steps that are put in place for problem-solving activity are aimed at bringing this desired result nearer.

The problem-solving model has two parts to it:

1. decision-making (or choosing courses of action to reach the desired end)
2. problem analysis (or listing and examining the many factors that hinder or facilitate reaching the goal)

It would not be quite accurate to say that counselling in mediation or dispute resolution is a problem solver. But some of the rules and premises of reaching some kind of solution or compromise would be the same as that for straight problem-solving, for example:

1. One rule is that problems with one root cause are as rare as two moons in the sky!
2. Another is that thorough awareness and accurate and clear information about the problem and its ramifications are necessary.

Planning the strategy step-by-step is a good idea, rather than trial-and-error interaction. It gives the client confidence in the approach, method and mode of functioning of the organization/ person she has come to. Strategy planning makes the activity of mediation with counselling appear more formal and professional, thus achieving one end—that of being taken more seriously than any exercise in advising that the client may have so far been exposed to. Dividing it into steps that do not have to be sequential but need to be set out systematically nevertheless makes it more lucid and coherent for the client.

In *planning the strategy*, eight small steps are listed as follows:

1. Assessing the problem with the client
2. Beginning at the beginning
3. New ways of looking at the problem
4. Setting some goals

5. Opening some possibilities
6. Exploring some choices
7. Seeing how these might be implemented
8. One concrete action towards the desired goal

The advantages with this step-by-step process in the problem-solving model, simple and simplistic as it may look, are several:

- It gives some concrete shape to the task by focusing the attention of all parties to the specifics of the task at hand.
- It provides focus points to be viewed by counsellor and client giving logic to the process.
- It enables the activity to proceed systematically rather than randomly.
- It gives a patient start to the activity—'let's begin from the beginning' approach.
- It provides the appropriate space for the client to tell her story.
- It gives the client the feeling that the activity is about working together.

Step 5: Reviewing the Information

By the time we are addressing the fifth step of the structuring of the process—*that of reviewing the information*—some information would already have trickled in. We would have got a fairly good idea of the problem, and further information would need to be systematically elicited and classified.

There are two ways this might be done:

- Working outwards from the nucleus or core issue or
- Working inwards from a general narrative to the core or nucleus

Exercise: Cases of domestic violence, wife beating and drunkenness could be looked at either by going straight to the core *and talking about the violence and beating and then moving out to other factors, reasons, effects and results; OR these could be addressed by talking about the*

reasons for and effects of the specific behaviour and then moving in to the actual behaviour, events and scenes of violence and drunkenness. Mediators/counsellors should comment on the merits and demerits of each approach.
Counsellor's Analysis:

> It becomes clear in such cases that the client's own anxieties decide the approach. Some women are so full of the hurts they have endured that they want to go straight to descriptions of the beatings they have endured and the humiliation they are subjected to each day. Some will lift up their blouses and show the blue and red bruises and cuts from the last bout of violence and as they do so there are already tears and sobs that have to be addressed. They then move on to how this affects her and her children's living each day and how the family image is *'matti paleet'* (in the mud), so she really needs to sort it out once and for all. Other women start from the general end of humiliation, public image, shame, sorrow, end-of-life syndrome and even suicide. They have to be allowed to go on that route for a while and then be brought to specifics with some connecting phrases: *'to phir kyaa hua'* (so what happened?) This part of counselling would have to be client-led.

The information-providing and reviewing process is crucial. It connects to those parts or features (can be called 'mini steps') of the First Set of Steps—the Structuring Process—enumerated in Chapter 4 (pp. 88–92) that relate to 'note making' and 'record keeping'. It also relates to the mini steps in the Second Set of Steps—Getting Started—also discussed in Chapter 4 (14, 16 and 17 on p. 92 onwards) relating to 'information gathering', 'communication skills and techniques', and 'asking the right questions'.

Step 6: Working Out the Ground Rules for All: Flexibility/Sacredness

The step relating to working out *the ground rules* for all pertains to the concept of flexibility/sacredness. For the activity to be of a meaningful nature and be capable of being likely to achieve its intended goal, it would need to be placed within a framework constituted out of the goals and purposes that the activity is aimed at, and it would need to follow such rules and procedures that will prevent the activity from becoming too unstructured, aimless and therefore unproductive. These rules and procedures need to reflect how seriously the activity is being taken by all concerned. They relate to the following criteria:

- The physical setting
- The general ambience
- Seating arrangements
- The decorum on the premises
- Dress code and appearance
- The manner and mode of address between clients and counsellors
- Language/including body language
- Noise levels on the premises

Each of these is as important as the other and needs to be discussed at length with potential counsellors to assess whether they understand the emphasis on each. Sometimes counsellors disagree about particular emphases that an organization might place on a particular feature of the ground rules. It would not be advisable to lay it down as a stricture; the resentment caused by this would make for an uncongenial atmosphere.

The importance of discipline generally and of particular ground rules specifically would have to be placed within the mediation/counselling context in which they are being used along with the wider social context in which the activity is being carried out. In traditional societies, where the age of a client is a factor for better interaction, there would be a need to instil some idea of deference to age in the counsellors' preparation and training. Young counsellors may have other ideas and would have to be allowed to vent their feelings on such subjects during training but at the end of it the necessity of giving age and other vulnerabilities their due place would need to be emphasized without compromises.

In a mediation-oriented forum, there may be several parties that may have been called in by the counsellor after the first session with the complainant. The importance of ground rules is crucial in such cases.

Exercise: A woman has been harassed for dowry and her marital relationship is on the verge of a breakdown. Accusations are bandied back and forth by the two parties: a daughter-in-law backed by her parental family and a son backed by his. The dispute has become ugly and is likely to burst the banks. The counsellor/mediator needs to set out the limits of each person's intervention and still get a total picture.

Counsellor's Analysis:

> I believe that after the first meeting with the client and a preliminary conclusion that more members of the family may neea to attend the session and the counsellor would need to spell out how many may come and how they would conduct themselves. Too crowded a room is inimical to the process and the question of numbers would need to be worked through between counsellor and client. When the collective session begins, the counsellor would need to take charge as amicably as possible and set out the rules for submission and interjection and state at the outset that raising of voices, bad language or commotion would be dealt with firmly. There have been cases where the counsellor has turned out a secondary party with the words 'when you think you can participate congenially let me know and we can bring you back'.

Step 7: Setting a Time Frame and Timetable

Setting a time frame and timetable is essential: The activity of mediating and/or counselling cannot be without a time frame that determines its duration. Once a particular client and a particular problem has been formally registered and placed in a counsellor/ mediator's list, some attention should be paid to planning the process in terms of time. It is recognized that counsellors and clients have their own agendas when it comes to laying out the time frame and process for resolving disputes or redressing grievances. The client is in a different kind of hurry; she wishes for a speedy solution if it is a problem that is damaging her and affecting her life adversely. Mediators/counsellors are in a different 'hurry' often out to prove themselves and their work as 'success stories' and to that end may rush headlong into the kinds of solutions that are detrimental for the client and for the cause of mediation/ counselling. It is necessary that time and the time frame are all suited to the best needs of the client.

'Hearings' have to be conducted so that the client can perceive patience and calmness during counselling sessions. On the other hand, the hearing also needs to be structured so that it does not allow for rambling and aimless talking and meandering arguments. Points of view must all fit into some scheme worked out between counsellor and client. Some problems bring their own deadlines, others need to have deadlines placed upon them and still others need to follow a relatively open-ended agenda. What problem falls into which kind of scheduling has to be methodically thought through without being dictated by personal or ideological agenda.

Exercise: A client has a problem with her 'in-laws'. They are preventing her from getting a job and clearly dislike her ways that seem to go against their somewhat conservative view of life and particularly the role of a wife. Each day is a battle and there is little support from her husband who seems to be caught in between a 'parents and wife syndrome'. Clearly the woman needs help, but sessions with her drag on as she spells out different incidents of each day to demonstrate the restrictions on her movements and style. How does a counsellor get across to the client that even though help is being given, there has to be a limit on the amount of time she can be given for providing details?

Counsellor's Analysis:

> Drawing a balance between allowing a client to express herself freely and not indulging her to the point where she is going all over the place with her narrative is a delicate exercise. A counsellor's patience must not be mistaken for casualness and overindulgence. Under no circumstances must there be a violation of the parameters within which the activity and exchange needs to be carried out, irrespective of whether that relates to the time factor or to the counsellor's person.
>
> The counsellor would have gathered at some point that the woman is anxious to corroborate her side of the story with as many instances of daily clashes as possible. She needs to suggest to the client that she has got the picture and that in the interests of

arriving at speedy and meaningful solutions it may be a good idea not to get enmeshed in repetitive detailing of events. For a counsellor reminding the client about a time frame also enhances her value in the eyes of the client.

To assist in how such situations are addressed proficiently, discussions about the cases that come before all the mediators/counsellors of a counselling group are a good idea to enable an exchange of experiences and views. Periodic meetings between counsellors to share case experiences help in determining things like the time frame and ways of trimming open-ended sessions.

Step 8: Determining Type of Counselling

Alongside straightening out all of the above in one's mind, there is a need to figure out whether the type of counselling we are embarking on should be *facilitative or directive*: The counselling that accompanies dispute resolution and conflict management can be of different kinds. Depending on the nature of the client and of the problem he/she faces the methods of counselling can be facilitative or directive. An important feature of the process is that clients need to be viewed as equal adults. The process of helping, whether in mediation or counselling, must therefore facilitate the client in arriving at agreeable choices which can be made without compromising the fundamentals of the problem that brought the client to the site in the first place. Acrimonious statements or patronizing remarks would nullify the spirit of the undertaking.

If a woman subjected to physical abuse by a husband or relative comes to a forum for advice and counselling after enduring and suffering in silence, it would be erroneous to suggest steps that compromise the reasons for her coming. To come even remotely close to suggesting anything that resembles endurance or suffering in silence would be a compromise of a self-defeating kind for the client. The client must be enabled to think through ways whereby the maltreatment is stopped, and gentle suggestions of police help and the law's assistance can be made. On the other hand, if the client is on the verge of steps that resemble suicidal tendencies as a result of the gross violence she suffers at the hands of a spouse or relative, the counselling would need to be stronger than facilitative. It would need to direct the client to seek professional help—both legal and medical—and counselling would be supplementary to this direction.

Step 9: Goal-setting (Intermediate and Final)

Goal-setting is an important step in the process of structuring the counselling. Open-ended sessions without markers in between to suggest goalposts are like rudderless boats that can go all over the place with no sign of the shoreline. They can cause uneasiness in both the counsellor and the client. It helps to give one's self and vicariously the client a kind of road map that at least indicates the 'highways' and the 'rest places' where indications of some achievement are expressed. All these should be thought through so that this step is not slurred over once the sessions begin.

Each session should have

- A time boundary
- A pattern (a beginning, a middle and an end)

It must be stated clearly that goal-setting and time constraints are not supposed to suggest a rush in terms of clock-ticking time-keeping. Preoccupation with the clock would be destructive to the cause. Time boundaries and patterns for counselling are intended to meet what might be termed the client's own expectations and anxieties. Clients come to counsellors in a state of expectancy and the time element forms not a small part of that expectancy. While a rushed clock-ticking structuring of the session might be damaging, an overstretched lingering laidback approach can be equally injurious to the client's mental/emotional state.

Step 10: Patterns of Recordkeeping and Note-taking

Thinking through some patterns for *'recordkeeping'* and *'note-taking'*: One of the crucial parts of counselling in mediation and conflict resolution is the method and nature of keeping records and making notes. A client's records need to be properly labelled and sorted. The importance of 'notes' and how they are made, classified and categorized are most important. It must relate to what the goals are and also how we have worked through the methods. It must also be remembered that the method of record-keeping has to be one with which the client is comfortable. Technical equipment (audio/video recorders) should be used only after consent has been taken from the client. In some environs, these methods can make clients (particularly those unfamiliar with the techniques) scared and uneasy. Simple and traditional women sometimes 'shut up' if machines are placed before them. All this needs to be thought through at the commencement of the sessions. It is a good idea to take notes but also pause and try to retain something in the memory so as to maintain a constant eye-to-eye contact between client and counsellor. Written records have the advantage of containing such notes and observations that may be made by the counsellor while listening and reflecting during sessions.

Incessant 'note-taking' can also cause anxiety to the client. Clients come to counsellors, whether they are coming for mediation or for counselling or both, with some trepidation. To make the experience more awesome and formidable than it already is would be counterproductive. The client must feel the objective is to give 'real' help and not 'textbook' help coming out of paperwork alone. The mediator/counsellor must be reflecting and seen to be doing so.

Exercise: A sample of how notes can be taken up for discussion among counsellors to see how these might be improved upon. Also verbal and written exchanges and their intermittency might be discussed.

Step 11: Evaluation and Stocktaking—Tools and Methods

An important component in the steps laid out in structuring the process of counselling in the context of mediation/conflict resolution is that of developing and then fine-tuning the tools and methods that will be used when it comes to evaluating the activity of counselling. Evaluation is not an easy exercise at the best of times and caution needs to be exercised in preparing the scales, measures, gauges, frameworks, etc., for evaluation. This is a preliminary thought process and many of the actual measures for evaluation would emerge after some cases have been handled and some interaction between counsellors and clients has taken place. Some guidelines could begin the process. Others could be developed later. Attention can be given to some likely methods although this is something that would be actually put into effect at the end of the process:

- Self-evaluation through 'checklist'
- Evaluation through questionnaires—by clients and counsellors
- Observations by senior experienced colleagues
- Feedback from clients on levels of satisfaction (both parties to a dispute)
- Discussions of cases in periodic collective counsellor meetings

GETTING STARTED

When it comes to the actual action of the counselling process—*Getting Started*—we homed in on six mini steps (see Chapter 4, p. 92) that relate to the actual exercise of counselling. These comprise those steps that take on board the first thoughts and concepts related to the 11 steps of *structuring of the process* and then transfer them to the actual engagement and interaction with the client in the activity of counselling.

Step 12: The Physical Setting

The first concrete visible step (in terms of the whole process—the twelfth) relates to the *physical setting*. The first impressions of a client who is seeking assistance/counselling begin at the point at which they enter the premises where they have been called. No detail is too small to affect the nature of the activity and its impact on the subject.

The entrance, the walk up to the location, the room where clients (even when they are illiterate) and families are seated while they wait; the place where they sit face to face with the counsellor; the colours they see around; the posters on the walls; the ability to have their children around or taken care of while in session; the smells, lights and sounds around; the physical comfort of where and how they are seated; the feeling of confidentiality that the environment elicits—these are some of the features of the physical setting that need to be attended to.

Making the client both physically and mentally comfortable is equally important. Village women may prefer to be seated on the mat/rug; the seating in the room should cater for all types of clients, and the counsellor should also adapt if necessary. Setting up the room is a crucial part of the preparatory process. It should create a feeling of warmth and security not excessive formality and fear.

Distractions should be minimal—by way of visual objects, sounds, interruptions, and the ensuring of privacy. How the seating is arranged should be well thought through to serve these purposes. It has been referred to as 'helping the client feel safe' (see Sutton and Stewart [1997: Chapter 3]).

Step 13: Introductions and Greetings between Counsellor and Client

Once the client enters the place where she has been asked to come for counselling, there is the question of 'introductions' that is usually begun with the asking of names. These need to be shaped to suit the situation. If one way does not get adequate response, another may be tried.

Exercise: It might be a worthwhile exercise to see how the adoption of one way as opposed to another is made and does it tell us anything about the counsellor. Here are several ways:

What is your name?

Name?

My name is 'so and so' what is yours?

Do you have a name?

Who are you?

It may be a good exercise in self-analysis to see if the most appropriate method has been chosen for purposes of Introduction

The introduction is important because there are likely to be all kinds of clients: confused ones, distressed ones, anxious ones and resistant ones. The style therefore should sense the type and addresses should be formulated accordingly. Different types of 'opening lines' need to be worked through—they should neither suggest that the process that is being embarked on is one where insurmountable difficulties will be ironed out and problems solved (it may not happen); nor should it suggest that the client is there for a chat (that would be to make the exercise too casual).

Exercise: The would-be counsellor might be set some exercises such as 'If a distressed woman enters with the opening remark "My husband has left me, what should I do?" what should your first response and your first words be?'

Step 14: Exploring the Problem of the Client

After preliminaries have been dispensed with, the next step is *exploring the problem*—the core of the whole process, but not necessarily the only vital part of the activity. Each step has a place as important as another—however, this step is the reason for the activity and needs to be very carefully begun.

Exploring the problem means initially two things: There are factual features of the problem that the client has come with that need to be stated and understood; and there are subjective features that come through sometimes without being actually stated. For each of these some techniques need to be developed: There are things to adopt and things to avoid and these can be listed as the counsellor perceives the need to do so both as a reminder for the next session and for colleagues faced with similar situations.

Factual information about the problem may sound simple on the face of it. Facts need to be presented and addressed in a manner whereby their different facets are distinguishable, that is (a) clear statement of the problem, (b) the chronological happenings or case history, (c) the highlights (like crises and unusual incidents) and (d) present position and state of play.

Subjective information often sounds charged with emotion, and counsellors tend to be dismissive of it for that reason in an effort to exhibit 'professionalism'. Subjective utterances have their own place in the scheme of things and need to be tucked away in a separate 'section' as indicators suggesting two things:

- Explanations of certain behavioural features of the client and
- Indicators of how redeemable a situation is (or is not).

In this part of the process — exploring the problem — the most important activity for the counsellor is *listening*. This may sound simple but is actually quite complex and demanding and forms the crux of the whole exercise. If the process of listening is not wholesomely laid out, it affects the goal of enabling and assisting the client to set out and present the problem. *Listening* will be dwelt on in due course to break it up into components and types that make its importance self-evident.

If there is only party that has come she should be asked if it might not be a good idea for the other party to the dispute or conflict to be present as well.

Exercise: A man and wife live with his parents. They have a child and the woman has been feeling the total lack of privacy in their relationship and the interference of the mother-in-law in how to run things. The husband is not strong enough to resist the unreasonable demands of his mother, is not responsive to the wife's protests and therefore not likely to come to any counselling session. What should the counsellor advise to remedy the situation (a) to get the husband to come and (b) to get them both to talk constructively without prejudice?

Step 15: Information-gathering about the Client and Problem

The vital step of 'information-gathering' is probably one of the most difficult, even as it gives the appearance of being the most simple. Those embarking on counselling somehow convince themselves as they sit with notepad and pen in hand and that all they need to do at this step is take copious notes as the client talks, talks and talks. Nothing could be further from the truth.

First, there is the client's story. What people tell counsellors is usually said in an anecdotal form, story-telling being as old a form as any used by all of us. Stories are a vital means of communication; what is made of them is just as important because it is an indicator of just how much understanding has come through as explanation for thought and behaviour.

It all began [she might say] when I refused to pander to his every need, to drop everything I was doing and rush to give him something he wanted (a drink, his cigarettes, etc.). He would fly into a rage and this happened day in and day out... till one day when I failed to respond, he struck me....

[OR]

We don't have a television and once my husband leaves for work and I have done all my household chores I really feel so bored. I knit and sew, but how much of that can I do? My neighbour used to ask me to come for a couple of hours in the afternoons and watch a popular serial with her. One day I went. Just that day my husband came home early from work and gathered that I was next door. He came there and shouted at me unmindful of the fact that he was in someone else's home. I was so humiliated. When we got home he was abusive and when I protested he struck me and I fell.

There are narratives here; the events and circumstances are recalled to reveal the source of anxiety and problem and form the raw material for understanding the person/life/problem. But there is also something that suggests that the client had strong feelings about her role as a wife, housewife and so on. Complaints about fetching and delivering what the husband demands or not being at home even when he is away at work have an ambiguity about them. They are expectations that are fulfilled without a murmur as a routine by the woman and regarded as innocuous demands on their own, but should they become the subject of protest, the woman's underlying resentments that lie dormant come seething to the surface and become a cause for a complete *volte-face*. Such narratives need to be carefully heard without too many lead questions so that the counsellor is well apprised about the layers within each story.

Here too the question 'what approach needs to be adopted' would arise: Should it be person centred, psychodynamic or a combination of several? Random methods are not a good idea when gathering information. Some of the information gathering is routine and includes the following:

- Description of the problem
- History of the problem
- Personal information such as age, marital status, number of children, etc.
- Living pattern
- Health and habits
- Additional information (distress signals)

Other information has to be carefully (tactfully) elicited without appearing to be rushing or overanxious. Experts have warned against a few 'slips' that often occur:

- Counsellors losing themselves in details of a story and letting go remarks like '*ye to bahut bura hua*' (that was very bad) and thereby missing the point about why the person is before them.
- Counsellors start identifying some parts of the story with their own experiences and respond prematurely with comments like '*mujhe sab pata hai aadmi log kya karte hain*' (I have a very good idea how men behave). They want to express moral disdain and anger.
- Counsellors probing details that the client is sometimes not happy to divulge and thereby succumbing to a weakness that can prove damaging to the goal, for example, narratives of forced sex by the husband are interrupted with questions like '*kya karta hai tumhare saath?*' (what does he do to you?).

Step 16: Attitude-developing (Shedding One's Conditioning)

Attitude developing is a part of the process the value of which can scarcely be minimized, and it relates to both the attitude that the counsellor has towards the client and to himself/herself. This may sound simple, but the questions it raises are both theoretically and practically important. They have been both a subject of debate among therapists and a matter of concern among those who see the mushrooming of counsellors as a sign that suggests a diminution in the importance attached to the professionalism that must accompany the activity of counselling.

This pertains to the whole question of 'how should one view the help seeker?' A debated supplementary question that is often asked is what the seeker of help should be called. A lot of discussion has surrounded this issue and the nomenclature 'client' that is universally acknowledged as the term best suited is still debated from time to time (see Lindon and Lindon, 2000: 14). To create some professionalism and formality in the whole exercise, the word 'client' has been retained even by those who wish to emphasize that this is a person-oriented activity that takes full cognisance of the individual person and the difference between individuals.

There are many ways in which particular attitudes develop in the minds of counsellors and affect how the counsellor views the client and how the ensuing activity unfolds. These need to be highlighted to suggest how they might be avoided:

- A negative outlook: 'What's the use: how do I know the person will really take heed of all this'
- Displeasure and annoyance at the client's periodic behaviour
- Inability to surmount a class/culture divide
- Being too chummy and losing sight of the objectivity of the activity
- Agreeing with someone against someone and losing objectivity
- Trying to control by giving direction to see something the way you see it
- Using clichés and platitudes and sounding like one is preaching
- Listening too passively
- Grimacing and frowning at the unpleasant parts of a narrative

These are only some of the real/small ways that can lead to the development of an inappropriate attitude on the part of the counsellor to what the client is trying to say. Connected with this is a larger issue: How exactly does a counsellor conceptualize his/her work? Is subtle disapproval ever a good idea? Is counselling a domain in which the therapist as the author of the ground rules allowed to express herself when she wishes? Is the activity one in which the two parties face to face are not really equals at all and the relationship is really asymmetrical?

To answer this means going into an academic debate between the traditional view of therapeutic intervention as pure professional and the modern 'democratic' view of therapists that think there is value in establishing a relationship in which the two sides are equal (the differing views in the two schools can be seen in the works of Carl Rogers and Hans Strupp). This equality can be interpreted as the counsellor's ability to say what she has in mind too. While the answer to the question of equality and professionalism may not lie entirely on one side or the other, if one did have to give more weight to one view, it would be to the maintenance of a fair degree of professionalism in the conduct of counselling to make it result oriented.

This may be problematic in societies where hierarchies and asymmetrical relationships abound and where the formality associated with professionalism would tend to overawe a 'help seeker'. But if the counselling that accompanies mediation and redress of grievances were to be so informal (and equal) that the client viewed it as a lightweight exercise not deserving of the seriousness it deserves, it would lose its meaning. If the time and energy dispensed by the counselling forum is not to be wasted, then gravity rather than levity should be the guiding mood.

COMMUNICATION TECHNIQUES AND SKILLS

Of all the features in the process of counselling, communication, with all its forms and content, is an activity that occurs throughout the exercise at each twist and turn of the interaction, at all times. So, even as it is being placed at the end of the list, it in fact is the beginning, the middle and the end. It is also the feature that is most affected by the individual, social and cultural aspects of the environment where counselling takes place. Information, thoughts and emotional experiences all have to be communicated for effective help to come about.

It has been said that a fish would be the last creature to discover the existence of water: because water is such an intrinsic part of a fish's environment its presence is hardly noticed. So, it is suggested, is communication. It is so much a part of life that we hardly notice it as something that is distinctive, different from person to person, from time to time. Only if one is aware of its significance can it be changed to meet the needs of the situation.

Whether we admit and realize it or not, we all look at the world and each other with our own 'coloured glasses'. This is not to suggest that we are full of biases and prejudices that we find difficult to overcome. It is simply to suggest that unless we are aware of them, our 'coloured glasses' are likely to influence the way we respond to situations in which we need to stay neutral and non-judgemental; and this is likely to influence our communication styles.

Communication is thus the area where 'techniques and skills' so often referred to in counselling and its professionalism take concrete shape. Most of these techniques and skills are in fact about communication one way or another.

Right at the beginning of the process of counselling in dispute resolution, one is not starting with a blank page. There is communication even before the first words are spoken: the body language tells a story at both ends. And it reveals through eyes, hands, feet, head movements, general posture, yawning, etc., and even before the facts and information are verbally exchanged, there are criteria of a relationship, such as the following:

- Moods
- Expectations and assumptions
- Attitudes

We are all aware that communication is verbal and non-verbal. The skills associated with verbal communication are of *form* and *content*. Aspects of *form* that need to be focused on are as follows:

- Tone of voice
- Volume
- Rhythm
- Accent
- Speed
- Turn of phrase

Being aware of one's style of talking and communicating is important; and each of the above-mentioned features should receive attention and be modulated or modified for very often there is a need to do so. This would only happen if counsellors have been trained by persons who have taken the pains to work through the essentials of these features of communication. This is not to suggest uniformity in conversing skills but an emphasis on the need to be understood with the least ire all around.

The content of *verbal communication* is best measured by the use of two gauges:

- That it is clear and simple and hence easily understood.
- That it is fetching appropriate responses from the client.

There are ways of ensuring that this in fact happens: an investigation into what language the client is most comfortable with would be required. Sometimes the client may be from a social background that is quite remote from that of the counsellor. It then becomes a case of 'stooping to conquer'; a few phrases from the client's dialect and a few reassuring remarks to make the client at ease (without compromising the formality of the activity) are sometimes a good idea. The counsellor does not then appear like an alien unlikely to understand the client's problem or predicament.

Body language is the most prevalent conveyor of *non-verbal communication*. Some aspects of it that can be elaborated upon when communication skills are being taught are:

- Facial expressions
- Eyes movements and eye contact
- Posture and hand movements
- Physical space between client and counsellor
- 'Space' — spatial and temporal (another way of saying avoid breathing down the neck)

Reference was made earlier to the feature called *listening* (earlier in the chapter on p. 123); as vital to the types of communications we are listing are the types of listening we do. How we listen is not as straightforward as we would like to portray. It has been classified into 'passive' listening and 'active' listening (see Sutton and Stewart, 1997: 45). Passive listening is nothing more than hearing, hence the phrase 'I hear you but I am not listening'. Such listening is ineffective because it fails to respond and communicate understanding without which the whole relationship of mediator/counsellor/client is also ineffective and purposeless. Conveying that one is listening may well have to be learnt and there are tips that can be kept in mind.

Active listening is of crucial importance if we are seeking cooperation from the client in helping her to surmount the problem at hand. Properly carried out it fetches a level of mature responses and behaviour from the client. Some common tips that are truly common but often get overlooked are as follows:

- Ensure that there will be no interruptions.
- Co-workers should not interrupt or make distracting noises that disturb ongoing sessions.
- Do not leave a session for any but the most pressing reasons.
- Erase as far as possible all unrelated thoughts from the mind once the session begins: no inner monologues of any kind, not even the worry whether the client will go away happy.
- Do not fiddle with fingers, jewellery you may be wearing, pen or pencil, do not tap table with fingers and do not fidget.

1. Equations between prisoners—a comfort for the elderly. State Jail for Women, Hyderabad (Copyright: Rani D. Shankardass)

2. Children old enough to remember where they spent their formative years, Rajahmundry, 2000 (Copyright: Rani D. Shankardass)

3. Prisoners washing personal belongings at the common tank at Women's Jail, Warangal, 2002 (Copyright: Rani D. Shankardass)

4. Informal counselling styles to make the client feel at ease, Hyderabad, 2002 (Copyright: Rani D. Shankardass)

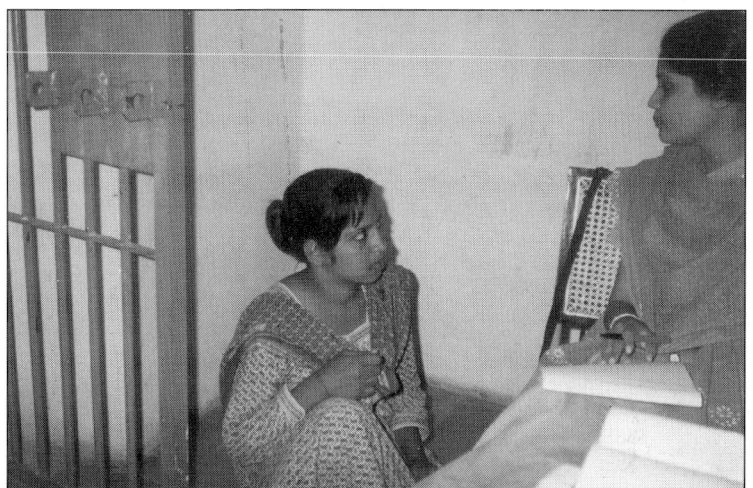

5. Another case of informal counselling, Hyderabad, 2002 (Copyright: Rani D. Shankardass)

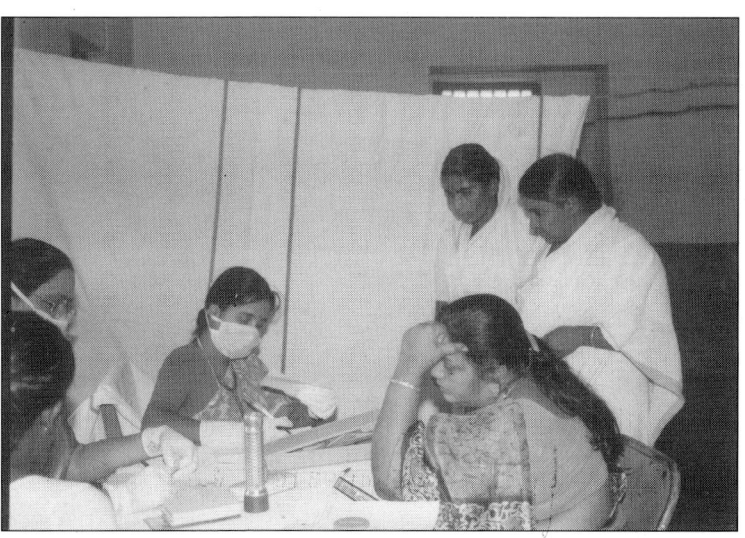

6. Medical camp organized by PRAJA counsellors at State Jail for Women, Hyderabad, 2001 (Copyright: Rani D. Shankardass)

7. *Rangoli* competition organized by PRAJA counsellors at State Jail for Women, Hyderabad, 2001 (Copyright: Rani D. Shankardass)

8. Inner courtyard outside the barracks in Women's Jail, Jaipur (Copyright: Rani D. Shankardass)

9. The sewing room in Women's Jail at Jaipur, Rajasthan (Copyright: Angela Clay)

10. Prisoner's private prayer corner—the solace when all else fails, Rajah-mundry, 2000 (Copyright: Angela Clay)

11. How old do they have to be to go home?
Rajahmundry, 2000 (Copyright: Angela Clay)

12. Convicts assembled to be addressed by officers, Rajahmundry, 2000
(Copyright: Angela Clay)

13. Age no bar? Rajahmundry, 2000 (Copyright: Angela Clay)

14. Emotional protest by agitated woman, Rajahmundry, 2000 (Copyright: Angela Clay)

15. Informal counselling for a woman 'in custody', Hyderabad, 2002 (Copyright: Rani D. Shankardass)

16. *Saari umar chakki peesogi!* [You will grind wheat forever in a jail!]: The age-old taunt for women offenders (Copyright: Angela Clay)

- Maintain eye contact with the client without making her uncomfortable.
- In cultures where women tend to look down, try to win over enough confidence to enable her to raise her head.
- If she is nervous ask if she would like water.
- Try to summarize after the client has spoken to give the client faith in your listening.

It is of benefit if the Counselling Unit has several counsellors working in it for some (senior counsellors) to sit in on others' sessions and then comment and discuss after the sessions (perhaps on appointed days each week) what was appropriate and what inappropriate in the session.

A vital part of the form of communication is 'asking the right questions'. There would be a set of questions that a counsellor needs to ask herself/himself and another set she needs to ask the client. The former are as vital to the process as the latter. The questions that need to be asked of one's self are related to how the client would view the counsellor and his/her style. These questions are simply like this list below:

- 'How do I look?' which means nothing elaborate, simply that the way one looks should inspire some confidence in the client.
- 'Have I developed my style of communication, that is, am I conscious of politeness, friendliness and attentiveness?'
- 'Am I uncomfortable when the client expresses her emotions and feelings?' This is important because sometimes persons are afraid of too much spilling of emotions from the client and cannot handle that.
- 'Am I judgemental? Do I allow my own views, experiences and moral stand to affect the manner in which I listen to the client and respond?'
- 'Am I affected by the client's background and style' (such as lack of finesse in language, bad posture, awkward body language, shabby dress, etc.)?
- 'Am I intolerant?' or 'Am I too indulgent because what the client is saying is something dear to my heart?'

- 'Have I paid sufficient attention to the specific condition of the client? Have I given due consideration to the fact that the client is uneducated, old, or too young, or upset and therefore impatient?'

The next set of questions would then be addressed to the seeker of help. These questions require both understanding and skill and cannot be blurted out as questionnaires in a survey. They need to be put with sensitivity and full understanding of the person. This means adopting a style and method in communication that is suited to the ends of the exercise of mediating and counselling.

A good starting point would be to ask the client, after the preliminary introductions: 'Where would you like to start?' This stage has often been referred to as 'Stage One' of counselling skills, and the one feature highlighted about this stage is *empathy* (not to be confused with sympathy which goes in another direction).

After a brief narrative, looking for a break trying to intervene to show some understanding of the basic problem is a good idea. If there is more than one person present, the next step might be to ask others to speak one by one, after determining how helpful it would be to call upon the particular person in question. While being patient, it would not help to allow speakers to go on and on and a polite 'I am afraid we will run out of time so let me recap' might be called for.

And so the session would proceed.

CASE ANALYSIS IN CONTEXT: MEDIATION AND DISPUTE/CONFLICT RESOLUTION

The case discussed later (dowry harassment and wife-beating) is one of thousands that come before a Counselling Cell that was set up by a national women's organization to assist such women in distress who were reluctant to go to police stations and courts at the first instance of dispute and/or conflict-ridden situations.

This cell located at a prestigious Women's Commission in India had on an average 15 to 20 women come to it for help and assistance in mediating disputes and counselling each day. While the Cell provided a much-needed service, it was unprofessionally run and certainly did not meet the standards of counselling that are universally recognized and required for a unit to be called a professional *Counselling Unit*. The case being recounted here was one of many of its type and is being discussed to demonstrate the nature of the situation/problem that was brought to the forum, what was done about it, whether the methods and conclusive actions were appropriate and if not what was really required in structural and functional terms for the whole exercise to merit the label 'counselling'.

As a non-government organization (NGO) that had researched the subject and accumulated information on how the activity was conducted at different locations, Penal Reform and Justice Association (PRAJA) offered to professionalize the Counselling Cell at this Commission. Penal Reform International (PRI), an international NGO, funded a year-long project specifically designed to make an in-depth study of several features of the existing Cell and then suggest measures that would bring it to the standards that were needed for it to be called a Counselling Cell. It was considered apt that the Cell be called the Complaints and Counselling Cell (CCC) because it was oriented towards receiving *complaints* and *providing counselling* when mediation, problem-solving and dispute resolution were being carried out for women who came to seek help.[2]

The case given below is a sample of one of the most prevalent problems brought to the Cell and has been selected for discussion both for the range of issues it covers and also for methodological purposes. An analysis of the existing Cell is also given to indicate what provisions for Counselling (and mediation) should *not* be. The counsellors (and in these particular cases they play a dual role that of mediation and conflict resolution, as well as counselling) that handled these cases were neither qualified nor trained in the appropriate skills required for the work, nor in the idea that counselling was a specialized activity and was not simply advice-giving.

This was the first time that the collection of cases at the Cell had been 'opened' for purposes of study and then systematically consolidated. The working team that collated the data, supervised the filing and classified the cases was comprised of a social anthropologist and a young lawyer as assistant. Both the documents and the functioning of the CCC were sought to be put in place in a manner that would transform it from a haphazardly run cell to a professional unit.

Over a whole year, the team first systematized the records, organized the counselling unit and finally prepared a training module for would-be counsellors. Unfortunately, not all of its recommendations were taken on board, primarily because several persons (official 'members') within the women's organization believed they were perfectly capable of taking on the role of counsellors and believed themselves to be suitably equipped to counsel all or any distressed women who came to the Commission. *They did not believe that attending to the distress signals of women required any particular skills or training in the art of counselling.* For these functionaries of the Commission, counselling meant listening to problems and giving advice that was akin to a solution. Such a simplistic view of the task of 'counselling' was regrettable because what could have been developed at that juncture was a professional training scheme that could have been put in place once and for all for would-be counsellors. 'Members' being at relatively senior levels in the organization considered themselves 'above' training. This is an attitude problem and a danger faced by many institutions in this part of the world: Senior functionaries consider themselves proficient in their work and therefore above any need for training which is seen as the requirement of the less proficient and competent. That training is a prerequisite in any field where there are special needs to be addressed with newer modes of functionality is not a consideration. Several service providing agencies (e.g. judges) often have the same attitude to training and believe it compromises their exalted status. In reality, training simply aims to bring the persons involved in the special activities in line with more recent thinking on the subjects and issues at hand and it brings into focus the primary objectives of engaging in the activity in the first place. It also sharpens the tools through which more sophisticated development in the field can be undertaken.

In professionalizing the Counselling Unit at the Women's Commission, it was first considered necessary for meticulous procedural steps to be set out that would form a part of the running of the Cell. This was necessitated by the fact that some individuals in the organization had little idea of what 'counselling' really was and erroneously believed that it was essentially about giving good wholesome advice, and that as mature women in the organization they were perfectly able to do that across a table if someone came with a problem, without any further ado. That was not a good beginning because (as we have clarified earlier in this book) *counselling is not merely advice-giving.*

It was thus necessary to set out what was a general procedure for carrying out the everyday activities pertaining to the running of the Cell, which was as follows:

1. That when a complaint was made, the *first* step was to be that the *'client' should give the complaint in writing.* This needed to be the regular practice for proper recordkeeping and referral in all organizations that have, or want to establish, a complaints and Counselling Cell.

2. That a 'case' was then to be formally *registered* and a *file* prepared and given a number for *recordkeeping* (an activity that had so far been somewhat haphazardly carried out—often cases did not come to the Cell first but got intercepted by functionaries who wished to conduct mediation, counselling and dispute-resolution themselves).

3. That a *centralized registration* process was another requirement (hundreds of cases were later filed as a part of the process of centralization of registration that had not been registered in the cell).

4. That *files needed to be organized systematically* (subject, theme, date and case wise).

5. That the *assignment of cases to counsellors* needed a system or procedure. The person in charge was neither acquainted with the activity of counselling nor familiar with the cases and counsellors. To cap it all, this person was a male and lived in constant fear that if he overstepped in ensuring

discipline or pointing out errors, he would be accused of sexual harassment at work by the women counsellors.

6. That there was *a need for principles and guidelines to be established* in relation to allocation of cases to counsellors both in terms of quantity of work and nature of the problem or case.

7. That *a time frame or timetable needed to be prepared* according to which counsellors would work—the paperwork was minimal and the fact that this was a good opportunity for an organization to be a centre for research and for providing future guidelines and strategies for intervention for distressed women had not come into the mode of operation at all.

8. That the *physical layout of the Cell or cubicles* needed to be redone because it was unsuited for the purposes intended. The Cell was housed in a long rectangular hall together with the administration and cash section. Six counsellors sat in separate open cubicles that were set one after another, close to each other, so that all that happened in one cubicle was visible and audible in the next cubicle or even further. Privacy (a vital ingredient of effective mediation and counselling) was totally lacking, which must have inhibited the complainants even if they said little about it.

9. That *quiet and calm was an essential requirement of the activity of mediation/counselling.* The noise level in the hall was disturbingly high at all times, and often became a din when several complainants were being heard by counsellors during the counselling, mediation, problem-solving and dispute-resolution sessions.

10. That *more space was required for counselling*: The existing cubicles of the counsellors were too small and neither cosy nor welcoming.

As a first step, a little redecoration (pictures, plants, posters, etc.) was undertaken and carried out. Counsellors' cubicles were provided with nameplates, and notices for clients were placed at several points for their assistance and guidance. Directions for where to register and where to wait were also put in place and a small waiting area provided where clients could wait with family members instead of wandering around wondering where to go and wait.

Case of Sumitra: Dowry Harassment and Wife-beating

This particular case out of the thousands that came before the organization for mediation or counselling has been chosen partly to demonstrate some typical cases that came before the Cell with a greater frequency than others, and also to highlight features of the Cell's methods of functioning (and malfunctioning) in dealing with such cases. These features highlight some typical problems and describe the kinds of women (the 'clients') and their backgrounds, their living realities and expectations, profiles of the counsellors, the manner of functioning of the counsellors and what they did in each case and what they should/could have done. The case (both history and sessions) has been elaborated to reveal where there were gaps and errors in handling in the particular context (women, the Indian social scene and the particular organization that was the venue for the counselling/mediation activity). All the names have been altered for reasons of confidentiality.

Most of the cases that came to this CCC located within the Commission relate to dowry harassment compounded by wife battering. Sumitra made her complaint in early April 2001 and the case was assigned to Mrs A. The *written* complaint was undated, as the counsellor did not bother to ask the complainant to put a date on the complaint nor did she do so herself. Most of the facts of the case are derived from this written complaint. Other details were described and narrated by the complainant during the course of the sessions, notations of which were few and scanty.

Sumitra was married in 1995 (according to Hindu rites) to Vinod Sharma, who worked in the Indo-Tibetan Border Police (ITBP). Vinod lived in a joint family. After just four days of being married, Sumitra's harassment began—her 'in-laws' began taunting her about the *dowry* that she had brought with her. It was 'meagre', 'inadequate', 'not commensurate with the status of the family' and so on. This was reason enough for some power to be exercised over Sumitra, and this was also the beginning of a process of control that becomes an integral part of a young bride's position in her in-law's family in South Asia. Sumitra was forbidden to go to her parents' home even if her father or brother came to fetch her (as is customary), and the refrain was that the father really needed to have given sufficient dowry if he had wanted Sumitra to be happy and free to go and come as she pleased. Sumitra's complaint stated that her father had mortgaged his pension in his old age to get her properly married and to give enough dowry. She feared for her father's health if he learnt of the taunts she had to endure for bringing insufficient dowry. This fact is significant for the context.

Sumitra's husband unfortunately did not consider his family's behaviour towards his wife as harsh or cruel or needing intervention. Fifteen days after their wedding, Vinod Sharma left for his (job) posting in Kashmir. In his absence, Sumitra's plight worsened: the verbal harassment turned into physical violence. With time the physical abuse increased and appeals for mercy and consideration fell on deaf ears. The entire family (parents-in-law, sisters-in-law and brothers-in-law) stood united in their hostility to an increasingly isolated and desperate Sumitra. Some relief came when after about nine months spent in the in-laws' house she was able to accompany Vinod to Kashmir, where Sumitra conceived. But there was no relief from the taunts about dowry and now the husband physically tormented her almost every night simply to assert authority and power.

After five months, Vinod was sent to Chandigarh for training. Sumitra was in the third month of her pregnancy and still at the receiving end of physical and mental torture. She had to be admitted to the hospital for treatment. In the eighth month of her pregnancy, Vinod brought Sumitra back to his parents' home (Delhi), where she delivered a baby (girl). She had a Caesarean delivery, but 'in-laws' brought her home from the hospital within three days of childbirth. The birth of a girl did not bring joy to the in-laws, who had one more reason to taunt Sumitra—she had not delivered a son. Antagonistic behaviour continued and she was deliberately asked to do the kind of work that was obviously dangerous in the post-natal period, due to which one day her 'stitches' split open, and Sumitra was soaked in blood and she fainted. While her infant child kept crying and howling, no help was forthcoming for either the infant or her mother. Sumitra clutched the child fearing 'they' might harm her baby. She was taken to the hospital late that night and left to sleep in the hallway; she was formally admitted after three hours. The mother-in-law was with her. Sumitra remained in hospital for almost a month unable to sit or walk in all that time. She told her tale of woe to the doctor and nurse who were moved and took charge of looking after Sumitra's daughter.

When Sumitra's condition improved, her brother-in-law (husband's brother) and his wife got her discharged from the hospital and took the mother and baby to their home in Mau and 'dumped them there'. The sister-in-law, Rajni, reluctantly agreed to let Sumitra and the baby stay in her house for a month showing no compassion or concern.

At the time of her writing the complaint, Sumitra said her daughter Pinky was four-and-a-half years old. Pinky contracted tuberculosis in Dehradun where Sumitra's husband was later posted and underwent treatment for nine months. Sumitra said that her daughter recovered physically but became a tense child as a result of having been subjected to physical abuse by her paternal grandparents. Rajni had little use for the mother and child and had a vested interest in removing them from Vinod's life, having manipulated Vinod into giving his earnings to her. Such a phenomenon is not uncommon in Indian joint families.

Soon after this incident, Vinod took Sumitra and Pinky to Kashmir. Vinod would often lock Sumitra and her daughter in the room for days and nights; and often women in the neighbourhood who knew of Sumitra's plight would come and rescue Sumitra and Pinky. When they returned to Dehradun the beatings and oppression had become unbearable. At that time Sumitra sent her daughter Pinky to Mau with Rajni. Vinod changed three accommodations after having been transferred to Dehradun. Finally they got living quarters through the ITBP, and Rajni brought Pinky to Dehradun to be with the parents. She continued to instigate Vinod against his wife and child, getting Pinky beaten under one pretext or another. On one occasion Pinky urinated and defecated as a result of the beating and when Sumitra went to rescue her daughter, Vinod and Rajni turned violent towards both Sumitra and Pinky. A neighbour heard the screams and went to the Commanding Officer's (C.O.'s) house and got the C.O.'s wife to intervene and rescue the mother and daughter. The C.O.'s wife arranged for a vehicle that took away Vinod and Rajni. Sumitra was badly hurt on the head, had black eyes and blood that had oozed out of her wounds had clotted at different places on her body. She was semiconscious. Sumitra met with the C.O. and told him her plight. The neighbours telephoned Sumitra's brother at the Indian Institute of Public Administration (IIPA) to get him to talk things over with Vinod. They believed that might make him relent and stop his brutal behaviour towards his wife. But nothing changed.

In fact Vinod's cruel acts increased after the intervention from her family and friends. His bizarre behaviour included acts like stuffing a towel in Sumitra's mouth and then beating her, or administering electrical shocks to her if she protested. When Sumitra's brother came to Dehradun (4 April 2001), once again at the plea of Sumitra's neighbours he went and met the C.O. and also discussed Vinod's behaviour with the Deputy Inspector General of Police (D.I.G.). They suggested that he take Sumitra back with him. She was called to the D.I.G.'s office and escorted by a constable to the taxi stand from where she left Dehradun with just the clothes she was wearing and without her daughter. Sumitra reiterated that all the things she had received from her father and from her in-laws at the time of her marriage were kept by the in-laws and Vinod kept the daughter with him by threatening dire consequences if she disagreed.

At the time of writing the complaint (April 2001), Sumitra was living in the IIPA hostel in Delhi where her brother lived. For some time she had been receiving telephone calls from her husband asking her to return at once to Dehradun so that they could go to Vinod's sister's wedding in the village. He threatened to kill Sumitra, her brothers and all the members of her family if she did not comply.

Sumitra pleaded that she had been very severely harassed and was physically and mentally at the end of her tether. She could not eat properly and was physically and mentally unwell. She requested that she be medically examined and that her husband and his family members should be legally tried for oppressing her. With a poor father who had done his best for a large family of five brothers and four sisters (Sumitra was the youngest), she was aggrieved that things had come to this tragic state.

On 24 July 2001, both the disputant parties presented themselves before the counsellor 'Mrs A'. Vinod came with his mother and Pinky, and Sumitra with her brother and his wife. There was thus quite a crowd spilling right out of the cubicle and the arrangement for sitting was clumsy. The parties came face-to-face without the counsellor having done any homework at preliminary meetings to be able to assuage their bitterness, anger and antagonism towards each other. There was a 'free for all' at this meeting. Tempers ran high, almost leading to fistfights and the counsellor was somewhat out of her depth on how to tackle the situation. Amidst the shouting and vituperation, the counsellor just sat there listening, making no move towards either discipline or postponement of the meeting. The discussion that should have taken place between Sumitra and Vinod with some dignity and decorum did not happen and both the husband and wife hurled all sorts of allegations at each other, with family members making matters worse with adversarial interventions. Vinod said that he had hit Sumitra only once and that Sumitra was being instigated to complain against him by her brothers. With tears in his eyes, Vinod told the counsellor that he had sought counselling in Dehradun too and wanted to resume a peaceful married life but that Sumitra (influenced by her brother and family) was not interested in that. Sumitra's contention was that she had suffered far too much at the hands of Vinod and his family and found it difficult to believe his words. Her wounds were deep and she was not ready to reunite with Vinod yet.

In April, Sumitra had already taken steps to have her daughter returned to her, and for that the counsellor had sprung into action and by powers vested in the organization wrote a letter to the Superintendent of Police (S.P.), Dehradun, asking him to rescue Sumitra's daughter from Vinod and hand her over to Sumitra. The counsellor had been told in reply that the matter of custody was one that could only be decided by a court and that police officials could only be asked to make enquiries about Sumitra's daughter. The counsellor's intervention thus did not result in any solution of the problem, and Sumitra's daughter was restored to her through the assistance of Vinod's senior officers when Sumitra went and met them personally (without the counsellor's intervention). Sumitra's daughter Pinky was handed over to her on 30 April 2001. Sumitra told this to the counsellor on 2 May 2001. The counsellor naturally lost face here and her credibility went down considerably in Sumitra's and her family's eyes.

After the communication between the counsellor and S.P., Dehradun, Vinod had asked a counselling organization in Dehradun to communicate with Sumitra's counsellor. The communication revealed that Vinod was going through sessions of counselling in a Psychiatric and Counselling Centre in Dehradun, that he was mending his ways (by quitting smoking and drinking and holding a steady job) and that if a meeting could be arranged with him before the child's school reopened so that the problem could be sorted out, it would be extremely beneficial for the child and the family unit as a whole and the marriage could be saved.

Up to that point, the counsellor had not considered it necessary to call Vinod or hear his side of the story. It was when Sumitra told the counsellor that she had received a letter from her husband telling her that Pinky's school had opened and she should join the school that she (i.e. the counsellor) decided to call Vinod on 24 July 2001. She also asked Sumitra to come so that all parties were present. That meeting again resulted in a commotion and the counsellor decided to terminate it and asked them to return on 6 August.

On 6 August 2001, Sumitra came with her daughter and as usual with her brother and his wife in tow. Vinod came alone.

This time the counsellor showed more sense and first met Vinod alone. Vinod (naturally) had a different story to tell: He said that he wanted to take his wife and daughter with him, but there were some facts he wanted the counsellor to know. He said that Sumitra's father (now deceased) had asked Vinod to loan him money to reconstruct the roof of his house. After the father's death, her brothers refused to repay the sum and also refused to have Sumitra return to Vinod.

The counsellor then called Sumitra to reveal to her Vinod's version of the facts. Sumitra was confused and emotional, and when Vinod saw his daughter Pinki, he also became emotional. He asked his daughter whether she was happy and the child said that the uncles and aunts constantly scolded her and that she was not given milk to drink. Vinod hugged his daughter and said that he would take her away and give her as much milk as she wished. The counsellor tried to tell Sumitra that without a job and income she would be totally dependent on her brothers, and they would soon tire of supporting her and she would suffer humiliation as well; and that now that that Vinod was going through counselling sessions, and had vowed that he would keep Sumitra and her daughter happy, she should move back with Vinod. He was now 'a good man'; he did not smoke and drink and held a steady job (he had been posted to Ladakh and wanted to take Sumitra and Pinky with him and start a new life with his family).

The counsellor then asked to speak to Sumitra's brother's wife alone. The latter told the counsellor that actually they were not happy keeping Sumitra, but they had no choice. She thought Sumitra was a selfish person and was taking advantage of her brother's kindness. The counsellor categorically told Sumitra that she felt that her (Sumitra's) brother's family was not likely to take the responsibility for Sumitra and her child for the rest of their lives, and that she would be well advised to reunite with her husband and go with him to Ladakh. Sumitra said she should think it over and return in two days (8 August) and tell her about her decision. All the disputants were asked to go home.

On 8 August 2001, when Sumitra and Vinod came to meet the counsellor, Sumitra said she was not ready yet to return to Vinod with her daughter; she wanted three months to think it through. The counsellor showed impatience and was upset that Sumitra was not heeding her advice, that it was not a good idea to depend on her brothers and that it was in Sumitra's and Pinky's best interests to return to Vinod. Sumitra, however, was adamant and said she would decide by January and in the meantime would try to procure a certificate from Vinod's senior officers about his so-called transfer to Ladakh. Vinod tried to reassure the counsellor and the client that he would make the certificate available as soon as he could and that he did want to start a new life and would turn over a new leaf, a statement that the counsellor seemed anxious to accept so that she could 'accomplish' a reconciliation.

The certificate was sent to the counsellor and Sumitra within 10 days of the 8 August meeting. Sumitra said she was still not ready to go with her husband. This statement was shown to Vinod when he came to meet the counsellor later that month. He wanted to take his wife and daughter with him, but Sumitra could not be contacted on the telephone.

The counsellor arranged for another meeting (23 August 2001) between Sumitra and Vinod. Sumitra came with her brothers. She told the counsellor that she would not go with Vinod and that her brothers had given a written assurance that they would take the responsibility of keeping Sumitra and her daughter, and also of getting Sumitra's daughter married. The counsellor was upset at this decision and retorted 'Do what you like!'.

On 3 October 2001, Sumitra's sister-in-law (Sumitra's brother's wife) brought a letter for the counsellor from Sumitra saying that as a result of the counselling and assistance provided by the counsellor (particularly the hazards of becoming a burden on her brothers and advantages that will accrue to her if she went back to her reformed husband), she had decided to be reunited with her husband Vinod. That she also realized that her daughter Pinky would need a father's love and care and that she wished to absolve her brothers from any responsibility of taking care of her and her daughter. The letter was signed by Sumitra and by her brothers. Sumitra also wished the counsellor to continue helping her and to keep in touch with her, which made the counsellor jubilant as she felt that *she* had achieved her objective, and announced as much with pride to other counsellors and to PRAJA researchers: She said her hard work had reunited another couple.

The counsellor asked Sumitra and Vinod to come in on 6 October 2001, and sign an agreement which stated that after thinking things over both of them had decided to live together again because of the counselling given by the counsellor (this was added so that the counsellor could show the agreement around as yet another feather in her cap), and that Sumitra was ready to go with her husband Vinod along with her daughter Pinky to the place of his new posting. Vinod took full responsibility for his wife and daughter and assured the counsellor that he would present himself whenever required to do so and would answer for his behaviour. Vinod also assured that he would visit his in-laws and meet Sumitra's brothers with amity.

The case was promptly closed, and no follow up was ever done. All in all it was a shoddy show, professionally full of holes. It was an appropriate focus for analysis and discussion in training for would-be counsellors.

For the counsellor, Sumitra's counselling process lasted about six months from start to finish. For Sumitra, the endurance test was spread over six years and this time frame was crucial for the manner in which each party looked at the events and happenings in this case. An analysis of the proceedings, the details and the personalities involved reveal several errors and aberrations in the process of mediation and counselling that violate the principles and guidelines that have been suggested earlier in this book. We shall briefly go through these one by one to highlight where the counsellor or the Unit as it was structured did not meet the fundamentals of counselling.

Beginning with the requirement of matching the counsellor and client, this step (*Step 1* in 'Structuring the Process') was not suitably met. The age of the counsellor and her training skills were not appropriate for the particular situation at hand. The counsellor assigned for Sumitra's case was an old (over 70 years of age) and somewhat frail woman, who also doubled up as a part-time 'counsellor' at mandatory counselling schemes at the local courts.

Her style of counselling was 'grandmotherly' advice-giving. She was not highly educated (had a Bachelor's degree) and had no training in counselling. She dressed sloppily and lacked alacrity; she was slow, tedious and excessively ponderous. Her body language suggested casualness and forgetfulness, and she made haste to just get the job out of the way as soon as possible. Her appearance did not inspire confidence because she believed there was no need to make an effort to look presentable.

Her idea of counselling being advice-giving, she was convinced that given her maturity and age she would give 'mature' advice. That this was about working with the client to arrive at a mutually worked out solution in which there was satisfaction all round and no one lost out was not an end she had in view. Non-conversant with modern theoretical developments and techniques (*Step* 2) that would make counselling the professional activity it is, she had little knowledge about how counselling was being conducted amidst professional groups. She conducted what she regarded as 'counselling', 'mediation', problem-solving and dispute-resolution by instinct—a sort of gut feeling about what she believed would bring some amicable and workable solution for the client and her problem. Age, a factor she considered her plus point, was more often than not a drawback: She could not empathize with a young woman's marital problems. She belonged to a generation that was told to stick it out 'till death do you part'. Her inability to see that counselling meant *professional* counselling, which in turn required a modicum of training, added to the inadequacy of her quite ordinary technique and methods.

She worked only half time at the Cell—three hours each afternoon. In the mornings she sat in the lower judicial courts, where she was meant to resolve disputes of a similar kind as part of the judicial machinery's new policy of 'settling' disputes outside court if possible. By the time she came to work to the next place she was quite exhausted. That was not the best arrangement for the kind of demanding problems that came to this Cell.

The counsellor had little understanding of the importance of 'self-reflection' and 'self-examination' (*Step* 3) in the counselling process. Unable to set aside her preconceived notions on most matters, she had her mind made up fairly early in the proceedings—almost as soon as she had read the complainant's first letter—and she had little patience with the client thereafter. Continuing counselling sessions was thus a futile exercise in her case. Her position on a dispute of the nature of Sumitra's was that married couples that came with marital problems always needed to be reunited. This was the aim and duty of every counsellor and she determinedly moved towards this preset goal in her sessions with the disputants. Self-reflection and self-introspection of her own values and attitudes were not her strong points.

That the case needed to be worked out through the problem-solving model (*Step 4*) and was not simply about consoling for loss or helping to cope failed to strike the counsellor. For her, all help-seeking situations needed one strategy: Bringing an ideal solution to the situation and in this case it meant reuniting the married couple almost at all costs. That this may not address the woman's suffering (the violence and a lack of love and care in the relationship) was of little consequence. When subtly advised (by PRAJA's counselling adviser) that she needed to revise her approach and develop her techniques and skills in counselling, she asserted that she had been 'counselling', mediating and solving women's problems for years now and knew what was required; she believed that her ability to unite warring couples had made her 'popular'. The counsellor also did not comprehend that during mediation in a dispute she may need to counsel not only the client but also the accused and the families of the complainant and the accused. She thus needed to be adept at handling counselling and mediation at different levels.

As the problem unravelled for this counsellor, almost the only issue was that this was a marital problem: the other details were marginal to the issue so that all the elaborate narrations made by the client that constituted important information were not really attentively analysed and put in perspective (*Step 5* to 'Review the Information'). Instead of reviewing all the information—both factual and subjective—given by the client, the counsellor had slotted just the broad facts into her scheme of things and proceeded with giving advice on how to handle the problem ('*handle*' rather than '*solve*'). This was unsatisfactory as an approach for the client, a much-abused woman for whom all the details were important and vital, and each hurt as consequential as the other. Mrs A's slow demeanour and lack of vigour clearly suggested she did not want to revisit questions and predicaments arising out of new information. The body language suggested casualness, forgetfulness and a wish to just get the job out of the way as soon as possible.

A step like setting out the 'Ground Rules' (*Step 6*) got missed, and there was little sense of just how she was going to set about conducting the process. Was she going to be very particular and almost rigid about how she saw counselling (which in her case was an erroneous fixed end product called *reconciliation*), or was she going to be flexible in carrying out the activity, taking things as they came and allowing for a few diversions and deviations now and then—these were not questions that were being asked or addressed. After the first interaction, she was not really concerned that things needed to be clarified between counsellor and client on the methods and procedures to be followed. For her, the feature about keeping the client involved all through the process was irrelevant: There was no need to create space for *negotiation*. For her, it was getting to the main problem (defined by her in one headline: '*marital dispute*'), and solving it according to the end (*reconciliation*) she regarded as best. That was how she saw a conclusion of the case. The client was therefore being *led*. As counselling or mediation this was inappropriate. So was the manner in which it was done, which was unlikely to satisfy all those involved in the dispute when there were no rules about who would be listened to and when, and how the interactions would be analysed and conveyed to the differing parties impartially and constructively. The client felt little assurance after the initial meeting that she was getting guidance from a 'qualified' person who would take it a step at a time.

The concept of time and timetable (*Step 7*) went awry right from the start. The counsellor called Sumitra for a meeting on 26 April 2001, almost two weeks after the complaint was made. Given the nature and intensity of the dispute between the wife and the husband and the 'violent' consequences of that on the wife, efforts should have been made to begin the process of looking for a solution sooner. A client needs to feel that her case is being dealt with a sense of urgency. The counsellor took too much time in starting the process; the absence of some systematic time frame for the overall process did not inspire confidence.

The counsellor did not also figure out and differentiate between the facilitative or directive model of counselling (*Step 8*). Her *modus operandi* was a one-way communication system where she talked more than she listened. She believed that once she had the information from the written complaint, there was little need for the client to make further input particularly about possible ways of resolving the matter. She did not feel the need for a two-way communication. Such an attitude clearly bordered on self-righteousness, inflexibility, lack of theoretical knowledge and awareness of the most basic ground rules of professional counselling, problem-solving or dispute-resolution. While the appropriate method was that in order to gauge all the dimensions of a problem the counsellor needed to engage in a dialogue with the complainant, with the accused and the families of both parties and get as clear a picture about the case as possible, this counsellor believed that the written complaint and the one face-to-face submission was enough. Building up trust in a two-way communication and with the constant involvement of the client to work out a solution in the client's interest was not her idea of counselling. Her style was somewhat overbearing—a 'mother knows best' approach. This counsellor gave Sumitra little chance to speak her mind out; interjections by Sumitra were regarded as 'arguing' and Sumitra fell in line out of deference for the counsellor's age.

The working out (with the client) of some immediate and long-term goals (*Step 9*—'Goal setting') had not been considered necessary. The sole objective (reconciliation) having been set, all other matters became marginal and had to fit into the main goal. Intermediary goals had not been worked out systematically, for example, having individual talks between counsellor and client, starting with a preliminary session in which they would talk and determine what the woman desired, having a session with the husband to identify some further objectives and what he had in mind, and so on. She had missed out on the kind of goal-setting that suggested taking each part of the complaint step by step and placing it within the client's own wishes and requirements, and then placing it against the long-term goal of the client's future in the light of present anxieties and wounds.

The next step was working out methods for recordkeeping and note-taking, not unrelated to the earlier point (*Step 9*), pertaining to how notes would be taken before and during the sessions (*Step 10*—'Recordkeeping and note-taking'). Before the sessions began, the counsellor needed to figure out how she would keep the record of the case and how she would take notes of the incidents and the personal feelings revealed therein. The records do not show any attempt towards making notes of the case or of taking notes during sessions or any comments either relating to the written complaint or the sessions as they proceeded. This was clearly a gap because there was a lot to note down. Sumitra had made a written complaint full of personal feelings. She had at no stage been encouraged to come *alone* to the CCC. She came with her brother and his wife. The counsellor would have known that this would be so given the fact that in marital disputes women in this society tend to bring their families along. In fact the entire family gets involved in such a dispute, and clarity of thinking for the client (and indeed the counsellor) becomes a problem as each family member begins to give advice in the presence of the counsellor. The counsellor should have had a few words with Sumitra *alone* even as her family waited in the waiting room partly to impress upon her that she needed to think this through with a little independence. The conversation with Sumitra should have been recorded including her feelings about the future so that when the collective meeting took place (which was inevitable) there would be a reference point for what others were saying. Details of words and emotions were not recorded at all. All in all note-taking was at a bare minimum in this case. Recordkeeping both about the sessions and about investigation of the background of the client (a feature that often affects the problem to begin with) should have been done in a counselling booklet developed for this purpose.

There were only scrappy notes attached to the original written complaint.

Evaluation is a routine that comes at the end of the process, but its method and preparation needs to be thought through before the activity begins (*Step 11*). This is because the process of counselling will be affected by how the entire process will finally be evaluated (i.e. what results it achieved, did it meet the purposes it was supposed to, was it within the rules and guidelines, did it transgress fundamental rules of counselling, etc.). So before the counsellor actually got started, she needed to have planned her methods for evaluation and assessment of the process and the results. We have no mention of any importance being attached to what the counsellor would do once the mechanical exercise of face-to-face sessions was completed. These constitute the features of counselling that underpin all the concrete steps enumerated earlier.

Some of Mrs A's methods (or lack of them) were discussed with her by our Counsellor Mrs H making it possible to see her reasons for following the process that she did. '*Parivaar ko tootne se bachana sab se zarrori tha aur mai yehi usko samjhati thi*' (preventing a total breakup of the family was necessary and that is what I was trying to impress on Sumitra). Being clueless about all the conceptual features and aspects of counselling that form its principles and guidelines, Mrs A began her first session on the wrong foot. She was all set to just try and reconcile the parties somehow, anyhow. Any evaluation of her sessions would yield the same result. It was unprofessional and therefore achieved what *she* wanted to achieve. It was never about enabling the client to exercise informed choices that would be for a long-term future for *her* and for her child. The fact that there is little comeback on the cases the Unit deals with is another flaw as far as evaluation is concerned.

In terms of the conduct of the sessions, Mrs A wondered why she needed to have a tidy table, may be a vase and a neatly stacked set of papers as opposed to the untidy pile that she did (*Step 12—'Physical Setting'*). How it helps the client in her predicament to face agreeable and reassuring in terms of ambience and atmosphere seemed irrelevant. Apart from the table of the counsellor being unprofessionally arranged, the seating arrangements had not been attended to and *no attention had been paid to ensuring privacy.*

Clearly the state of mind of the client was less of a priority: there was a problem and it needed a solution. The persona of the client faded into the background. To add to that the client was young and the counsellor considerably older. Acutely conscious of her seniority and the deference it demands in Indian society, she did not think she needed to make any special effort to make a relatively young client comfortable by greeting her with welcoming words of assurance. In her view, the young client needed to show respect due to an elderly person and there was little that was expected of the counsellor by way of courtesies. Each time the client came and said *'Namaste'* (greetings), the counsellor would say *'Chalo baitho aur jaldi se batao ki ab kya hua hai tumharee samasya ka.'* (OK. Sit down and tell me quickly what has happened about your problem.) Being at an obvious position of advantage—age and her position as counsellor—both of which could be turned into power arrangements, Mrs A needed to balance those advantages by making the effort to make the client feel at ease and able to express herself freely.

Having read the written statement, the counsellor somehow felt there was not much the client needed to say. She felt she already knew all that the client was seeking and what she needed. Hearing things from the client herself was regarded as superfluous and there was no record of what impact the physical presence of the client had on the counsellor. There is no description of the client or of her communications or responses. Did she weep? Did she show anger? What was her mental/emotional state? What prompted her in April after six years of being tormented to decide to come for mediation to the Unit? Was there a discussion about how she viewed marriage and how the counsellor viewed it? Exploring the problem with the client just did not happen (*Step 14*). Nothing in the notes suggests anything that indicates why the client decided she wanted to be counselled or helped, and what she was expecting from the exchange or interaction. The absence of dialogue on a matter so personal that needed confidential discussing was a gaping lacuna.

Once she was in possession of the basic facts, as stated in the complaint, the counsellor did not feel the need to get further information about the case or about the client's problems from the client. The counsellor believed that counselling was 'giving good advice' and that given her age she was more than equipped to do so once she had the basic facts. The client's subjective feelings were given short shrift and the counsellor's one-point agenda of reconciliation at all costs loomed large at every juncture. That the information needed to be set out in a systematic way to gauge to what extent the client wished to move in any particular direction, or that it was necessary to assess how much the client was wounded and hurt in the happenings that constituted the complaint was not seen as fundamental to 'information gathering' about the client and problem (*Step 15*). The subjective features therefore got hidden amidst the bare facts set out in the statement submitted at the start.

One of the biggest flaws that underlay the whole process in this case was that of developing the right attitudes and shedding one's conditioning (*Step 16*). This 'step' is more like a backdrop in the whole process and needs to be consciously worked at by a counsellor not only for each counselling activity but also for each individual session of a particular counselling process. There is no evidence of the counsellor doing a self-assessment of how she may be conditioned by the values of her generation or by the customary view towards marital problems within the society in which the client and counsellor were located. It was evident from interactions she had had with other counsellors that Mrs A believed that reconciliation was the best remedy for marital problems and any other route could only be second best. Expressing so much keenness that Sumitra return to Vinod (regardless of all other considerations) and being in a hurry to reach such a goal were the consequence of never having been told what 'counselling in mediation' really entailed: the shedding of inbuilt attitudes and the need to face the client with empathy and without prejudice.

And all through the sessions, the development of appropriate 'communication techniques and skills' (*Step 17*), a feature of counselling that should run like a thread through the entire process from beginning to end, was absent. The counsellor was not prone to losing her temper or showing undue impatience. Her patronizing attitude was commensurate with her belief about the advantage of her age. She also believed that attributes of authority and power were a part of counselling and to perform the task of mediating in disputes meant that she needed to use that authority to achieve a concrete result. Methods, techniques, attitudes and skills were not within the framework of the counsellor's *modus operandi*. Conversations and communications between her and the client (and family) took on the hue of talking down to them rather than talking with them. This was partly due to ignorance on the part of the counsellor about the importance of communication skills in the process of counselling, and partly due to a 'know it all attitude'. She believed that just reaching a solution (some solution) within the precincts of the Cell, and conducting a few 'successful' sessions under her belt was all she needed to do.

SUMMING UP

It needs to be mentioned that the counsellor's intentions were not questionable here nor was any malevolence intended when she gave the instructions she did either to the police department in Dehradun or to Sumitra. She was simply untrained and ill-informed and it was the organization's responsibility that persons handling such delicate tasks receive a minimum of training to qualify as counsellors. She was picked to be counsellor because she was working as a guidance counsellor at a local court and asked to be involved at this prestigious Commission as well. Neither the Commission nor this counsellor had grasped adequately the principles of professional counselling.

What the counsellor was doing here was making a decision for the client. It has been suggested earlier that this is a temptation that a counsellor must resist because it leads to *four obvious errors* that really have no place in a counselling programme, particularly in the social context that this counsellor was working in. These four errors are as follows:

1. *Deciding for a client* instead of facilitating the client in making the decision for herself. This is particularly important for a client who has been accustomed to having decisions made for her and landed in the trouble she is in.
2. Giving the impression to the client *that there is really only one ideal option* before her and any other option would not only be second best but almost inferior.
3. Failing to take a *long-term view* rather than find a short-term workable solution.
4. Failing to take some *initiative in empowering the client* given the social context in which such women, as the counsellor was faced with, are made to live without any power over even their own lives leave alone those of others. Such a perception needed skills of understanding and communication that the counsellor did not possess.

The question of empowerment assumes more importance in some contexts than others and as a feature of counselling in mediation, problem-solving and dispute-resolution was completely ignored by this counsellor who made no attempt to explore with the complainant, Sumitra, possible ways in which the latter could work towards being economically independent (she was a graduate). The counsellor's aim very obviously seemed to be just to send Sumitra back to her husband (see Figure 5.1 for a diagrammatic representation of Sumitra's case).

FIGURE 5.1 Diagrammatic Evaluation of Sumitra's Case

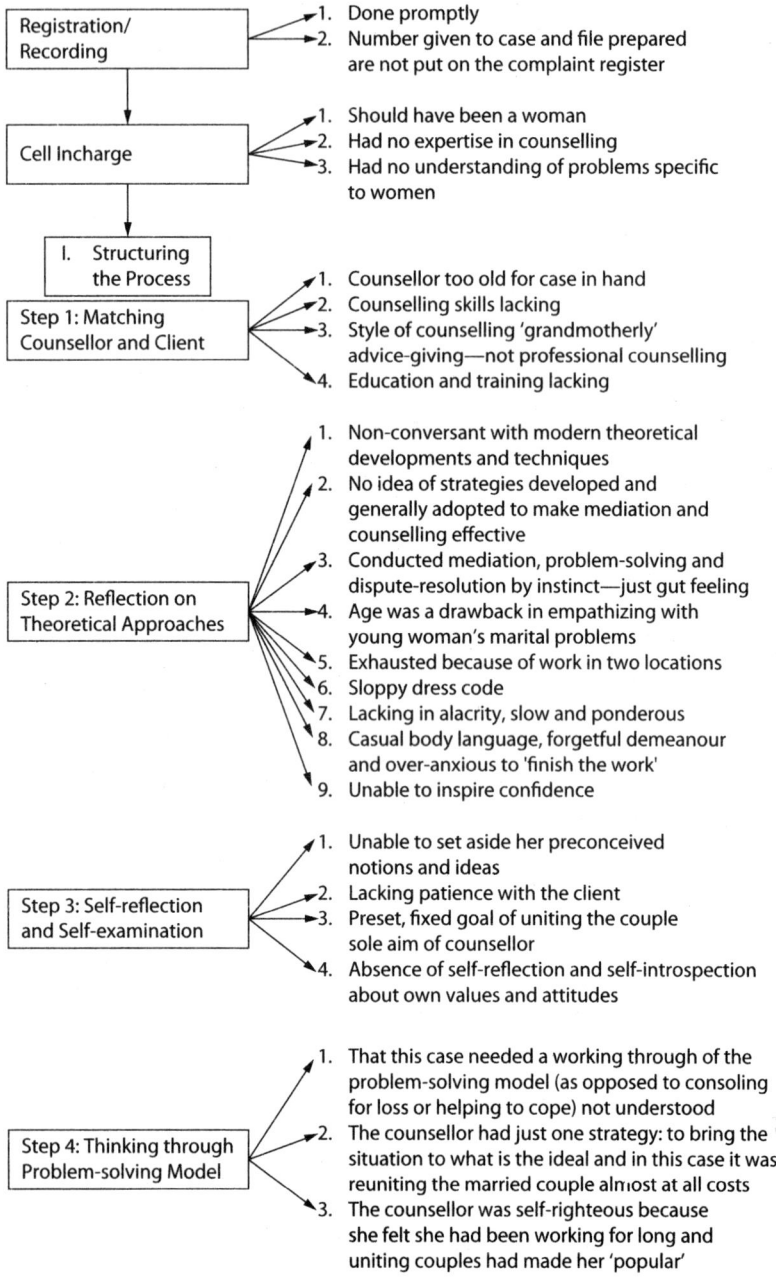

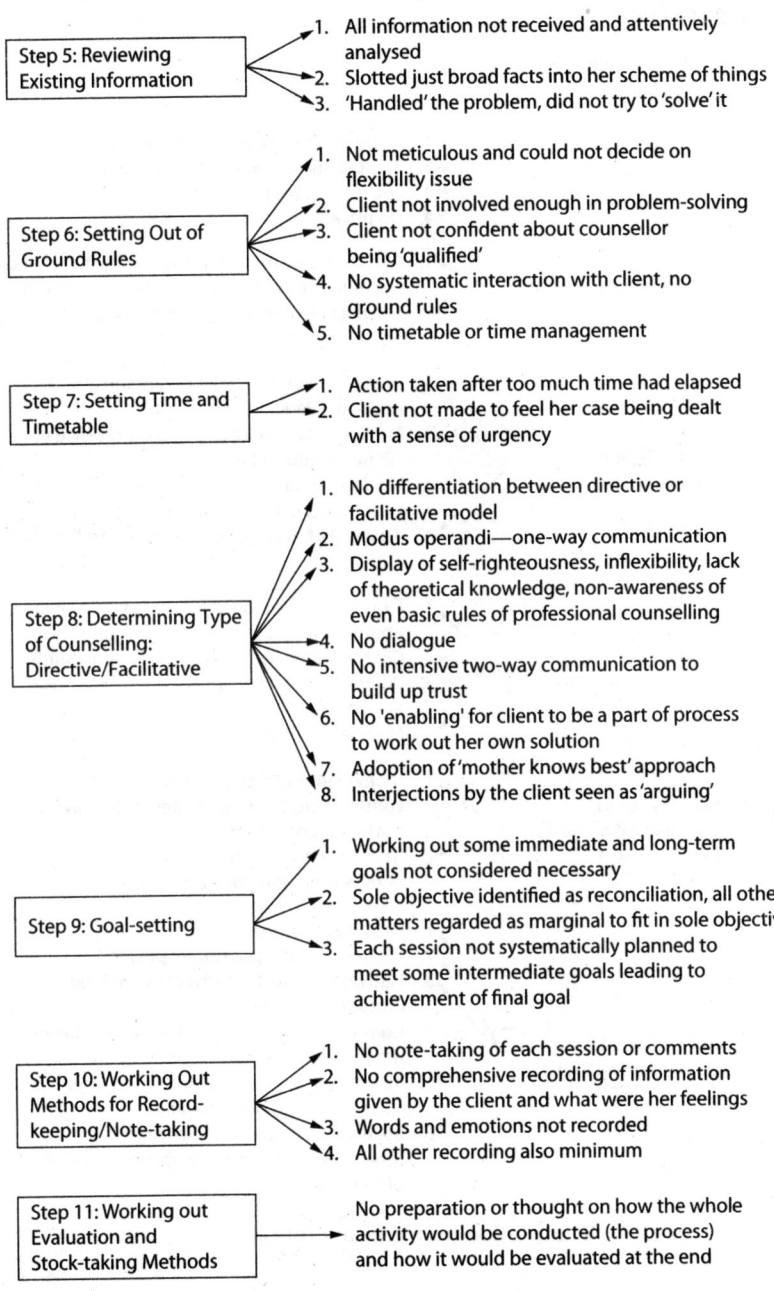

Step 5: Reviewing Existing Information
1. All information not received and attentively analysed
2. Slotted just broad facts into her scheme of things
3. 'Handled' the problem, did not try to 'solve' it

Step 6: Setting Out of Ground Rules
1. Not meticulous and could not decide on flexibility issue
2. Client not involved enough in problem-solving
3. Client not confident about counsellor being 'qualified'
4. No systematic interaction with client, no ground rules
5. No timetable or time management

Step 7: Setting Time and Timetable
1. Action taken after too much time had elapsed
2. Client not made to feel her case being dealt with a sense of urgency

Step 8: Determining Type of Counselling: Directive/Facilitative
1. No differentiation between directive or facilitative model
2. Modus operandi—one-way communication
3. Display of self-righteousness, inflexibility, lack of theoretical knowledge, non-awareness of even basic rules of professional counselling
4. No dialogue
5. No intensive two-way communication to build up trust
6. No 'enabling' for client to be a part of process to work out her own solution
7. Adoption of 'mother knows best' approach
8. Interjections by the client seen as 'arguing'

Step 9: Goal-setting
1. Working out some immediate and long-term goals not considered necessary
2. Sole objective identified as reconciliation, all other matters regarded as marginal to fit in sole objective
3. Each session not systematically planned to meet some intermediate goals leading to achievement of final goal

Step 10: Working Out Methods for Record-keeping/Note-taking
1. No note-taking of each session or comments
2. No comprehensive recording of information given by the client and what were her feelings
3. Words and emotions not recorded
4. All other recording also minimum

Step 11: Working out Evaluation and Stock-taking Methods
No preparation or thought on how the whole activity would be conducted (the process) and how it would be evaluated at the end

(Figure 5.1 contd.)

(Figure 5.1 contd.)

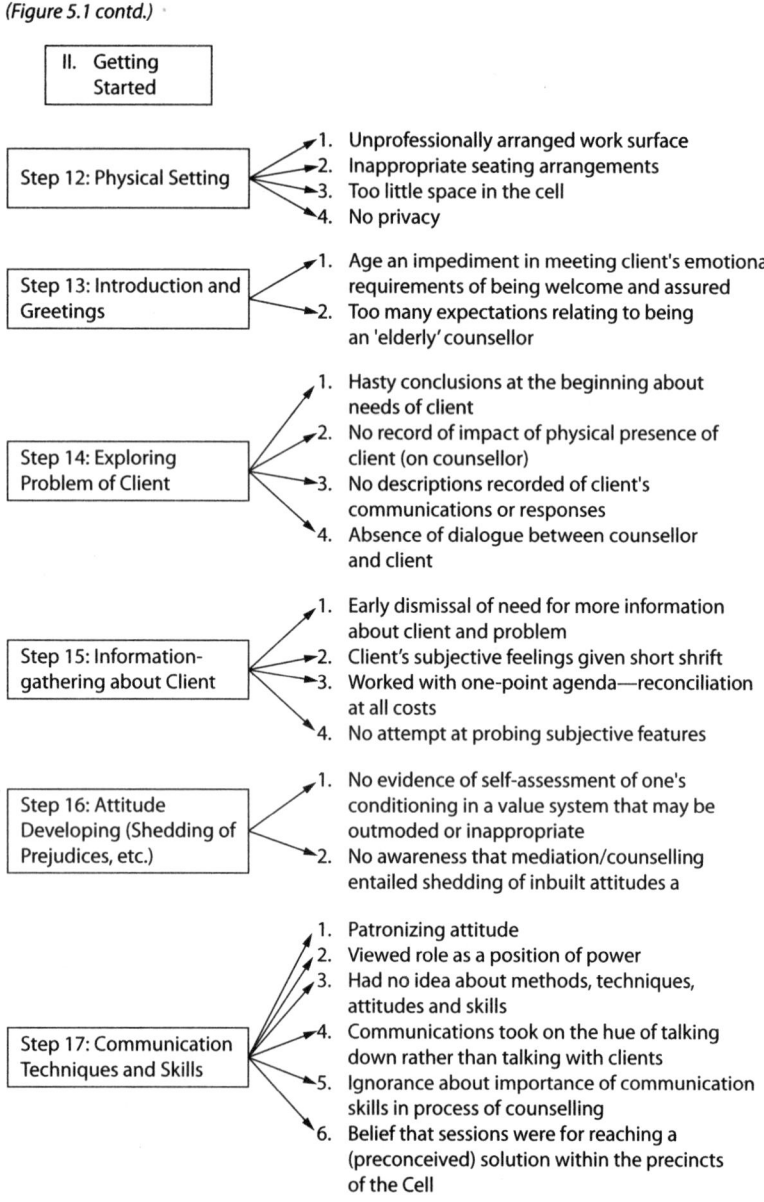

II. Getting
Started

Step 12: Physical Setting
1. Unprofessionally arranged work surface
2. Inappropriate seating arrangements
3. Too little space in the cell
4. No privacy

Step 13: Introduction and Greetings
1. Age an impediment in meeting client's emotional requirements of being welcome and assured
2. Too many expectations relating to being an 'elderly' counsellor

Step 14: Exploring Problem of Client
1. Hasty conclusions at the beginning about needs of client
2. No record of impact of physical presence of client (on counsellor)
3. No descriptions recorded of client's communications or responses
4. Absence of dialogue between counsellor and client

Step 15: Information-gathering about Client
1. Early dismissal of need for more information about client and problem
2. Client's subjective feelings given short shrift
3. Worked with one-point agenda—reconciliation at all costs
4. No attempt at probing subjective features

Step 16: Attitude Developing (Shedding of Prejudices, etc.)
1. No evidence of self-assessment of one's conditioning in a value system that may be outmoded or inappropriate
2. No awareness that mediation/counselling entailed shedding of inbuilt attitudes a

Step 17: Communication Techniques and Skills
1. Patronizing attitude
2. Viewed role as a position of power
3. Had no idea about methods, techniques, attitudes and skills
4. Communications took on the hue of talking down rather than talking with clients
5. Ignorance about importance of communication skills in process of counselling
6. Belief that sessions were for reaching a (preconceived) solution within the precincts of the Cell

Source: Author's adaptation from relevant sources.

NOTES

1. A *Johari window* is a cognitive psychological tool created by Joseph Luft and Harry Ingham in 1955 in the United States, used to help people better understand their interpersonal communication and relationships. The concept has also been called the 'Johari House' with four rooms. Room 1 is the part of ourselves that we see and others see. Room 2 is the aspects that others see, but we are not aware of. Room 3 is the most mysterious room in that the unconscious or subconscious part of us is seen by neither ourselves nor others. Room 4 is our private space, which we know but keep from others.

   Treating each square as a quadrant, an exercise is performed whereby subjects are given a list of 56 adjectives and they have to pick 5 or 6 that they feel describe their own personality. Peers of the subject are then given the same list, and each pick 5 or 6 adjectives that describe the subject. These adjectives are then mapped onto a grid.

   Adjectives that are selected by both the participant and his or her peers are placed into the *Open* quadrant which represents traits of the subjects that both they and their peers are aware of. Adjectives selected only by subjects, but not by any of their peers, are placed into the *Hidden* quadrant, representing information about them their peers are unaware of. It is then up to the subject to disclose this information or not. Those adjectives that are not selected by subjects but only by their peers are placed into the *Blind Spot* quadrant and they represent information that the subject is not aware of, but others are, and they can decide whether and how to inform the individual about these 'blind spots'. There are adjectives that may not be selected by either subjects or their peers and remain in the *Unknown* quadrant, representing the participant's behaviours or motives that were not recognized by anyone participating. This may be because they do not apply or because there is collective ignorance of the existence of these traits.

   The 56 adjectives that comprise the list from which the selection is made set out alphabetically are as follows:

   - able
   - brave
   - clever
   - dignified
   - giving
   - independent
   - kind
   - mature

   - accepting
   - calm
   - complex
   - energetic
   - happy
   - ingenious
   - knowledgeable
   - modest

   - adaptable
   - caring
   - confident
   - extroverted
   - helpful
   - intelligent
   - logical
   - nervous

   - bold
   - cheerful
   - dependable
   - friendly
   - idealistic
   - introverted
   - loving
   - observant

- organized
- quiet
- responsive
- sensible
- smart
- trustworthy

- patient
- reflective
- searching
- sentimental
- spontaneous
- warm

- powerful
- relaxed
- self-assertive
- shy
- sympathetic
- wise

- proud
- religious
- self-conscious
- silly
- tense
- witty

2. The year-long research and documentation on the 'Project on Mediation, Counselling and Conflict Resolution resulted in a 137-page report that was compiled by Saraswati Haider, PRAJA's Project Officer, and was submitted to the Commission. Unfortunately it only gathered dust on their shelves. See Report 'Creating a Window to Redress Women's Grievances', PRAJA/PRI (2002).

Chapter 6

Women in Prisons

South Asian countries are both diverse and similar in their social characteristics. Language and religion, two main features that underlie the differences in the various countries (Bangladesh, India, Nepal, Pakistan and Sri Lanka) do not dilute the essential similarities that underscore the way of life of this region. Tradition and culture are held in high esteem and 'progress and development' notwithstanding a common thread that runs (deep) through the entire region is the shared histories and common social codes that determine how individuals, groups and communities are viewed both by themselves, by each other and by the rest of the world. Nowhere is this more evident than in the way gender issues have played themselves out. For better or worse, since time immemorial, sketches and images of women drawn for interest-oriented goals and purposes have become sacrosanct enough to find a place in all areas of policy formulation and decision-making in the body politic of this region.

Women's experiences in the criminal justice system provide fertile territory for analysis and change at the interface between social mores and legal institutions, notwithstanding the fact that the codes that form the backdrop of the formal penal system go back in essence to the colonial period and have seldom been considered in need of change. In some parts of the South Asian region (India for instance), laws and statutes have created myriads of new offences—'crimes'—still punished with the same penalties set out in the Penal Code of 1860. While there is hyperactivity in creating new offences, the attempts at altering the penalties and thinking of alternatives to existing punitive measures are sluggish to say the least.

Despite the mistrust and misgivings about the clout that feminism has had in the changes surrounding women's lives and perceptions of their roles and positions in society, the contribution of feminist activity as a mover and shaker in the world of women is undeniable. The role of NGOs has had a similar effect in exploring why women are viewed the way they are, particularly when they face the 'equal' and 'neutral' machinery of the State.

Of relevance to us here is a glimpse into how women face the criminal justice system and whether their experiences connect with the 'equality and neutrality' claims made by the system. This begs a question of course: Is equality for women 'sameness' (corresponding exactly to) or 'suitability' (appropriate for)? No attempt at a perfect answer is any match for the real experiences of women observed and documented by NGOs in the region we are concerned with. As they face the criminal justice machinery from the time of accusation to investigation, charging, and sentencing to police and judicial custody, there is much that is unsatisfactory and unacceptable for accused women. The search for 'other ways' has a miserable history. It needs to be reviewed and reactivated.

One of the most damaging features of the criminal justice experience for women is the prison, an institution that will just not go away no matter how much the damage it causes is demonstrated to governments and policy makers. For some (and they are but a fraction of imprisoned populations), locking up may be necessary for the security of the rest of society. For women (and other vulnerable groups), it is a severe punishment that needs a hard second look. The wounds are more often than not invisible and therefore insignificant. The NGOs that have worked in women's prisons in South Asia are struck by the general indifference of the official machinery to the mental state of those who stay within walls and behind closed doors for months and years and come out worse than when they went in. The recommendation for Counselling Units in prisons (especially women's prisons) seemed an obvious response even as it was not an answer to a wider question of alternatives.

Not much has been either done or written about the need or the methods of counselling women locked inside prisons, particularly in South Asia and similar tradition-oriented societies (in Africa for instance). This is surprising, and yet not so. Surprising because of all the women that need counselling of one kind or another (and there are indeed many *kinds* of counselling that are required in such a context), women in prison would surely be the one group that would stand out as an obvious choice. *Not* surprising because women in prison are not a top priority for those who do have women on their agenda. And if imprisoned women are seen as in need of attention, it is their most basic needs that are considered worthy of focus and not counselling and/or emotional/ mental help or repair which would constitute an indulgence.

When women enter prison, they are 'doubly deviant, doubly damned'. There is scarcely any other group of persons in any society that is measured by a yardstick that has changed so little over time or place. Rhetoric and declarations notwithstanding, nothing evolves when it comes to the way women in our society are measured and judged. There are prototypes, stereotypes, models and ideals in every society for the way women are supposed to look, present themselves, behave, act, perform and carry out all that has been laid out for them (their roles), and woe betide the woman who seeks to cross the role boundaries carefully drawn up for her. Pointing to a mere 0.5 per cent of any region's population to disprove this generality or suggesting a long list of women as achievers or 'movers and shakers' to demonstrate that these roles and expectations have changed does nothing for the ground reality that is being stated here. And nowhere does the stereotype of what a woman is (quite conveniently merged with what she should be) become more apparent than in a women's prison.

Speaking of stereotypes, ironically there is a stereotype of the imprisoned woman as well which is as much in need of being shaken off as any other stereotype. Constructing stereotype images of women 'inside' is dangerous because these women are not in a position to resist the constructs imposed on them. Even without contact with women prisoners (who may or may not have committed offences) or direct knowledge of prisons, self-styled experts are able to flaunt views that pass for knowledge about these subjects. A scrutiny of this misinformation and constructed knowledge is vital if manipulative methods are to be avoided. Some studies have tried to do that but not gone far enough. And a study that seeks therapeutic interventions for imprisoned women needs above all to set a few things straight in order *not* to be considered manipulative and controlling.

Assuming that there is a modicum of information and knowledge about women in the prisons of South Asia and similar environs for would-be counsellors to work in the prison, caution about the 'misinformation' and half-truths masquerading as knowledge is a first step.

Two aspects of these women that need to be straightened out before there is any talk about how they might be helped and assisted with coping with as damaging an institution as the prison:

1. There has been an attempt towards a *portrayal* of offending women that seems to suggest that there is a qualitative separation between the 'general' women in any society and the offending women in that society. It is the contention of all the researchers associated with this book that that is both false and fraudulent. The women who offend and find themselves in prison come from the same 'stock' of women outside; and the attempt to prove that the 'offending woman' is a separate breed from other women needs to be countered at every turn. It has been suggested (in studies conducted elsewhere on women and offending women) that the idea of a continuum for studying women (and that would include the offending women) in which the issues that relate to women generally are addressed seems far more sensible and cogent than the idea that there is a divide and offending women fall one side of the divide and 'normal' women the other side.

2. The *knowledge* that is paraded as expertise about offending women is tainted. Why women offend or commit crimes (potentially an overrated area of study) becomes a dangerous exercise if the objective is to label them as *offending women* instead of understanding them as *women*. Building stereotypes to determine the causes of their deviancy, and then moving on to what might be done about it is nothing less

than manipulative. 'Experts' (from different areas of study and theorizing—medical, psychological, legal, etc.) proclaim they already know all about these offending women and what they are (inherently, biologically and sociologically) made of; and therefore they are in a good position to suggest how these women might be managed and controlled. Nothing could be further from reality, as the experts have scarcely taken cognisance of the women's subjectivities and accounts of their own experiences. Instead, armed with 'the expert knowledge' with which they look at these women, they in fact ensure that these women have been muted even before they can speak.

The slate on which the counsellor writes her script when she embarks on so sensitive an area of activity as counselling women in prison should therefore first be wiped clean of old scribblings and jottings (that may have had an agenda of their own) before new ideas from the information freshly provided are put on the slate.

To set out a process for the counselling of women in prison in the South Asian context (and other developing societies) is not to automatically place all the steps set out earlier (in Chapter 4) in the prison setting and get on with playing out each step in this different context. The context is a world apart from other contexts, and any mechanical transfer of either approach or techniques would be to reduce the importance of the mission. Much needs to be said about just how unique and different from other contexts this one is and how convoluted is the logic that dictates its modus operandi.

Germane to the issue of structuring the activity of counselling in a prison is the entire question of the need for counselling people in prison. *What is the urgent need for counselling in prison and where is it aimed?*

- Is the objective *preventive?*
- Is the objective *curative?*
- Is the objective *palliative?*

All of these questions beg another question: What is it that happens in a prison that needs any of the above objectives of the preventive, curative and palliative to be sought? This question of all questions brings us to the crux of the matter of prisons and prisoners and the perceptions about them that are rife with misinformation, misunderstanding and misguided notions of the functioning and achievements of jails in general and women's jails in particular.

It might appear like putting the cart before the horse if the counsellors are already told what *does* happen in a prison rather than they discover it in the course of their activity. But this is a statement that needs to be made for counsellors by those who would supposedly have enough information and perception at their command to begin the whole process by stating some facts about the effect of imprisonment on most prisoners:

- Prisons damage people in visible and invisible ways.
- Prisons damage some people more than they do others.
- The damage that prisons do have repercussions that go well beyond the prisoner and the duration of their stay in a prison.

Related to these facts observed and verified by research (see Shankardass, 2002) are the additional truisms stated in international standards agreed to by all countries around the world and forming the goals of prison reform:

- Imprisonment does not make a person into a non-person.
- Offenders are sent to prison *as* punishment and not *for* punishment.
- Prisons are institutions of the State that has the responsibility to run them according to acceptable rules and standards.

Neither the effects of imprisonment described above nor the truisms stated thereafter are features that those who manage prisons are consciously aware of at an operative level. Most prisons in India and certainly women's prisons seem to be managed almost by habit and reflex and are therefore mismanaged. Most of the personnel manning the jails have never been called upon to answer for the mismanagement, and those who are living in them are more unaware of what a jail should be than can be imagined. Without the transparency that must accompany the proficient running of any institution, the state of mismanagement usually continues until there is a concerted effort from some direction (usually pressure from the civic or international community) to change this state of affairs.

Temporary do-gooders, also called '*mithai* (sweets) distributors', are not likely to bring all the problems of the prison to the forefront of society's gaze. Whatever work/reform/change is sought in women's prisons needs proper understanding of what is happening inside and needs to begin with learning some things and unlearning many others. Counselling is regarded as one activity through which some of the intended changes can be achieved, and therefore those involved in counselling need to go through a wide and deep learning process first. It would begin with information-oriented observations. The learning would need to cover the following areas that should be thoroughly delved into and discussed:

1. *Why prison?* Counsellors should engage in the debate about whether prison is the best way of punishing those who violate 'criminal laws' and should *all* violators get this punishment?
2. *What is a prison?* This should suggest some physical features of a typical women's prison in the region. (Are most women's prisons in India and indeed all of South Asia similar physically and conceptually?)
3. *How does a prison function?* At different times of day, at different locations — admissions, barracks, kitchen, activity areas, toilets and *mulaqat* (visiting) areas etc. — and for different groups (age, physical condition) on a daily basis, and at specific activity times (admissions, meals, recreation, education, visiting).
4. *Who is in the prison?* Detailed information of everyone inside a prison is essential for anyone who is looking at any

change-oriented activity, which would include staff, prisoners, those who come to visit prisoners and those who come to provide services (deliveries, repairmen, inspecting teams, observers and social workers, etc.).

5. *What happens to them inside?* This would need to be imbibed through different voices—prisoners, staff, observers, families, social workers—and it will become clear how different voices give such different perceptions of what happens inside that one is left in disbelief.

Vital to the counselling process these issues need to be imbibed before the '17 steps' process is set out for the conflict resolution model of counselling. They precede the process that in this context could then be said to have 18 steps, starting not with 'matching the counsellor and the client' but with understanding the custodial environment in its entirety.

The two main categories that are more or less permanent in a prison are the prisoners and staff, and each of these categories has its own perceptions of how they view things; they also have their own sets of difficulties and problems that are (*a*) related to their being in the closed environment called a 'jail' and (*b*) peculiar to them because of the nature of their particular positioning in the setup.

The first category that needs to be discussed are the *prisoners*, who supposedly constitute the raison d'être for the prison and are the object of all the rules, regulations, routines and rituals that surround the running of the prison. For a would-be counsellor or for those who are training would-be counsellors, knowledge about the subject and the terrain is equally vital.

The second category that needs a different kind of counselling are the *staff* of a prison. Staff problems often get missed in all the prison-oriented work that is done both by the managers and the non-governmental groups that come to assist with the inculcation of better standards and good prison management.

Armed with the fundamentals of counselling and with adequate information, knowledge and learning about the above five questions set out earlier, the counsellor would have to go through the exercise of structuring and charting out the process whereby the activity of counselling would be carried out in this one of the most unique of social/institutional environments imaginable.

It might not be out of place to repeat here the first reminders the counsellor would be required to administer to herself to draw the right balance between form and content development:

- *The theoretical position from where she would come to counselling*: These would relate to theoretical models of personality, causes of behaviour, etc., which the counsellor would need to clarify in her mind so that as she proceeds she is clarifying her theoretical emphasis. The theories about personality or behaviour that form the counsellor's standpoint for instance would in turn be constituted of further theoretical formulations related both to counselling as an activity and to imprisonment as a phenomenon (and to the subject's prisoner status).
- *The most suitable approach to counselling in the context (behavioural, psychodynamic or humanistic)*: Should the (present exhibited) behaviour of the person be the prime focus, or should there be intensive delving into the past for explanations of the present, or should the client's gender and the influence of the social structure in which she is positioned be a point of focus?
- *The specific problem(s) faced by each prisoner*: This aspect is what would form the centre of the counselling process and would therefore need to be identified at the outset.
- *The most pressing needs of the particular client*: These would be determined by both of the first two points listed above (theoretical understandings and approach), and would be further determined by listening to the prisoner's own voice.

Exercise: Making a note on all of the aforementioned points by each counsellor might be helpful and a reference to earlier definitions of counselling set out in Chapter 3 would be of assistance in this exercise.

The 'Structuring of the Process' of the actual activity of counselling with its 11 steps (and there may be a need for more if the situation demands) must thus be preceded by all of these thought processes and considerations before it is actually given practical shape in the form of stage-by-stage implementation. The prison being an environment with a difference, and an almost abnormal environment, all preconceived notions about who and what is inside the prison would have to be set aside before some kind of method is devised to determine the kind of counselling needed by the imprisoned inside. Appropriate assessments of the kind suggested above would assist in leading up to the actual counselling process.

Inevitably this would be linked with two additional features of the special situation that would need immediate identification:

1. *Is there a type here? Are 'imprisoned women' a type since they are all prisoners?* Or are there many types given their differing backgrounds, personalities, offences, needs, etc. The counsellor needs to give very serious thought to this question and put down some of these thoughts after some preliminary introductions with prisoners.
2. *Is there a trend and type in the complaints or problems that these women have* since they share a common environment and have the same routine, or are these also many and varied given the differences of personality and backgrounds?

The answers to these almost conflicting questions, highlighting different facets of a woman as prisoner, lie somewhere in between 'yes' there are similarities among women as prisoners, but 'no' there is no 'type' that can be labelled *the typical woman prisoner.* And 'yes' some of their problems are alike, but 'no' there are some that are so fundamentally different from the problems of others that any slotting of problem types would be both dishonest and dangerous in terms of the help they seek. This needs to be carefully thought through and the theoretical underpinnings that lie at the heart of the counselling process brought back to the forefront for understanding the need to avoid oversimplification that may have an agenda that goes against the grain of the aims of counselling.

It is only after all this thinking, pondering and contemplating has been done that the would-be counsellors can claim to have the disposition and mental apparatus to handle the counselling of women prisoners in prison.

In setting out the steps that form part of the process of structuring the activity of counselling earlier we set out 17 steps that were divided along the lines of 'Structuring the Process' and 'Getting Started'. They form the broad guidelines, and cannot be rigidly followed if the environment demands something more. This has to be kept in mind as the process unravels and the activity takes shape. Prior to the first step, all the thinking, rethinking and putting the counsellor's own mind into the right gear to do justification to the subject and the activity is essential.

In the prison environment, 'matching the counsellor and the client' (*Step 1*) would have to be handled somewhat differently from other counselling environs. It is assumed that those who have been assigned this task or been chosen for it would be informed about some prerequisites.

1. *To be adequately equipped to handle the demands, stresses and strains of the prison environment* and the sometimes unpleasant incidents that may occur in the course of their work whether with prisoners or staff.

2. *To be acquainted with prisoners' problems* as thoroughly as possible. This would be necessary in view of the difficulty of having a large number of counsellors working within the prison, given the prison's constraints and limitations. The chosen counsellors would need to have adequate skills and the appropriate disposition to know what to look for. Matching counsellor and client in this context would therefore mean that the would-be counsellor apart from having been appropriately chosen would need to *get* matched and become *suitable* for the purposes for which she is needed here.

Exercise: The counsellor should be asked to note down the first five things that come to her mind about prisoners just by looking at them

'collectively'. The counsellor might also be asked how she is equipped to address these features about the prisoner.
Counsellor's Analysis:

The first five things that come to mind are:

- The prisoners hardly ever smile.
- Most of them come from relatively poor backgrounds.
- Some are too old and feeble to be here.
- There is something unreal about children being in prison.
- Prisoners don't have much to do to while away the hours.

The whole atmosphere is formidable and unreal because it is a cage, and people don't belong in a cage. It is not an easy atmosphere to work in because there are already too many rules about movement. But I have told myself that they are here because something unpleasant happened in their lives and the law has only one way of dealing with what they did—'locking them up'. I believe that the best way of addressing the prisoners' dispositions would be to address some of the (above-mentioned) features that have struck me at first glance. I think I can do that. I feel confident about befriending them. It is possible some would keep me at a distance at first—but I can be patient and will try different ways. What I have to be careful about is that I don't break any of the rules under which we have been allowed to function.

Unlike the counselling for dispute resolution, this is about *counselling prisoners who are often not even sure what help they could possibly expect in prison.* All that they know is a dull routine and many instructions that have to be followed. Their ultimate wish is to be out of the prison and reunited with families, which of course is neither in the hands of the prisoner nor the counsellor nor indeed the prison managers. It is therefore a unique situation and one that has no parallel in the world outside.

After all the preliminary reflections (described earlier), the counsellor should be in a position to form some idea of the theoretical approach (*Step 2*) that she would need to follow in dealing with the client. A few conversations and observations down the road (with prisoners and staff), it should become apparent what should be the best way to deal with the clients as and when they come for counselling. Sometimes the client's present predicament (being in prison) may be more appropriate as a lead to better understanding about her and the most suitable form of assistance. It may be necessary in some instances to discreetly go back into the client's early experiences and search for reasons for her consternation. Some reasons for the chaos and confusion in her mind may lie in her cultural context (the customs and religion of the client), and the prescribed role this has entailed for her. While the approach may end up as a combination of several of the approaches stated earlier, it is necessary for the counsellor to be aware of her approach so that the counselling is not directionless and the step-by-step activity actually appears to be planned and designed and not chaotic. So the question here would be 'how shall I approach this client: through her present, her past' or 'what lies beneath?'

Exercise: A woman remarried after the death of a first husband. She had two children from her first marriage. As the daughter grows up she is sexually abused by the stepfather. If the wife intervenes and protests about his behaviour, he violently attacks her. On a particular occasion there is a physical struggle and the wife extricates the daughter from his clutches and strikes him and he dies. She is in prison and her daughter is outside with relatives. She is in a total mess, does not communicate with anyone and is very bitter. What kinds of different (theoretical) approaches would a counsellor use to address the woman's state?

The 'psychodynamic approach' would probably be a good starting point and going into the woman's past would have to be carefully done, each step being embarked upon with her full consent and cooperation. There may even be a need to go further back than her married life. The experiences in her parental home and with her first husband may also need to be delicately drawn. The present need being how she should cope with all that happened and where it has brought her; clearly the observations and surmised reasons for her present behaviour then would need to become the subject of the interaction between the client and counsellor (behavioural approach).

The significant feature of developing the appropriate approach in this setting is the position of the client—in prison—being one from which she cannot remove herself or be removed at the behest of any one agency, least of all the counsellor. How she is helped (apart from being extricated from the environment) is very important for her and every detail needs to be worked through to arrive at the right kinds of approaches. It should be reflected upon and discussed among counsellors.

In this context, the need for 'self-awareness' (*Step 3*) cannot be emphasized enough. This is an unusual environment and these are people whom we do not associate with in our normal living. The words 'prisoner' and 'offender' conjure up all kinds of images in the average person's mind. Each case that comes up needs a brief self-awareness exercise. This is quite crucial in the light of the stark location and the trite nature of the logic that usually determines the help offers that are thought of for prisoners. The need to reflect about the environment in prison or jail, and about the women that are there as prisoners (albeit for legally justifiable reasons), is vital at this stage above all. Tainted images and stereotypes and the biases and prejudices pertaining to those inside have to be consciously brought to the surface and addressed in this reflection.

The awareness we are talking about is reached easily for those facets that lie in the conscious and are reflected in obvious functionalities of the person. Others may lie below the obvious reachable surface—the subconscious—and may have to be thought through and analysed. (See Figure 5.1 and note on Johari's window in Chapter 5.) The aim is to reach the 'knowns' and as many 'unknowns' as we can to give fair counselling.

All our proclamations to the contrary notwithstanding, for an 'outsider' working in a prison and with prisoners is not an experience that comes as naturally as working with students, patients in a hospital or the general assistance-seeking distressed woman. The woman prisoner carries a baggage with her of a life that ended up in her offending against the law which society/state has made for social order and security, and which we all subscribe to. To get involved with so many women who have offended and violated this law is something that brings us face to face with a pattern of life that we believe is alien to ours, and that we have not really needed to give much thought to. This is the moment when one's own life patterns need to be looked at: the elements of security, safety, smooth living, problem-free day-to-day existence. All these reflections of one's own life and the accompanying mental make-up is helpful in better understanding of those whose fractured lives lead to situations that the 'normal' person who is about to engage in counselling has probably never faced. Or if they *have* faced such situations, then the subjectivity that may accompany an appraisal of the client's problem also has to be consciously thought through.

Looking at one's self to assess one's own strengths and limitations means an awareness seeking at two levels: (*a*) of *social attitudes* and (*b*) *personality traits*. The questions one would address to one's self to measure one's capability would thus be done at many levels:

- How equipped am I to understand the scenario I am faced with?
- Do I have some preconceived ideas about women who offend?
- This is a case of violation of the Dowry Act: Have I got some inbuilt leanings one way or another on this matter?
- Do my religious/ideological beliefs enter my thought process when I seek answers?
- Am I a prisoner of my own beliefs and class mores?

These and many similar questions would need to be put to one's self before beginning to be engaged with the client. In training for counselling, personality assessment tests can be set to focus on this issue (see Annexures for samples).

In Chapter 5, on counselling women who come for mediation and dispute resolution, we already set out several *personality traits* that might be worth analysing in one's self. We listed some that are the most prevalent in situations where the counsellor and client have little in common socially. The counsellor can be any or most of the following:

- Overbearing
- Dogmatic
- Opinionated

- Head strong
- Self-willed
- Bigoted
- Narrow-minded

In the prison environment, anyone who is not prisoner or staff is for all practical purposes an outsider in a very real sense. She is an outsider in other ways too, loaded as she may be with preconceived notions and views pertaining largely to social attitudes towards the backgrounds of the women who are in prison. The fact that they are offenders, and that their offences might grate on the values that most of us have been conditioned into believing to be sacrosanct and righteous is a difficult hurdle to surmount. There are *prostitutes* (called 'sex workers' in some regions) who have been brought in under the Immoral Traffic (Prevention) Act (popularly known as 'PITA'); there are *women who have kidnapped children*, others have *killed daughters-in-law*, and still others have *assailed a spouse*. Some yielded to the temptation of making quick money by *selling liquor illegally* or grew poppies and became *small-time drug peddlers* for making money because they lost jobs. One woman allegedly pushed two children into a well because the village wizard told her that it was necessary to be done to ward off the evil spirits that had been responsible for the death of her only son. Someone is there on charges of *vagrancy*, and yet another for *theft* on a train. A range of activities that are constructed as criminal by the State from time to time bring more and more offenders into prison, for example, cheating in examinations is made a crime and brings many young people into jail. The counsellor is hardly likely to have met such a range of persons and activities all at the same time and in one place. It is an overwhelming experience and needs serious contemplation.

The counsellor needs to address the first range of questions to herself, which are as follows:

- Am I having problems accepting the 'type' that comes before me?
- How do I look upon people of this 'type'?

- Do I need to shake off something before I begin, or acquire something else before embarking on this activity?
- Is there an element of hostility in how I view them because (a) their backgrounds are so remote from what I am accustomed to and (b) because they have committed such weird 'crimes'?
- Or do I have it in me to empathize with their frame of mind and even while I disagree with their actions can I take them into a more positive frame of mind?

When class, caste, religious and community divides are harsh and rigid (as they are in the region we are discussing), for people to *cross the divides* is not an easy exercise. Many a do-gooder who thinks she can assist in counselling women in prison fumbles, and then bungles up things because she believes that her good intentions and lofty do-good spirit is adequate for the work. Nothing can be further from the truth. Crossing age-old barriers and conditioned attitudes is sometimes more difficult than climbing a mountain!

All of these aspects is in addition to one's own capacity to tolerate aggressive behaviour, brusque replies, silence, cockiness, etc., on the part of the client. These would have to be thought through for they are experienced. If a counsellor is not able to handle these, she should clearly withdraw from such activity. Egoists and acclaim-seekers have no place in this activity and can cause more harm than good, almost as much harm as the ignorant and ill-informed. After all, it has already been suggested that the activity of counselling requires the client and counsellor to be equals in a way. That means they are different in many personal and social ways but they are to deal with each other as equals without subservience coming into the relationship, with no talking 'down' and patronizing or condescending attitudes.

It becomes necessary fairly early on to think through *the model* that needs to be adopted to help the counsel-seeking woman (*Step 4*). In the earlier counselling scene (that accompanied mediation and conflict resolution, discussed in Chapter 5), it was the problem-solving model that was advocated and discussed. A problem would inevitably be defined as a difficulty or hindrance in what is viewed as normal activity by a person. It can be either related to another person or to a situation that arises from the actions of another person, or is the result of a person's own inability to cope with 'things' as they exist in her life (such as abject poverty, ignorance, social limitations, physical or mental disabilities, etc.).

Can the problem-solving model of counselling be advocated for women in prison or is there something else that is required for this special different environment? The same model as that discussed for mediation is clearly not applicable as it stands. Women that come for mediation or conflict resolution have been driven to the counselling site because a specific 'problem' became significantly irksome and insurmountable and needed a 'solution' that would address the problem at least partially to bring back some order in their lives. *The situation with women in prison is markedly different.* Even if the general definition of 'problem' fits their condition somewhat, the biggest problem for them is that they are locked up and all other problems arise from that. Their pasts and futures are inextricably linked to their being in the prison.

The 'problem' of being locked up has inherently two insurmountable difficulties within it: (*a*) it is not a problem for which the counsellor can offer (or is there to offer) a pointed and direct solution and (*b*) it is related to experiences about which the client may be in denial and counsellor and client are therefore 'not reading from the same page'.

The model that the counsellor therefore needs to build for this specific purpose is essentially a '*therapeutic model*'. It is a model that is at the same time wider and yet perhaps more limited in its reach than a straightforward problem-solving model, so that while it does solve a lot of problems for the client, *its primary target is not a specific problem* (identified as lying at the root of the distress). Therapeutic counselling for women locked inside a prison is aimed at their personal selves and at features that relate to the prison experience. The purpose is to lighten their personal load at each level. The focus at the personal level is an attempt to see just what the client is experiencing as a result of being plucked from her habitat and brought to the most alien of places—a prison.

Some of these experiences relate to happenings prior to coming to prison and are aggravated by the strange and unfamiliar surroundings. At the prison level, the attempt is to determine just what features of prison life have the kinds of negative results that necessitate the need for counselling and therapy inside.

Essentially then the therapeutic model is both enabling and effective in this context: It enables both the client and counsellor to identify (together if possible) all the things that trouble the prisoner as person, and then to set about correcting those that can be corrected or assist in coping with those that cannot be changed, with as little damage to the person and personality of the prisoner. While change is intended, there may not be any specific problem-solving of the kind aimed at in the mediation model. If a woman is in jail and has left behind children with the extended family (because only children below six are permitted to be with mothers in the prison) then her main grievance and problem is being parted from her children. That is not a problem that the counsellor can solve. The woman can be reassured about the condition and well-being of her children, and visits by children can be arranged so that she is at ease on that front. She can also be counselled to accept her predicament and learn to lessen the damage that this whole situation would have on her personality and on her present and future ability to 'make it'.

While the eight strategic steps of the problem-solving model may not be replicable here (see Chapter 5), there would still be a need to work through some steps that would assist with the therapeutic model. As the aim is the change of the person's capability and 'cope-ability' rather than a radical change of the outside scenario, some agreement with the client on the nature of the therapeutic model is in order, for it avoids misleading the client into believing that something more will be achieved.

No matter what our own ideas and perceptions it may be taken as a given that, particularly for first time offenders, entering the prison is a 'shock' regardless of age or any other factor.

Exercise: Observe newcomers and first-timers when they are admitted into the prison and note down their actions and reactions to the ordinary routine activity of their admission.

FIGURE 6.1. SELF-REMINDERS OF A COUNSELLOR

- Do not allow their prisoner status to affect the spirit or style of counselling.
- Collaborate with them in their own personal change.
- Avoid even the semblance of an adversarial relationship; it is anathema for counselling, especially inside a prison.
- Take the client seriously; she may be poor, ignorant and imprisoned but is still a woman.
- Take it slowly and don't rush them.

Counsellors therefore have to go very easy with them; their (private) world has fallen apart regardless of their guilt or innocence in the eyes of the law. While the law is meting out the punishment that is within its power to do (i.e. imprisonment), there is no other agency that has the right or authority to mete out any other punishment in addition to that. That having been clarified by the counsellor to herself and her client, a few further self-reminders would need to precede the sessions (Figure 6.1).

It may also be a good idea to explain to the prisoner-client the rudimentary ideas behind the therapeutic model being adopted (as opposed to the problem-solving one, which has less relevance in the context). The client may appear too unsophisticated to be addressed on this issue but it is still a good idea to do so in the most simple and easily comprehensible style and language. It may be a psychological move or quite simply a confidence-building one but is still worth pursuing as a step towards inclusiveness regardless of the simplicity and plainness of the client. It also gives a professional start to the process of actual interaction that should begin after the preliminaries have been thought and worked through. The client is put at ease with the sharing attitude and the 'process' of counselling in some concrete form can then begin.

Unlike the step in the problem-solving model where some basic *information* must be obtained for working through the next few steps, in this model we let the information trickle in as effortlessly as possible at this stage (*Step 5*). Care needs to be taken not to exercise any kind of moral pressure since there are likely to be sensitive issues that may be inextricably intertwined with the client's mental disposition. Whatever information comes through, it needs to be discreetly taken note of in order to develop the detailed process of information gathering undertaken later.

What is probably coming through at this stage even with the minimal interaction is basically what is 'bugging' the client and through her communication style (verbal and non-verbal) some idea of her personality (shy, quiet, afraid, aggressive, cantankerous, deliberately provocative, etc.). Some note should be taken at this point about some of these first-encounter features of the client, as the counsellor is making her way towards setting the stage for interacting, communicating and connecting directly.

With clients who are not in charge of their lives, there would be a need to refrain from being daunting and intimidating. There is a difference between the model developed earlier for mediation counselling and counselling prisoners in jails because the clients are different. They come with different expectations, the objective of counselling is different, the pressures on both sides are different and the expected outcome is different. Counselling in dispute resolution may well be for women who are in dire straits for specific reasons, but they are still women who have a semblance of normality in their lives. Expecting them to conduct themselves according to rules and time frames would not hit them hard as they are there for some result for which they would abide by ground rules. Counselling imprisoned women entails being mindful of their fragility and of their every emotion. And yet some sense of purpose and a framework is necessary to inspire the client to feel they are being taken seriously as persons and not being patronized. Creating an ambience, making a timetable and setting out some ground rules (*Step 6*) suggests this is not a casual exercise of sympathy and purposeless enquiry.

In the mediation mode, the attempt had been to work towards the following steps and to formalize (without intimidation) the locale and atmosphere. Attention was paid to

- The physical setting
- The general ambience
- Seating arrangements
- The decorum on the premises
- Dress code and appearance
- The manner and mode of address between clients and counsellors
- Language/including body language
- Noise levels on the premises

While most of these remain the same for women in custody, the emphasis is different. Dress code and appearance inevitably gets adjusted to meet the client half way, as the prisoner is not in a position to observe any dress code and can at best be encouraged to be presentable to give her a feeling of going somewhere special (even if it is just a room in the same building where she spends all of her days and nights!).

The physical setting, general ambience and seating arrangements for counselling is the first part of the preparation, and this raises some issues and problems. Should the counselling site or room be set up with a general concern for good appearance with furniture—chairs, tables, etc.—or should the arrangement be of a kind that the prisoners are accustomed to, that is sitting on the floor, etc. This becomes an issue for well-known reasons. Prisons in South Asia (and that can be extended to several developing countries) are minimum facility environments clearly for two reasons: (*a*) that the women that are brought here are for the most part from economically backward and uneducated backgrounds and (*b*) that it is therefore believed that 'what they don't have at home they don't need to get here'. The physical surroundings in the prison are therefore almost devoid of furniture and of facilities for storage. While this is the ground reality and prompts the thinking of those who run prisons, the view of those who are seeking changes and reforms is that there cannot be a letting up on the basic minimums that are agreed now as 'minimum standards' and must be followed at any cost. In the provision of food, clothing and shelter, it is clearly understood, recognized and propagated that there cannot be any compromising of the minimums that are agreed as basic requirements for a human being. The reformer cannot have double standards.

Those who are in the business of wanting to set up a Counselling Unit to assist those who need therapeutic assistance belong generally to the same genre (in ideas and reasoning) as the above-mentioned reformer. So if counselling requires some formalism, physical standards and rules of conduct, then there is really no reason to compromise standards only because the clients come from humble backgrounds and most of them are not likely to complain no matter what they are provided. The logic may need some modification (not necessarily leading to a compromise with standards). In this specific case if a counselling room were set up with urban furniture in a setting where women would be awestruck and uncomfortable sitting in upright chairs because they are unaccustomed to it, then such an arrangement would run contrary to the purpose and hence requirement of the Unit. It is a question of making the women 'at home', whatever it takes to do that. It is sometimes possible to find a middle path where the (mental) comfort of the women and the (standard-oriented) principles of the counsellors (who wish to be 'correct' on both fronts) can be amalgamated.

For the Counselling Unit in prisons on which some of the experiences of this book are based, the physical setting materialized after some thought was given to several different aspects of the activity.

- What would the women be comfortable with physically and mentally?
- What would be most conducive for the atmosphere that was required for the work?
- What would not compromise the professionalism that was being underlined as essential?

In one example of finding the right balance between the correct form and the required ambience, something quite appropriate was worked out: there was a literal compromise between sitting on the floor (which the women did all over the prison in their cells, when they ate, when they watched TV, etc.) and sitting in high chairs. A nice rug was placed on the floor and some low cane *mooras* (little stools, 'pouffes' or hassocks but made of pliable cane and reeds) placed randomly on the rug to give the air of informality and choice to the client. The women responded well to these and felt both 'at home' and duly catered for. Posters relating to women's and children's health adorned the walls and for the literate some mission statements were pasted alongside.

For a category of persons (women prisoners) that are living by strict rules, regulations, instructions, commands and directions each day and all the time (even when they sleep), it seems ironic that even as they come for counselling (comfort seeking and a little letup on the regimentation) we are talking about rules. These *ground rules* are not intended to be harsh or regimental in their intent and are there to suggest to the client that both sides need to be bound by rules for systematic conduct of the sessions. They are also needed to indicate that there needs to be a modicum of behavioural requirements in order to project it as an exercise with some discipline.

Because it is a jail, some features of ground rules that pertain to other settings have to be put aside for the prisoner-client: rules such as coming by 'appointment only' cannot be strictly adhered to. Prisoners are already constrained by other schedules and a 'drop in' system may sometimes have to be adopted, provided of course no one else is already in a session with the counsellor. Another kind of flexibility that can be adopted is that the counsellor may sometimes have to go to the client if such a situation arises, and it may considered necessary to do so for reasons of age, infirmity, acute depression and tension or a general framework of hostility that has built up in the woman and that needs to be addressed. (It was followed in the case of a woman in Hyderabad who had phobias and obsessive compulsive disorder [OCD]).

All other rules of language, greeting, volume, etc. remain the same. Trying to bring prisoners who have lost track of the general niceties and manners pertaining to human interaction back on line or track is an aspect of suggesting that they are being treated at par with women 'outside'; that they are not being treated as aberrations and abnormal persons.

Ground rules for language and non-verbal communication are vital. Many prisoners who may already not be quite so well mannered and courteous to begin with as a result of the backgrounds they come from become harsh and callous as a result of the severe and brusque manner in which they are handled by the staff. The importance of being civil and polite has to be re-inculcated into their functioning. Not unconnected with this is the fact that staff too need a session with the counsellors perhaps as a group (group counselling will be discussed at the end of the chapter).

There is no process of formal registration as in the cases of mediation. Clients come and their details are noted and filed, but the idea is not to have too much preliminary paperwork. The intention is to put them at ease and to work towards the mutual aims of both counsellor and client. The features of 'time frame and timetable' (*Step 7*) that apply to other counselling modes are not rigidly applicable in this context. No one is in the kind of hurry that was suggested for the (problem-solving) mediation model. Having set out the limitations and boundaries of the counselling that is to be imparted, it is implied that neither the client seeking help nor the counsellor offering it would be on a rigid timetable.

There is a feature of the prison in South Asia that is peculiar to the region: this is the physical openness of the prison and the open spaces like verandas and courtyards where there is considerable movement of people—both prisoners and staff and indeed of social workers who are able to meet and observe prisoners and staff in the process. As a result, there is likelihood of counsellors getting added glimpses of clients outside of the Counselling Unit. If after one session the client stops coming, the counsellor is able to move about the prison and therefore can by autosuggestion encourage the client to come again for her own good, but there can neither be any cajoling nor pressure. The time frame is therefore determined by what the counsellor believes is the goal for a particular client, and only that, but is also modifiable given the nature of the prison structure and functioning.

Even if rigidity is not imposed for the time, some structural steps would have to be set out so that there is a modicum of formal procedure that can be observed as the session proceeds, such as:

- Gathering some personal details.
- Assessing the problem that is most intense.
- Assessing the personality to determine the coping factor.
- Sizing up the nature of help that is possible.
- Sizing up how much cooperation will be forthcoming from the client.

While these may not really constitute a timetable, they do suggest the barest minimum that must be sought from the client, no matter what it takes (in terms of time or effort). This will also be of assistance in determining what type of method could be followed to get to that point.

Whether the counselling process and steps should be 'facilitative or directive' (*Step 8*) will clearly depend upon (*a*) the kind of personality the client has, (*b*) the kind of difficulties the client thinks she is facing, (*c*) the kind of preliminary assessments the counsellor is able to make during the first encounter and (*d*) the nature of first interaction with the client.

Some challenging cases throw counsellors at the deep end, and there is a need for collective consultations to determine the best way they should be handled. One such was a client 'R' around whom much debate and discussion took place that then took the form of an exercise that the counsellors and others were asked to address.

Exercise: A young girl 'R' is being bullied by seasoned prisoners and in addition to other adjustment problems related to her age this is something that she just cannot cope with. She retaliates by being brusque with prisoners and staff and when pushed too hard she is abusive. 'R' even attempted suicide on a day that she was running a fever by swallowing all her five days' medication at once. Her mother and older sister (accompanied by two children) are in the same prison but are at their wit's end about how to handle this teenager. *'R' is too tense and unwilling to talk and yet needs help. How should she be counselled?* Several factors need to be taken into account in approaching such a client. In most prisons in South Asia the average age of imprisoned women is about 35. Those who are very young (under 20) are either indirectly involved in offences (whole families get picked up and thrown in jail when 'dowry deaths' occur) or have been picked up for 'immoral trafficking'. Then there are women much older in the 60s and some even over 70. This category has increased since the incidence of arrests and convictions under 498A and 304B went up.[1]

The case of 'R' is unusually curious. She is a convict in the women's prison for two years with her mother and older sister and two little nieces aged two and five. Her father, brother and brother-in-law are in the men's prison—all for a 'dowry death' in which her brother's wife died. She is generally a playful, sprightly and talkative girl who moves around the prison cheerily without any sign of self-consciousness. The counsellors determined through their own methods that she was underage (14 years old) when she was brought to the adult prison. Details of her case and its ramifications are given in Shankardass (2012). Counsellors investigated her case thoroughly and exposed several incongruities in the way it was handled. Through their intervention 'R' was finally released. Whether it was a solution or not is difficult to say. But equally uncomfortable was the (convenient) answer that the justice system had arrived at when faced with the problem of an innocent underage girl (she was not convicted) whose entire family was going to prison for a 'collective' act of causing a dowry death. We have observed other cases where for want of suitable alternative arrangements children (over 6 and below 18) have been kept in adult prisons with offending mothers. A blind girl of 12 accompanied her convicted mother to prison in an Uttar Pradesh (UP) jail because there was nowhere else she could be sent for care. One wonders if the course of justice may not have been better served if an alternative punishment had been found for the mother so that the 12 year old was not 'punished' alongside. The effect of such decisions on minor girls is devastating and needs careful examination. Counselling 'R' when she was going through her rebellious phase was challenging. When the counsellors approached her in the courtyard she turned her face away. Everyone was treated as an enemy. Every day one or another counsellor searched her out just to befriend her. Simultaneously requests were made to other prisoners not to be impatient with 'R' when she spoke rudely. 'She is going through a bad phase and is only a child even if we have made her wear the white *saree* with the border that convicted women wear.' Some responded positively, others scowled and said they would not take nonsense from a slip of a girl.

Counselling was carried out in this case with facilitative and directive skills. The client had to be encouraged to communicate. Her age was the guiding factor in developing communication in the absence of any offence committed by her. The exercise was one of enabling the 'child' to cope and also ascertain what it was that made her so impatient in her dealings with others. The attempt was also to link up the behaviour patterns of others (through information gleaned from her accounts) in order that those 'others' could be brought to the Counselling Unit. There was a need to assure the child that while the counsellor made enquiries about the treatment meted out to her, she needed to behave better ('directive') and that it would be in her own interest to do so. In such cases merely being facilitative is not enough. If there has been a gross misrepresentation of age by the establishment, the counsellors would inevitably get involved in enquiries and examination of records and perhaps medical checks to ascertain the truth, which they did. Meanwhile the damage to the person 'R' needed to be minimized.

'R's' counselling was somewhat informally conducted, given the errors that the system had committed in her case. She did come to the counselling room eventually, but most of the interaction with her was in courtyards and verandas to avoid tension and anxiety. And yet specific goals had to be achieved in her case so the activity could not be random and directionless. Slowly but surely she (and her mother) had to be informed about the flaw in the system that had allowed a 14 year old to be falsely implicated in a dowry case so that she could be housed with family in the prison. That was a primary goal for counsellors and it was made clear to the family, the staff and the prison managers. Strangely the mother was not excited about it at all. That put counsellors in a quandary but they were not about to relent. The client was kept fully apprised of what the counsellors had in mind and the family was given some idea of 'road map' (see Chapter 5, p. 118). Intermediary goals of calming 'R' down and getting her well so that she did not feel suicidal again were a challenge.

Even if some prisoners come to the Counselling Unit just for a 'change', it should not be objected to by the counsellors. In a prison situation, 'providing relief' from the monotony of routine and the drudgery of being at people's beck and call can well be considered one of the goals of the counselling service. Prisoners' predicaments are unique and exclusive to their circumstances and an opportunity for emotional sharing is an oasis in the desert.

Problem-solving and solution-finding as life's permanent goals need to be highlighted to suggest that running away from smothering the problem gets us nowhere. It is a good idea in this context to supplement the activity with some puzzles and games that are brief and involving, but not taxing and demanding. Joining dots in a picture or looking for the clown in a jumbled up picture—these could be briefly tried and the suggestion made thereafter that everyone needs to be engaged in problem-solving and solution-finding at most times in life: small problems or big problems, there is always the need to seek ways. The objective should only mildly relate to what the client may have done as part of the process of solving her problem in life (this would mean only a passing reference to her offence and not a discussion or judgement about it).

Even as the time boundaries are not to be rigidly adhered to, some attempt at avoiding rambling and being focused on achieving some change should be made. This should be shared with the client—questions periodically need to be asked together with the client: Where are we headed? Do you feel we are going some-where with this? Is some goal visible here? The client's own views about goals and purposes could be ascertained.

In the region that is under discussion (South Asia with a spe-cific focus on jails in India), the paucity of information that relates to women in jail and the near absence of recorded versions of hap-penings and 'voices' relating to these women, the need for a clear methodology for taking notes and classifying the information systematically can scarcely be overemphasized (*Step 10*). Haphaz-ard note-taking is not a good idea: It makes for poor understand-ing of the client and the goal that is in view. There needs to be a method determined by the object in view. Some of the guidelines for developing this method could be set out for use on a semi-permanent basis:

- Data and facts relating to client
- Descriptions and other interesting personal details (physical observations)
- Her first utterance (it might assist in establishing future starting points)
- Body language and any specific idiosyncrasies
- Level of articulation and expression
- Self-expressed anxieties or other distress
- Observed indications of distress
- Idea of the requirement of the client
- Some indicators of what steps might be taken for a start
- Time record (with details)

Having said all this it must be remembered, as stated earlier, that excessive note-making can cause anxiety and tension in the client's mind and defeat one of the purposes of prison counselling, that is reducing stress. The client must feel the counsellor is listen-ing and thinking about her above all.

How does one measure the effectiveness of the process and the results of counselling as a therapeutic intervention in a pris-on? Evaluation is difficult for some contexts and those who insist on having objective tests for measuring impact of some activities in a prison, for instance, would have to revise their expectations. Impact of counselling in a prison is often so subjective it would fail the most effectively devised objective tests. Measuring and evaluating is tough in a prison. There are so many features that need to be evaluated—from counsellor and client satisfaction to assessment and environmental change, each feature would need differing yardsticks and it would be difficult to decide what the crucial features of each aspect of counselling are, each of which would need a particular yardstick. Sometimes an effect could be as simple as noticing that a prisoner who was earlier dull and gloomy now smiles and talks! How is the smile in her face to be measured?

With so many different features and not all measurable by the same yardstick it might be a good idea to try and list them and work through some key features that could be highlighted in each to see where things were before and where they are after the process of counselling. Feedback from the institution's workforce can also be used as one important component of the evaluation.

Thus, that list can contain any or all of the following:

- Counsellor's self-evaluation on content, methods and (perceived) outcomes.
- Client's feedback through questionnaires.
- Feedback from client's companions through behavioural changes.
- Feedback through staff reactions.
- Observations by experienced members.

It may help to get some input from external evaluators who have some idea of the subject (which here means all three: prison, counselling and evaluation). However, it must be kept in mind that too clinical an evaluation in this area of work is neither desirable nor possible.

Talking about 'Getting Started' at this stage is not really incongruous. The steps are not meant to be sequential steps (see Chapter 4, p. 92) and need attention at various points in the process of counselling—some at the beginning, some at the end and some at all times, all along. The steps in *this* section that are entitled 'Getting Started' are steps with which counselling does actually begin. These steps relate directly to the actual (physical) activity of counselling and may well need the supplement of the other steps (from the list of 11 set out earlier) like getting the ambience right, note-making, self-awareness, etc.

So when the actual sessions need to begin, all the tips and safeguards discussed earlier need to be checked out (*Step 12*): Is the location neat and inviting? The counsellor's first impact is at the entrance to the location. Is the door unpleasant? Is there a curtain? How private is it? Is the client visible from outside when she is in the counselling room? Does she feel secure and assured of confidentiality? Do the posters there on the wall suggest (particularly for the illiterate) what the location is for and what the counsellors are there for? Are the smells pleasant? Is there a flower vase that adds colour to the room? Even if the room is small is it cosy and inviting?

These are some of the physical manifestations of the preparedness that must be attended to and put in place in order that the very first step in the direction of a counselling process is positive and pleasant. No matter what the socio-economic background of the client, the personality and behavioural characteristics, and the nature of her offence and the problems associated with it, the 'welcome' sign needs to be there in the ambience, even without the words being written at the door.

We have already described the possibilities of seating options that would make clients of all manner and type comfortable, and comfortable here means 'at ease' or as referred to earlier 'helping the client feel safe' (Sutton and Stewart, 1997). Given the nature of the client and the subservience that has been inculcated in her in the environment of the prison (and probably where she comes from), the first feeling she would appreciate is that of being treated with respect. A polite gesture indicating that she may sit in front of the counsellor on the types of seats provided for *both* is reassuring and encouraging for the client. The counsellor should not have her back to the door so that she is the one with an eye on the entrance. Any entry or interruption can thus be monitored by the counsellor who is able to gesture that the interruption is not welcome.

Provision for water should be there, and in the event of 'tears' something to wipe the eyes. Notepads and writing material should be at hand and there should be no fumbling once the conversation begins. It is often a good idea to tell the client something about the counsellor's background and general interests and if possible her expertise to conduct this activity. If the counsellor is being assisted by another person, or if there is an intern present, it would give the client great self-respect if the client's permission were taken for the presence of another person in the room, albeit with reassurances that she is part of the team.

'Greetings and first words' (*Step 13*) are of immense importance for the start of the interaction between such unequal persons. The inequality arises partly from the one being free and the other a prisoner and from the social divides that present themselves before both parties to the relationship in this particular context. The counsellor is an educated, relatively well-informed and socially well-placed person who has sensitivity and understanding both of the society and the institution in which she has decided to work. Most of the women who will appear before her are likely to be from relatively poor, uneducated and ignorant families and equally likely to be part of a conservative family scene where the rules are laid down by the men, and women are expected to follow the roles set out for them over the ages.

The form of greeting that is used will reflect this difference. Clients that come from well-placed homes and environs will extend the customary greeting of their social origins (these may be of a semi-religious nature reflecting the community from which they come). Others may just enter in silence and it would be for the counsellor to speak the first words, which are usually the asking of the client's name.

Exercise: Counsellors in training may be asked to list out various options of 'first words' and the different choices may be taken up for discussion to discuss the suitability of each. For examples: 'So what is your name?', 'Who are you?' or 'Come sit down and tell me who you are?'

Trite as this may sound to some, the mode and manner of introducing and deciding the first spoken words has an impact on the client. In the context of a prison, this has a special meaning. Torn away from what was once normal living, a woman is now full of trepidation and uncertainty and even if she has come of her own volition she is the unequal component in a relationship where the effort should now be to suggest that she is an *equal* in more ways than one. The greeting has significance for her.

Because the client is more than likely to be somewhat ill-informed about many things that pertain to the institution of the prison, in the introductory exchange a general 'chat' about the prison and what it is all about (all over the world) and how it does need improvements, etc., may not be a bad idea. Prisoners who come for the first time are often in a state of shock and some words of comfort that suggest that the counsellor does not think the prison is a great place would not be taken amiss by anyone (staff in particular). It may reassure the client that the counsellor also has a vision of prison reform.

The basic idea to put the client at ease whatever it takes within the bounds of the environment and the task at hand. This is uncharted territory in most South Asian prisons, and women prisoners who may sound aggressive and brazen outside would have difficulty being treated as normal (and equal) in an otherwise hostile environment. Putting her at ease (for counselling purposes) would be difficult and would take some trial-and-error attempts that can then be listed as effective or ineffective depending on the client's responses.

Unlike in the mediation situation ('Exploring the Problem' in Chapter 5, p. 122), there may be no specific problem or predicament and therefore opening lines like 'So what seems to be the problem?' are not always a good idea. They give the client a feeling that the Unit is only for solving specific problems and since she may not have had a specific issue in mind she may not wish to continue. Inviting them to talk about their lives in prison will fetch enough responses that will lead to further points of entry into their difficulties. Prisoners have some pet themes that can get them talking and inevitably the general leads to the particular. Suggesting for instance 'It must be tough here?' or 'This place can depress you, can't it?' or 'I know that nothing is normal here but what is the worst part of being in prison?' are questions that fetch answers that could fill a book if steered properly! However, since we want to get to the person and personality of the client, we need to make our way into her difficulties as soon as possible (*Step 14*).

On the other hand, there may be clients with some very specific problems some of which may be disturbing and soul-destroying, and these would need to be carefully listened and attended to and handled. This stage is really a build-up to the next stage that has concrete dimensions to it: Exploring means preparing the stage before really using it. Facing the client in the first instance enables the counsellor to be prepared for the following activities:

1. Broadly assess what is 'bugging' the client.
2. Observe the client's communication style and body language.
3. Note some of the client's obvious personality traits that can be analysed within the time.
4. Work out how she would like to develop her own communication skills and techniques.
5. Put into place all the tips that she would have gathered from the '11 steps' and reflect on an appropriate approach to the way the client should be counselled.

After a few general questions, the 'information gathering' (*Step 15*) should begin in earnest. Up to this point the counsellor should avoid picking up her notebook to do the scribbling and frantic writing that we are all prone to do in any exercise in which recordkeeping and information-gathering is vital. Once the name, personal details (age, marital status, etc.), family details, origins and finally offence details have been procured, other information will come in bits and pieces. Unlike the mediation model of questioning, this is not a specific-problem-solving situation where the narrative will flow smoothly. Women who come for conflict resolution have narrated their stories a hundred times before they came to the counsellor and probably talked as many times about their stories to friends and family. Women in prison have only made factual submissions earlier (whether about themselves or related to their offences) mostly before a relatively hostile official machinery, manned by intimidating personnel, who far from giving a sympathetic ear have in all likelihood reprimanded them for not standing straight! Now the same information is asked for in a spirit of cooperation and with a quite different agenda. This spirit should come through right from the start (without an innuendo that there is a fundamental divide between the official machinery and the Counselling Unit in terms of style and intent).

Notes would begin about now to assist the gathering of information, and as the counsellor moves towards the client's story and narrative the need to set out (classify) the information within some system will arise. Some counsellors keep pens in different colours to suggest that their own observations are in one colour and the narrative of the client in another colour. While taking notes is vital, at no point should it be a preoccupation nor should 'active listening' be lost sight of. Points made earlier (in the 11 steps set out as part of process) about listening, active listening and listening with self-awareness need to be put into action now.

There may be junctures in the client's narrative when the counsellor has hunches ('this is a blatant lie', 'this is so inconsistent with what was said earlier' or 'this woman is in total denial'). These can be put down as points that need to be clarified later (and tactfully) with the client.

Apart from recording what the client says as a narrative, there should be some special method of noting down other 'problems'. There could be a note on prison difficulties and a separate one on the past that precipitated many of the present difficulties and problems. The two should not be indiscriminately mixed even if the intimate relationship between them is to be worked upon when an intervention is sought.

Accounts of the 'description of the problem' and 'history of the problem' will both inevitably relate themselves to the offence and lead finally to the prison experience. Contrasted with the earlier counselling context, there are a few tricky parts to this one that sometimes the 'best' (meaning here simply long standing in experience) counsellor may have difficulty with. The details of some accounts are so gory and horrific that keeping a straight face is not easy. This is the tough part. Women have killed. Equally they have had the most dreadful things done to them. It is not for the counsellor to judge which of the acts might be more appalling. The women are here as prisoners and they will (should) not be here forever. It is in the fitness of things that they need to get hold of themselves to live the rest of their lives with some normality.

What attitude the counsellor has towards the client, her past and present and the reasons why she is here will affect the quality of the counselling she provides. Not paying attention to how crucial this feature of the process is leads to a general diminution of the quality of professionalism that is being emphasized again and again as a prerequisite to effective and meaningful counselling. A counsellor has to remind herself that viewing the client through the wrong kind of glasses is detrimental to the counselling process and to the client (*Step 16*).

One of the reasons why Counselling Cells and counsellors seem to mushroom with such rapidity and dismissed as commonplace 'advice providers' is the scant attention paid to the essential qualities that are being highlighted as the 'soul' of real (professional) counselling:

- Rising above one's innate prejudices
- Curtailing one's temperamental traits
- Looking at clients from their own standpoint
- Avoiding a moral high-ground based on social positioning
- Holding back from doling advice too readily

These are only some of the general safeguards that need to be brought to the surface at each point in the process. In the case of prisoners who are in a unique position of disadvantage ('doubly damned'), a counsellor can find myriads of reasons for always being right when she pronounces on the prisoner's accounts and narratives. A counsellor can easily feel smug about advice-giving simply by virtue of being neither an offender nor a prisoner. This feeling is not easy to eradicate from the mind because it is not consciously thought out. 'Outsiders' often enter a prison in one of many frames of mind: feeling generous and charitable, altruistic, condescending, patronizing, over and overtly sympathetic, bountiful and all of those features that convey that they are 'givers'. But to be a good counsellor none of these is the vital ingredient, for it is a skill and a mission that needs to be imbibed and trained for. Many attitudes and postures that have been learnt by the counsellor (as a person) over the years for effective functioning in the class to which she belongs may have to be shed at the prison gates if she is to fit into the role of counsellor. This includes the way she dresses, talks, smiles, moves around, looks at people or sits as they sit and eat as they eat.

Referred to as *Step 17* in our process ('communication-techniques and skills including verbal and body language'), this is not one single stage or step: It is the very essence of the whole process and the single most important feature of counselling as an exercise whether for problem-solving or alleviating distress. Even as we always place and discuss it at the end, it is a feature of counselling that is its main tool and present from the beginning, at the middle, in the end and beyond. It is the one factor of counselling that can make or break the whole endeavour if not professionally handled. All that was said in earlier 'steps' about body language, active listening, skills and techniques and verbal and non-verbal communication relate in the ultimate analysis to this area—the vital tool for implementing all of the ideas that constitute the process.

Communication happens through all the ways that we can possibly think about: through eyes, hands, feet, posture, yawning, nose-twitching, lips-pursing, pencil-fidgeting, shuffling or even total silence. We have already described the nuances of verbal and non-verbal communication and rather than repeat them here it would be appropriate to glance over them again in Chapter 5 (pp. 127–132). Sometimes observations of this kind seem so obvious that a likely response from a would-be counsellor might be: 'Are you teaching me to walk?' Yet it is surprising how the most obvious tips for effective communication are the ones that are constantly slurred over and make for bad interaction. Nothing is obvious in this field, for if it were, half the things written here might not need to be said.

The one feature about communicating with women in prison that needs special attention is how much the counsellor is learning as she goes along: insights that she never dreamt of would now come her way and provide the opportunity for a depth of understanding of human nature and behaviour that would stand unparalleled. If a counsellor thought she was privileged for one reason or another, the privilege of being allowed into the lives of women who have had experiences of a kind that need to be known but are not, or that need to be understood and are not, is something to think about. The introspection that would accompany such thoughts would lend a measure of understanding and concern to the whole mission and justify the need for this little developed area of work.

Two specific points that need to be highlighted in this particular context of counselling in the prison: one is the kind of *language* used in the prison by prisoners and staff that passes off for natural and normal and that is nothing short of abusive; and the other brought about by insensitivities of routine is a certain *loss of femininity*, of the quality of being a woman that *seems* not to be important (but in fact nothing could be more important and hence the signs of an internal struggle in most women of trying to cope with this). The development or perpetuation of these relates in turn to specific features about the prison in general and women's prisons specifically that were mentioned earlier: one is the opaque nature of the prison and the other is the living realities of most of the women inside.

The kind of communication skills that would need to be developed to handle areas of sensitivity such as these is a matter that should be almost separately covered by counsellors who are structuring models for communicating with women who are as remote from their own experiences as any one will ever get. 'How to communicate on especially sensitive issues' needs to be included as a separate section of the 'Communication step' in counselling women in such special locations as the prison. It would be a measure aimed also at recovering a section of women who (already excluded) get further alienated from the mainstream when loose vocabulary, bad language and insensitive allusions to their bodies and bodily functions are the usual manner of dealing with them. This is considered 'OK' for their 'kind' (which of course is loaded with innuendos of caste, class and the usual symptoms of 'otherness'). Prison is one place where the question 'is counselling intended also to reform' comes up once again and needs to be faced unhesitatingly.

CASE ANALYSIS OF COUNSELLING IN CONTEXT 2 : WOMEN IN PRISON

The prison (and more specifically a women's prison) must be the one place without doubt where the value and need for counselling needs little justification. This relates to several features of the subjects, women *and* prisons, and it also requires handling of the several strands that form the picture called 'women and the prison'. The stories (cases) that form a part of this picture are not intended to be 'touching' narratives of helpless creatures that are locked up and miserable because they are being badly managed, roughly handled and brutally treated. Some of these imprisoned women appear almost as tough as the constables or warders who handle them each day. The difference in the toughness of the two categories is that whereas the warder's or constable's toughness is supplemented by some power and authority that she is expected to (and definitely does) exercise for the smooth running and security of the prison, the prisoner's *toughness*, often a defence mechanism, if exhibited, is more likely than not to get her into more serious trouble. How these equations get played out in effect in the prison scenario is a matter of much concern for those who believe that as an institution of the State the prison, like all State institutions, needs to be managed according to the same principles of 'fraternity, assuring the dignity of the individual' laid down in the Preamble of the Indian Constitution.

A prison is not an easy institution to manage, not only because it is (falsely) believed to be filled with undesirable criminals who must be abnormal people if they have violated State laws, but also for other reasons:

- It is opaque and surrounded in a mystique that is scarcely ever fractured.
- Its opaqueness allows for both slackness and disregard of proper rules of governance.
- It is filled mostly with persons who are poor and powerless and don't really count.
- It is regarded as a 'stepchild' amidst other state institutions, and both staff and prisoners suffer as a result.
- It does not attract the kind of staff that other institutions do. ('Who wants to work in prison where all you do is open and close locks and count the number of persons all day long?')

All these features can be multiplied several-fold if it is a women's prison. This is because of the following reasons:

- Women are ill-informed about their legal and human rights and more likely to be manhandled.
- When women commit crimes they are dubbed criminals *and* sinners.
- Women are inarticulate and inept at formulating demands for what it due to them.
- Once imprisoned they have little support from families even when they are the prime carers in the family.
- Being less individualistic and more collectivistic, the experience of being wrenched from the collective is acutely traumatizing.
- Coming with one kind of oppressive experience, the callousness in the prison regime causes acute distress and anxiety often leading to a breakdown in mental health.
- A prison experience reduces their chances of fitting back in the one environ where they felt they 'belonged' — the family and community.

These are only some of the many difficulties that women face when incarcerated, over and above the physical deprivations of basic needs and amenities required for a life of decency.

Some of the most common mental disorders that women suffer from (even outside the prison) are accentuated and deteriorate in the prison. That these need being addressed is an understatement. That they have not been considered worthy of attention is probably more accurate. Because attention to mental health is minimal in most societies, attention to women's mental health even more so, the problem has not even been investigated. It is easier to identify those with severe mental illnesses and 'medicalize' the problem, so that drugs and other 'treatment' can be imparted; one can then boast of a curative line of action that yields results. But common mental disorders or mental distress (anxiety, some forms of depression, panic, etc.) that need other interventions is an area that has been glossed over because these disorders are not considered 'serious' enough (even if the sufferer is falling to pieces emotionally and mentally).

... supportive of this difference between mental distress and illness is the increasing awareness of the association between distress and social circumstance in the case of women. Research into the causes of women's distress is noticeably absent in India, with most studies seeking only biological explanations.

When psychiatry (as epidemiological intervention) is resorted to all too readily, any suggestion about the need for encouraging studies on sociological data about women's deprived social experience as an explanation of mental distress is not likely to be given importance. (Davar, 1999)

This is where counselling comes in as the most suitable intervention. Safe, sound and supportive it addresses those very gaps in women's lives that that are never considered worthy of exploration: because they are too ordinary, too banal and not dramatic enough.

The case discussed here seeks to illustrate some features of the distress women in prison experience and suffer, and the interventions that are offered to address that distress. They have not been picked for any demonstrative agenda. They are samples picked on the basis of the following differentiating factors:

- Different age groups (very young and very old)
- Different offences

- Different sentences
- Different backgrounds
- Different personalities

This is one of almost five hundred cases that formed part of the records of the Counselling Units that were set up by the NGO PRAJA in the several prisons where women's experiences in prison (and prior to being imprisoned) were investigated and analysed. The whole initiative towards counselling as an appropriate intervention for distressed women came about as a result of the many studies of imprisoned women's lives that had already been undertaken in prison, by talking to the women and their families, and going backwards and forwards in time into their lives. Origins and backgrounds had been investigated and those who were released (often through our interventions) were followed into their new lives to observe changes if any (Shankardass, 2012). Counselling was the follow-up that seemed to emerge almost as a requirement, and while not every woman came to the Unit (some were shy, some hostile), those who did made it a worthwhile exercise all round.

Case of Saloni, Arrested under the Immoral Trafficking (Prevention) Act (PITA, 1986)

The Counselling Unit set up by PRAJA in this particular prison was carefully worked through by following the standards and procedures set out in the 'rulebooks' as closely as possible. Prisoners here come from all kinds of socio-economic backgrounds, are of all ages and differ quite fundamentally from one another in personality traits. The room provided for counselling by the prison administration was small and had a small toilet attached, primarily for the counsellors' benefit, but counsellors did permit prisoners to use it if and when necessary. The seating arrangements were made with a view to providing options: chairs around the table that the counsellors used, and a carpet area with cushions thrown around for those who were more accustomed to and comfortable with sitting on the floor. There were appropriate pictures on the walls and flowers to add colour to an otherwise drab room. Two women (prisoners) had actually volunteered to paint the room before the decorations were put up and even made *rangoli* (decorative designs made on floors) outside the room the day the Unit began functioning.

Ever since the passing of 'PITA' more and more young girls have been picked up by the police and brought to prison. Some are bailed out in a few days, some languish for weeks but either way they form a category apart, not because there is something inherently peculiar about *them*; it is the way they are viewed by prisoners and staff, and the manner in which they become the butt of crude jokes, snide comments and side glances that in turn make them either withdrawn or more brazen than they really are. Acutely conscious of how they are viewed, they develop attitudes and postures that get them no sympathy or understanding, adding further to their disjointedness from the social environ in which they live.

Saloni was one such girl and meeting her and eventually getting her to talk at counselling sessions was both a challenge and a learning curve for her counsellors. Recounted here are both her story and her counselling sessions to suggest the delicacies and complexities of the encounters between counsellor and client in this particular setting and context—prison. Most of her narrative is in the first person. In the prison, most of the information about personal stories is received perforce from one source, the other players being unavailable or even unknown. Factual information relating to the case comes from records and files.

When Saloni first came in she kept standing and waited to be told to sit down. Her expression was one of resentment and a defiant sort of sadness. It was difficult to ascertain how to break the ice and the first question that came to the counsellor's mind was 'How old are you?' Clearly that was a bad move that only brought a retort:

Why is my age of so much concern to you? Surely you want to know what I am here for, how did they catch me, and what I do in the prison day in and day out. I am really not interested in a long conversation with you the way others here are. You asked everyone to come to your room so I am here and this is probably my last visit.

No amount of retraction helped; she was convinced the counsellors wanted to make her a statistic in their book and wanted to give her moral sermons about life. Assurances that the exchanges would be confidential and might help her in some way were brushed aside:

I really am not interested. I have done and do what I think had to be done and my reasons and compulsions would neither be important nor indeed comprehensible to any of you because for you all we are just a type, and I know how we are viewed as a 'type'.

She made her way to the door and no amount of beseeching helped. She was gone. The bewildered counsellors looked at each other in dismay and perhaps with some guilt about their strategy. Being put to the test in the early stages was not a good position to be in. The predicament was how to get her back without pressurising her. Every day at least five or six women came to the Unit but not Saloni.

And then about five days later, the curtain of the room was lifted and Saloni stood in the doorway. The counsellors were already busy with another client and had to follow the rules: 'Could you wait till we've finished this session? You might wait outside in the veranda for a few minutes.' Saloni let the curtain drop and left. There was discomfort in the room that this may be another lost opportunity. The session ended in 10 minutes, and the counsellors got up to take another round of some 'barracks' where there were elderly women who could not really come to the Counselling Unit. As soon as they opened the door to go out there was Saloni standing in the *veranda* waiting to be called in. The relief could be seen on the faces of the counsellors and they came right back to their chairs.

As she came in from the veranda, the Counsellors noticed she had a limp and also that she had some difficulty bending her knees as she tried to sit down.

I am sorry I was so sharp with you the other day. I really get weary of the constant barrage of questions that come my way. It's because of the nature of my offence: sex work! It's not just a curiosity about my offence but the inquisitiveness borders on disdain and contempt and then I don't even want to begin to talk.

The senior counsellor offered her some water and said: 'So are we still suspects or would you like to have a free and frank chat with us? Everything you say here is strictly confidential you know.'

Saloni whispered:

I have not had a free and frank chat in years and don't really know what that means anymore But I still need to know why you are interested. I'm not sure just how much time are you able to give me, because my story is a long and tedious one and not very pleasant either. And how would it help you or me in the big picture?

The counsellors tried to make all the right moves this time, neither pushing nor interrupting and she unravelled what had clearly been a burden she had been carrying for far too long. Every now and then there were a few false moves on the part of the counsellors.

She volunteered her age (22) at which the counsellor said 'Holy Moses!' which startled Saloni. She asked why they had exclaimed and said this was just what she meant when she said that people's reactions put her off so much that she withdraws into her shell and just does not wish to converse.

'My mother sent me into this work, although you people wouldn't call it work', she said. 'So now you are horrified aren't you? You see what I mean about people's preconceptions.'

Concealing one's emotional reactions to the horror of other people's lives was not an easy task for the counsellors. They did betray a sense of horror and she was agitated. She was clearly tired of even beginning to explain and justify to someone, anyone, why she does what she does. The counsellors were unable to contain their sense of shock at her statement that her mother had sent her into this work. Their reaction causes some dissonance. The senior counsellor suggested a break. She was anticipating some serious revelations and felt entangled in subjective sensitivities. Maybe they should resume the next day she suggested, a risk at best. Saloni provides the solution herself: 'I may not be here tomorrow; after all we do get bailed out you know.' And so they proceeded.

My father was a mechanic and worked in a garage and earned enough to provide us the basic minimum. He left us for another woman when I was eight; my brother and sister were five and three then. For a few years I attended primary school, before all the problems started. There was a teashop run by a couple across the road from my father's garage where people from that locality came for tea. The routine was that twice a day the wife would cross the road and deliver tea to all the garage employees. She often sat and chatted with them and soon my father started a relationship with her.

There were long pauses in Saloni's narration and the counsellors were always reluctant to push her.

My mother worked in the house and was a hard-working woman. She slogged each day to make sure we were well fed and clothed and she dreamt that all of us would go to school. I went to school for about three years. I still remember her doing my braids and sending me off to school with a black slate and some notebooks.

There was silence again, and there was a wistful look in Saloni's eyes; she was fighting back tears. She had clearly not reflected on that past in a long time and it was painful.

One day my mother passed the garage when she was out on an errand and she saw my father cosily seated with the woman enjoying tea and *samosas*. She was upset but didn't accost him just that day but decided to see if there was more in it than met the eye. She didn't go out too often so by the time she went that way again the relationship had developed enough to anger the woman's husband as well. My mother didn't see my father at the garage and when she asked his mates where he was they gave an all-knowing smile suggesting he was probably at the tea-stall owners' house. The tea-stall owner who was sitting right there reprimanded my mother and asked her why she couldn't keep her husband in check. My mother was humiliated beyond belief. I only know these details now because my mother told them to me years later when I accosted her about what she had done to me.

Saloni's eyes filled up again and suddenly she said, 'I would like to stop now and come back later perhaps. It is getting too much for me.'

The younger counsellor opened her mouth to say something and was stopped by her senior. They all watch Saloni limp her way out, and along with a hundred other questions one that engaged them then was—How did she get that limp?

Saloni did not come the next day and the counsellors were worried: if she is out on bail that is the end of the story. Meanwhile they attended to other women with equally pressing problems. An old woman of 70 was in the barracks, suffering with OCD and really needed professional and medical help. But above all she needed to be released and the counsellors were drafting letters to the authorities giving details of the woman's symptoms, corroborated by the staff who were happy to help.

Saloni comes in two days later, looking pretty in blue and she actually has a smile on her face. 'We have been granted bail and I hope to be out tomorrow', she says excitedly. The counsellors expressed delight and she sat down. It was up to her to resume her story. The counsellors had learned to wait.

> There is something I want to say. I get this feeling that you are really disturbed by what I have said so far. As I pondered over this I got the feeling that you are truly concerned about my future. The truth is there is no future for me from where I am looking at it but who knows!

Not knowing how they should respond to this, the two counsellors ask her if she wished to resume her story. She replied in the affirmative, and the session resumed.

Counsellor: You were saying that your father was having an affair with another woman. How did your mother respond to what your father was doing?

Saloni: She had gone to the tea-stall owner's cottage and caught the two of them red-handed. She just slipped away home and cried her eyes out. When he came home she confronted him and there was a big fight. She called him names and he was doubly abusive. When things got out of hand he struck her hard and she fell. I remember it well because it was a stone floor and within minutes she was bleeding profusely. He picked up his things and he left. I tried to pick up my mother and she struggled to the bed and sobbed for hours. Nothing was cooked in our house that day and my siblings were crying incessantly perhaps from hunger but also from the terror created by the shakeup. The next morning there was a dramatic change in my mother. She got up at the crack of dawn, swept the house, cooked a meal, fed us all and after clearing up asked me to watch over my siblings and not open the door for anyone. She went away presumably for errands.

She returned after sunset and I had been petrified. After we ate our evening meal she sat me down and said to me: 'From today you will have to look after your brother and sister. I will be working for a few hours each day to earn some money and I am afraid you will not be able to go to school. Your father has let us down and I cannot forgive him. If I had done what he did he would have killed me without thinking twice about it. But that is a woman's fate.' She was soft and mellowed that day and wept for all of us. I also wept—I was heartbroken that I would not be able to go to school. That was the end of my childhood dreams.

The counsellors listened with patience and unease and Saloni continued her narration.

As the years passed by, my sister and brother grew older and when my sister turned six I decided to teach her a little. When I turned 13, my brother was 10 and my mother felt that he needed to go to school, otherwise he would never get a job. So he was sent to school. Of course all this cost money and we didn't have enough so I told my mother I could earn something at odd jobs. She refused as if she was offended and I was angry.

So you can see that fateful day when my father let us down our lives changed dramatically. It only sank in gradually as I became older just how fundamentally things had changed. Years passed by and I grew restless at my powerlessness. Soon I began a hunt for work. With my mother at work and my brother at school, I took my sister along to look for something that would fetch us some money. My sister was sworn to secrecy and finally I did find something: A cleaning job for two hours not too far from our house and the woman there would pay me ₹75 a month. I had no clue whether that was a fair amount, but I took the job and carted my sister along to work each day making sure to return before my mother and brother returned.

One day I was washing the dishes at the woman's house and a large glass bowl slipped from my hand and broke. All hell broke loose. She said it was a very expensive bowl—'cut glass' she said, and was I blind or what. She picked up a rod and beat me mercilessly on my back and legs. After a while I couldn't stand and then she threw me out. I couldn't walk so my sister rushed home to see if someone could bring me back. There was no one there and I just sat on the road waiting. My mother came an hour later and took me home. She was livid. I thought I would get another thrashing. She did scold me but also kept crying as she did. She kept asking me why I had set out to work and whether I believed that she would let us starve.

The counsellors had their answer about her limp and had already begun to feel uncomfortable with the intensity of Saloni's experiences. The senior counsellor had trained the juniors not to show emotions that would jeopardize the exercise no matter what, but they too were young and often showed sympathy, horror or anxiety and Saloni could sense it.

As time passed, Saloni and her family continued to live frugally but with everyone getting on in age and with increasing needs there just wasn't enough. The mother lost her job because the employers got someone else and the family was plunged in darkness again. For a while it seemed to them there was no light at the end of the tunnel. After a few weeks a woman who lived near Saloni's family home, and had clearly watched the family's activities, came and asked the mother if she would like to work in the guest house that they had. 'We might even have a job for your daughter but we'll talk about that later', she said.

I was sixteen by then and ran the house as my mother resumed work. We were on our feet at last and for two years it was relatively smooth. But good times have never lasted for us' [*Saloni sighed*].

Another catastrophic day came soon enough. My mother got hit by a car when she was returning from work and was badly injured—broken bones and deep cuts and bruises. She was hospitalized for weeks and when she did come home she was disabled and could only walk with support. The guesthouse owners did pay for her hospitalization and treatment but our mother was crippled for life.

The woman from the guesthouse came to see my mother one day to ask how she was and to assure her that if she ever needed anything she should send word. She then asked me to go and make some tea for her and she began talking to my mother in hushed tones. She did all the talking and my mother listened quietly and with a grave face. I had no idea what was said but it was obviously serious stuff.

There were awkward silences when Saloni was narrating her story. Sometimes a counsellor would ask her to continue, sometimes there would be a gasp or grimace and Saloni would look up and pause wondering what had happened. The senior counsellor would indicate to her colleague to wait and not express herself. Saloni was conscious of the tension around and would grimace if there was as much as a sigh.

'You see' she said breaking one of many embarrassing silences that punctuated her story telling:

... the guesthouse is one of many that have sprung up in many cities where small businesses are thriving and businessmen come in and out of these guesthouses every day. In the evenings, part of the entertainment arranged for them is the company of young girls, and that company is what the lady was arranging with my mother. My mother didn't tell me till the next day what it was all about and when she did I was numb. My mother tried to underplay the whole thing by saying that all I was required to do was serve drinks and dress nicely and just be around the bar and lounge. But I was old enough and wondered whether my mother was being generally naïve or was she so callous that the offer of ₹10,000 a week had made her totally insensitive to a daughter's feelings. She said she would never be able to resume working herself and even if she did it would take her six months to earn that kind of wage.

One of the counsellors got up to turn on the fan for breeze—she was perspiring and very uncomfortable. The interruption made Saloni stop again. She put a question to the counsellor: Do you think I had a choice in this matter? Tell me.' When there was no response she said:

> I have viewed my mother in so many different lights. As a child she was my sense of security. She fed me, cared for me and was everything that the mothers around me were. As I grew older, and my father left us, I pitied her and therefore loved her differently. I felt she needed something special to compensate for the hardships she was facing. I pitched in at every turn and got myself the job that left me lame from the thrashing. And now I was facing another picture of my mother, a picture that perplexed me and made me wonder. I can't say I hated her then. I was confused. But once she sent me away and I had the experiences I did I developed the strangest feelings towards my mother.

Saloni then started revealing the details of her first week at the guesthouse, and was red-faced by the time she finished. It was a sad tale and strangely enough she spelt out all the gory details of her encounter with a shoe salesman who raped her violently and ruthlessly. Her tears were unstoppable and clearly this was the first time she had told the details of her story to anyone. She had the water that was offered to her and dried her tears with her *dupatta* (long scarf draped across shoulders). The silence in the room was uncomfortable, and no one seemed equipped to handle the dramatic outpouring of this 22 year old. She was distraught even though she had been in and out of guesthouses for more than three years now.

> That was the day I crossed over and it was also the day that I first experienced the emotion of hate for my mother. I kept asking myself why she had done this to me. The following day was when I was going home to see my mother to give her the money the lady had given me. I hated going home and hated everyone around me. I went home in an auto-rickshaw and was sick to the stomach. I hurt so much between my legs and felt so sore I couldn't walk straight. My siblings were so overjoyed when they saw me they hugged me

and we cried holding each other. They had no idea where I had been and I took refuge in their hugs knowing they would get fewer and fewer with time. I went inside to my mother and wished her, and no I did not give her a hug. It was the strangest meeting between a mother and daughter and one that I will never forget.

Overcome with emotion and bewilderment, the younger counsellor suddenly said, 'You should have reprimanded her and asked her why she did this to you?'

Saloni looked at the counsellor and had a wry smile on her face. She continued with her story and described how she gave her mother the envelope with money and how the mother could not touch it out of fear, shame and a host of emotions that she saw on her mother's face. She got up to make tea for Saloni and as she limped back with a stick in one hand and the precariously balanced teacup in the other, Saloni felt a flood of emotions—pity, rage and bitterness among others—and when the mother finally sat down, she said her: "Why did you do it mother?"

She couldn't look me in the face and after a long silence she covered her face with her *saree pallu* [one end of the saree] and wept, as I have never seen her weep, not even when my father left. She kept saying things in between her sobs and what came through was that she realized that she had put me on the road of no return. I was already so benumbed by my own experiences over the last 24 hours that there was no room in me to contain my mother's remorseful feelings. That was the last time I saw my mother.

Saloni looked at the counsellors and it felt like the narration was over. The younger counsellor interrupted again and said something at which Saloni glared at her. Turning to the senior counsellor, she said:

I am condemned for life aren't I? I go through hell each day and the irony is that in prison women who have taken someone's life are not so condemned as I am. I hear staff say of them 'They acted due to compelling reasons: they will never kill again!' But no one will ever say that to and of me. All I hear is *'dhandha karti hai besharam!'* [she trades her body, shameless creature!]. When I was arrested, you should have seen the way the arresting policemen handled us. Even stray dogs are treated better. They went to each room and pulled out the girls, and one of them was in bed with a guy when they barged in. You should have heard their comments. I can't get myself to repeat them to you. They did the same thing when we arrived at the police station—taunts, heckling, lewd comments and deliberate brushes with our bodies—I can't describe it. It was assumed that we were the 'type' that was used to all that!'

The counsellors were fidgeting now and were so flabbergasted and bewildered that they didn't speak although Saloni had now finished her narrative. This was a tough case and the underlying questions were endless. Saloni broke the silence again and posed the question that has no answer: 'Will nothing wipe my slate clean?'

The counsellors had handled cases of women who had killed spouses, terrorists who had attacked people in villages, drug users and drug peddlers, mothers-in-law who had caused dowry deaths, mentally challenged women who had killed children— but the challenge posed by this case was mystifying. It was not the harrowing story so much (there had been several harrowing tales of women experiencing domestic violence who eventually took matters in their hands) as much as the dead-end syndrome that resulted in uneasiness, discomfort and embarrassment.

Saloni was clearly tired from going through such a long verbal journey and the counsellors in their turn were mentally exhausted from the winding trajectory of Saloni's predicament. It was difficult to ascertain whether Saloni actually considered it a predicament. Saloni left hurriedly because it was lunch hour and then returned just when the counsellors were winding up later that afternoon. There had already been a discussion about her for an hour or so. Will she go back to the guesthouse? Will she return home and see how things go? How will the rest of her life play out? What will happen to her when she gets older and is not wanted by the 'employers' and can hardly cater to the kinds of needs that the establishment would wish for her to fulfil. Was she thinking that far? When she posed her next question is when the counsellors figured the hint of uncertainty in her mind.

'I am scarred for life aren't I? This is like a tattoo—it is for life. There are no erasures and no closures.' Looking at the counsellors, she said,

We are coming to this problem from two different and very complex directions—you from an ideal that we all start our lives with, and I from a ground reality that is now so far away from the ideal. I can see you are disturbed because you are trying hard to match the two standpoints. But I know (and so do you) that it just isn't going to happen unless I could be transported to another planet. But that can't be can it?

She was right. There was hardly any meeting point and it made the counsellors desperate. She left with a sad face and the room was filled with a strange gloominess and negativity, suggesting failure all round. It looked like this was her last session. Counsellors did not push for further sessions unless the client wished them. The only silver lining in a case like Saloni was her questions after the session that day. Clearly she had not shut the door on thinking about the rest of her life, even as she told herself there was no alternative.

The senior counsellor could not allow Saloni to go without voicing some hope.

Nothing is impossible Saloni; things change and I am not talking just about change at your end but also at our end. We are also to blame for our rigid attitudes when things go wrong for our young girls. May be in time attitudes of others will change and people will try to give young people who have got into a mess another chance. Who can tell? So never say never!

The next day Saloni turned up looking pretty and cheerful.

I have got bail and all of us arrested that day are leaving. I just came by to thank you for listening and giving me a ray of hope. May be some day things may change. You are right: Never say never! I am going to keep my eyes open for the opportunity if it comes when it comes.

She folded her hands and said 'namaste' and went away.

SUMMING UP

Unlike the counsellors in Sumitra's mediation case in the Counselling Cell (Chapter 5), those in Saloni's case had had their preliminary training and there was one senior ('trainer') counsellor and one new (trainee) counsellor at all the sessions. While comparisons would be inappropriate, given the completely different environs, contexts and consequently requirements of the situations at hand, a quick run-over of the procedural aspects can be made to assess the sessions.

In the prison environment, the requirement of matching counsellor and client (*Step 1*) needs to be and was handled somewhat differently from the other counselling scene. It is assumed that those who have been assigned this task or been chosen for it are well informed about the demands posed by the unique and unreal environment that is the prison. The counsellors in this case had worked on other projects in prisons and were familiar and comfortable with the demands of the prison world. They had studied the prison, prisoners and above all had had long sessions with prison authorities and staff to know the hazards of going down the wrong road when dealing with those 'inside'.

The young junior counsellor did start out with some preconceived notions about this particular prisoner. Her moral conditioning slipped through now and then during the sessions and while she did not express her horror in words, her body language and facial expressions did betray a lack of empathy with the client. After each session the senior counsellor discussed this problem with her and advised restraint.

Figuring out the appropriate theoretical approach (*Step 2*) had not really been thought through, primarily because there was no available 'material' to go on. Most of the factual and other data and details came with the subject and unfolded during sessions. They were subjective and it was not prudent, given the sensitivity of the problem, to ask too much. The approach was therefore developed as the sessions unfolded and the bottom line that was worked through before sessions was that too many probing questions should not be asked.

The task was sensitive, and the counsellor's self-awareness (*Step 3*) was a problem. In discussions after sessions it was apparent that innate prejudices did creep in from time to time, especially when the question of 'how can we help her' arose. It was obvious that the environment (prison), the client (sex worker) and the uncomfortable narrative all posed problems that had to be teased out after each session. There seemed an urgent need to consciously shake off particular attitudes mentioned earlier (prejudices, hostility, negativity, stereotyping people, etc.). In short, the positive frame of mind took a while coming. 'Crossing the divides' had presented a problem, but some discussions down the line a change could be perceived (see discussions on prostitution in *Step 5* later).

There was little difficulty in choosing the model to be adopted—therapeutic—given the intensity of the experiences narrated and the state of the client (*Step 4*). While the intention of counselling in the prison is to help the prisoner cope with the 'hostile' surroundings, in this case the history of the client before coming to the prison was seen as a scar that posed problems for the counsellor and client. The inability to enable the client to explore solutions was a problematic that stayed till the end. It seemed clear even while it was not stated that the counsellors could not really provide solutions. Therapy lay in listening and understanding and not pretending to have pat answers to the personal problem at hand which was not prison related but pertained to what had happened earlier. What the counsellors were able to talk about at the end was something they thought they would never get down to: the future. While it was posed as a question, it stemmed from her statement/question 'I am scarred for life aren't I?' Counsellors did not give a definite answer to that but did suggest that the client think about where she saw herself years from now. It was when the client came back to thank the counsellors that they realized they had made some contribution in bringing the future into focus. She said may be some day she would get out of her mess.

Information in this case was not seen as 'paper information' and review of information was done as and when there was enough to review (*Step 5*). The punchlines in this particular case came slowly and the counsellors let the story unfold at the pace the client set. Counsellors were sensitive to the 'alien' experience. They had observed comments and attitudes of other prisoners and staff to offenders who had come to the prison under the PITA violation and had prepared themselves sufficiently so as not to betray their innate feelings.

There was one interesting aspect of this subject that received particular attention in the course of the discussions between counsellors and has a special bearing on attitudes and outlooks towards it. Acutely aware that this was a theme that was part of a sensitive debate the world over, counsellors sought clarifications amongst themselves about some of the aspects of the subject. What exactly was prostitution was the question that was candidly asked by the junior counsellors of the senior? How did the law address this concern?

It was interesting to see how the concern for a young girl who sat before them made the counsellors sit up and take notice of the problem that they had never had to confront directly. The discussion was an education in itself for all of them as they went through all the words that are related to prostitution, but may or may not be prostitution. Historically there were courtesans and 'escorts' in all societies, so what was their status? Then there are words like 'whore' and 'hooker'—where do they feature in the vocabulary? And what about 'call girls'? An interesting perception was the way the counsellors looked at portrayals of women as courtesans in films that were considered near classics in their view. 'Is *Umrao Jaan* regarded a prostitute?' 'And what about *Pakeezah*—is that film about a prostitute?' 'And *devadasis*? Who are they?' These were not really irrelevant questions coming from young counsellors who had had a disdainful attitude towards all the women they met in the prison brought in under the PITA law. All this was before they actually heard the individual stories about these young women, some of whom were younger than they were.

That there were several dimensions to the problem became obvious. It could be addressed from many social angles: sex, gender (above all gender inequality), exploitation, perpetrators and victims, social customs, traditions and norms, and ethics and morality. Then there is State and the law. The world over, the debate has had all of these features and the counsellors settled for the fact that much of the debate now was about how the society and the State (law) viewed the issue. Both could give (or not) any of the words related to prostitution the pejorative they had, just as both could analyse it in its many manifestations and decide which of the issues related to it needed being addressed through the law and how.

How society and the State view prostitution differs from country to country. Society's views and related to it the State's come from all the cumulative attitudes to women, their sexuality and how society has viewed this sexuality down the ages. As with so many social issues in our society, it is not possible to start the discussion on this subject with a clean slate. The status of prostitution in the law differs—permitted as legal but regulated (as a profession) in some countries and regarded as illegal in others, prostitution is also indirectly outlawed when it is not prohibited in itself but other activities connected with it are illegal (pimping, soliciting publicly, running a brothel and sex-trafficking).

Part of the counsellors' discussion also focused around issues of principle: 'How is this a concern of the law at all?' Or is it really 'the society talking all the while even when the law makes the statements'. Otherwise, said one counsellor, how is the penalty for prostitution so harsh in many (Muslim) countries (stoning, death) and not so harsh in others. 'All morality is subjective', one said.

The law supposedly takes charge when someone is exploited and victimized, when violence and/or force are used (including duress and threat) or when the social order is threatened which includes the principles of human dignity and freedom. The last concern relates to what is called 'public order crime', a category in which even if there is consensus between the service provider and the buyer, and there may not be an accusing victim, the State takes charge on behalf of society referred to as secondary victims and declares certain activities illegal and punishable. Where it draws the line varies from region to region, and from society to society, causing confusion about public perceptions of certain acts and their morality and legality (separately). Drugs, alcohol, prostitution and gambling fall into this list among others.

Then there was the discussion about making some acts (for which more and more prisoners are being sent to prison) legal: foremost among them are taking drugs and prostitution. The problematic in these two offences is that the trade in them is steeped in and surrounded by innumerable illegal, abusive and dangerous activities. It is then asserted that if these acts were made legal, the 'black market' racket and abuse would diminish. This has its own problems. It does little for the individuals who engage in the activity (drug users or sex workers), and only creates two areas of operation—one legal and the other illegal. And as far as the counsellors were concerned, their focus was the individuals who are hauled up by the justice machinery for offending one or the other part of a law that makes either drug use or sex work legally unacceptable.[2]

The counsellors were getting a sense of the distinctions. Prostitution was seen as having two dimensions—as the act of women providing sex for money and as a business or trade of providing women (and children) for sex. A blanket legalization process would not address both dimensions. Decriminalizing the activity *may* save women from the brutalities they are subjected to by the racketeers and by the State machinery that nabs them when they are caught for illegal acts, but whether it would help women and children who are bought and sold and abused as part of the trade of prostitution is doubtful. That activity would carry on at two levels—legal and illegal.

Counsellors were getting a sense of the complexity of the problem and of the need for deeper insights into issues that they had treated with a simplicity that was dangerous.

Given where the prisoners are coming from, the adherence to some of the features relating to ambience and atmosphere had to be modified. Making the client comfortable meant physically and mentally comfortable. The prison setting being intimidating to begin with, an extra dose of kindness and courtesy was observed that conveyed the mutual respect that was needed to enable the client to communicate. A suitable setting and ground rules (*Steps 6 and 7*) are always a good idea but not if strict adherence to them makes a client ill at ease. No pressure was put to observe a rigid timetable. The physical surroundings too had to be casual and less intimidating (some of the women prefer to sit on the floor and rugs were thrown around to enable them to have that choice).

Whether the counselling should be facilitative or directive (*Step 8*) cannot be predetermined in a prison context. Every effort was made to be more facilitative than directive and several features played a role in deciding how to conduct the session. Age, background, lack of confidence, fear, shyness, hostility, mistrust, and despair—all of these had to be taken on board and every now and then a little prompting had to be done to enable Saloni to focus on the issues at hand. The whole experience of narration was also seen as a catharsis for the young girl and interruptions were few and far between. After the initial encouragement to talk, counsellors were forthcoming with their reassurances—a hand on the shoulder when there were tears, a little pause when she was overwhelmed, offering water when she sobbed—the counsellors consciously observed the gestures that had been suggested to show active participation. The client was encouraged to communicate—that was the underlying feature of the session.

One factor that did get missed out was how the client should cope with the taunts of others. Offenders under PITA were out of their depth on this front: determining what made Saloni so impatient in her dealings with others was not addressed. It had been talked about that there should be an attempt to link up the behaviour patterns of others (through information gleaned from her accounts about other prisoners and also staff) with the emotions of offenders like Saloni in order that those 'others' can be brought to the Counselling Unit. That did not happen. A stumbling block was the attitude of members of staff who were judgmental and vicariously responsible for the postures that other prisoners took. There was often more sympathy for women who had killed their husbands than for women who were brought 'in custody' as 'sex workers' under PITA. Addressing this issue was seen as part of the training programme that counsellors were preparing for staff.

It was difficult to have a clear idea about the setting of goals (*Step 9*) in this setting, particularly when the mission in this case was primarily therapeutic and secondarily result-oriented. If goal-setting was a mutual act between counsellor and client, the particular case posed problems. Some prisoners are happy to come and be in the Counselling Unit for 'a change'. Saloni was not here out of curiosity—she was bursting emotionally and wanted to vent but needed reassurances that she would not be judged, mocked or preached to. It was clear that there would be little by way of problem-solving of the bigger issues (i.e. life's future course) and more in the way of intermediary goals, that is, coping with life and with taunts. Even as the time boundaries need not always be rigidly adhered to, some attempt at avoiding rambling and being focused so that some change, even if minimal, is achieved. This should be shared with the client—questions periodically asked need to be asked together with the client: Where are we headed? Do you feel we are going somewhere with this? Is some goal visible here? The client's own views about goals and purposes could be ascertained.

One of the most important parts of the process—taking notes and classifying the records—had to be adapted to the needs of each session. This part of the methodology is particularly important in the prison environment where data and information have two meanings. The first one is the facts, figures and procedural details that are obtainable from the records and from staff. The other is information of real-life happenings and 'voices' of the counselled women of which there is a near absence and which are most important for counsellors and their understandings. In Saloni's case, caution was exercised in the area of note-making. Given the reluctance and diffidence with which she came to the Cell, the vision of pencil and paper and frantic note-taking would have been intimidating and caused anxiety and tension. Reducing tension being an important objective, any preoccupation with notes would have been counterproductive. Most of the notes were made after she left the room at the conclusion of a session. The client did feel the counsellor was listening and thinking about her above all.

Descriptions (body language, utterances, facial expressions, nervous twitches, quivering voice, tears and sobs) were all put into the record to be analysed at the end of the entire series of sessions.

Could one work out some way by which the process and its results could be measured? Developing some tools for evaluating the whole exercise (*Step 11*) to determine when one is getting it right or getting it wrong was not easy at all because there were too many personal dimensions that took centre stage in the exchanges. As mentioned earlier, from counsellor and client satisfaction to effective assessment and environmental change, each feature would have needed differing yardsticks and it was difficult to decide which features of each aspect of counselling needed a particular yardstick. Sometimes an effect of counselling may not be very conspicuous or remarkable; it may be as simple as a calm, peaceful smile instead of agitation or misery. How could the smile on her face be measured?

With different features forming a part of the process, and not all measurable by the same yardstick, it just seemed a good idea to try and list them and work through some key features that could be highlighted in each to see where things were before and where they were after the process of counselling. The nearest one could arrive by way of evaluation was each counsellor's self-evaluation on content, methods and (perceived) outcomes, feedback from client's companions through behavioural changes, and feedback through staff reactions.

External evaluation not being a possibility, given the constraints posed by prison rules, the counsellors reminded themselves that too clinical an evaluation in this area of work was neither desirable nor possible.

Steps relating to physical setting, ambience, ensuring privacy and confidentiality, pleasant smells and visuals (posters, flowers, etc.), seating arrangements, 'introductions' and exchange of greetings (*Steps 12 to 17*) were followed meticulously to make for a safe and welcome environment for Saloni. There were moments when she looked around even as she was thinking or formulating her words, and it is assumed that the pleasant surroundings were conducive and therefore positive. The nature of this exchange was one involving persons in an unequal relationship in more ways than one. Putting the client at ease was a major concern because the client's mental state unravelled somewhat slowly and gradually and with each revelation further steps were put in place to make the experience less odious than it was at the beginning.

It has been stated earlier (in setting out *Step 17* in Chapter 5) that aside from body language, active listening, and verbal and non-verbal interaction and exchange, communication happens through many other gestures, motions and signals, discussed earlier. We have already described the nuances of verbal and non-verbal communication and rather than repeat them here it would be appropriate to glance over them again in Chapter 5. Sometimes observations of this kind seem very obvious. Yet it is surprising how the most obvious tips for effective communication are the ones that are constantly slurred over and make for bad interaction.

The one feature about communicating with women in 'custody' that needs special attention is how much the counsellor is learning as she goes along. There will be insights that she never dreamt of that she would now have and that would lead to a depth of understanding of human nature and behaviour that would stand unparalleled. If a counsellor thought she was privileged for one reason or another, the privilege of being allowed into the lives of women who have had experiences of a kind that need to be known but are not, or that need to be understood and are not, is a feature of this specific experience that is something to think about. The introspection that would accompany such thoughts would lend a measure of understanding and concern to the whole mission and justify the need for this book.

NOTES

1. Sections 498A and 304B were inserted in the Indian Penal Code in 1983 and 1986 respectively.

   IPC Section 304B: This Section of the Indian Penal Code was inserted by a 1986 amendment. The wording of the law states:

   Section 304B. Dowry death

   (1) Where the death of a woman is caused by any burns or bodily injury or occurs otherwise than under normal circumstances within seven years of her marriage and it is shown that soon before her death she was subjected to cruelty or harassment by her husband or any relative of her husband for, or in connection with, any demand for dowry, such death shall be called 'dowry death' and such husband or relative shall be deemed to have caused her death.

   Explanation: For the purpose of this sub-section, 'dowry' shall have the same meaning as in section 2 of the Dowry Prohibition Act, 1961 (28 of 1961).

   (2) Whoever commits dowry death shall be punished with imprisonment for a term which shall not be less than seven years but which may extend to imprisonment for life.

   IPC Section 498A: Section 498A was inserted into the Indian Penal Code in 1983 via an amendment. It reads:

   Section 498A. Husband or relative of husband of a woman subjecting her to cruelty.

   Whoever, being the husband or the relative of the husband of a woman, subjects such woman to cruelty shall be punished with imprisonment for a term which may extend to three years and shall also be liable to fine.

   Explanation: For the purpose of this section, 'cruelty' means

   (a) Any wilful conduct which is of such a nature as is likely to drive the woman to commit suicide or to cause grave injury or danger to life, limb or health whether mental or physical) of the woman; or

   (b) Harassment of the woman where such harassment is with a view to coercing her or any person related to her to meet any unlawful demand for any property or valuable security or is on account of failure by her or any person related to her meet such demand.

This section is non-bailable, non-compoundable (i.e. it cannot be privately resolved between the parties concerned) and cognizable.

2. There was a suggestion from the Supreme Court in 2010 that because of the proliferation in the 'sex trade', it may be a good solution to legalize sex trade. The two-judge bench admitted that no legislation anywhere in the world had successfully managed to stop the sex trade, and legalizing it would allow the appropriate authorities to monitor it and provide rehabilitation and medical and other aid to those involved in it. This suggestion, however, has received a mixed response from activists working with sex workers in India. While those like Dr S. Jana, the man behind the formation of 65,000-strong sex workers' forum, the Durbar Mahila Samanwaya Committee (DMSC), have welcomed it, others fear that such a move would only encourage traffickers and the prostitution mafia.

Chapter 7

Selecting and Training Counsellors

Perhaps, this chapter could have come before we elaborately set out the requirements of good counselling and the detailed process ('17 steps') of counselling. Upon reflection, we considered the appropriate place for the choosing and training of counsellors to be after the vital ingredients of counselling (accumulated, adapted and modified for the region and the context) had been catalogued and discussed. And the reason will become evident after some of the contradictions surrounding counselling in India (or indeed all of South Asia), alluded to at the beginning of the book, have been placed squarely before the reader. These contradictions relate to both the subjects of this volume—counselling and women.

But first a discussion about counselling. Unfortunately in most parts of the 'developing' world, counselling is an underrated, fragmented and completely unregulated undertaking. Having said that, it must also be said that counselling has 'caught on' as an ingredient of good personnel/human resource management and has been slotted, albeit mechanically, into the composite structures of all kinds of organizations—educational institutions, career guidance, industry, finance and banking, hospitals, etc. Termed 'counselling', what really goes on in such places is an advisory service not to be confused with 'counselling' as it has been developed and fine-tuned for serious 'coping' problems and issues (such as the ones discussed in this book). The label 'counselling' is misplaced and inappropriate in such (advisory) contexts. Where it does have a legitimate role, it is amateurish and unprofessional such as at the locations (as the Women's Commission) where we observed firsthand how counselling was being carried out and discovered how haphazard and mismanaged it turned out to be. It is amongst such experiences that the idea of writing this treatise arose, thereby addressing at least partly the problems, issues, complexities, intricacies and difficulties of real counselling for individuals and groups in personal distress.

The question was of letting the counselling that existed carry on with no moorings, *or* assist by providing, even if in skeletal ways, some kind of *navigation* for conducting the activity according to accepted and acceptable principles. This book makes no pretences of anything beyond filling the somewhat big gaps in the state of the art of counselling in the so-called developing world. With counselling shops opening up at the speed that they are, there is an urgency to highlight both the principles and the required skills for those 'shopkeepers' who are earnest about carrying on their trade with some discipline. It needed to be impressed on them that counselling is not (as clearly set out at the beginning of the book) just any kind of help or guidance-providing activity; it is a special kind of help-giving, and the skills required need to be imbibed through systematic training. That of course begs a question: 'Where should the training be obtained or provided?' That was almost as difficult to answer as the question posed at the beginning of the book: 'What is counselling?'

There are no (recognized) courses in counselling in the regions we are concerned with. Even if counselling is becoming a fashionable activity because it is recommended in industry and professions for better personnel output, there is no equivalent for counsellor training akin to what exists in the West. Having said that, counselling in the rest of the world has gone through its own problems and as one writer informs us about counselling courses in Britain, for instance:

> Most of the British university-based courses have been running for less than ten years, with staff who are often struggling to demonstrate the academic respectability of their discipline within a sceptical college environment. (McLeod, 1995)

If that is the situation in Britain, from where most of our understandings of counselling presented in this book have come, we would not be far wrong in saying that in India and all of South Asia nothing exists that can even vaguely pass off for training (of professional counsellors). Shortcomings discussed in texts and other sources on counselling relating to the problems of training of counsellors in western society can be multiplied manifold for traditional and/or developing societies where fashions catch on but not the qualifications that should go with them.

TYPES OF TRAINING FOR COUNSELLORS

Formal training has to be clearly distinguished from courses that are short term and that can last from a week to a few months, or maybe even few years. *Short-term training* is a form of 'professional development' rather than 'formal training'. Formal training is what is run or recognized by an authorized body (e.g. in Britain, it is the British Association for Counselling and Psychotherapy — BACP) and is of sufficient duration to include theoretical understandings, practical work, skills development and other features. In countries where counselling is developing into a profession, such courses can be located in independent institutes and universities that provide education and training-based courses. Counselling courses also take place in voluntary agencies and while they can fill the gap, it is these that are felt to need both regulation and a relationship with what is being done at recognized counselling locations.

There are online courses in counselling offered by various institutes in several countries. Some that we consulted and are familiar within the UK are within universities and others are short courses from distance-learning colleges, providing the basic knowledge and skills for beginning counselling activity that may then be enhanced according to the specific requirements (context and location) of counsellors. The courses give recognized diploma-equivalent certificates.

This is something that needs to be mentioned for the region under discussion (South Asia) where there is no such thing as a *recognized* counselling course and where counselling continues at various locations as if it were professional and recognized, but is not. In such cases there is a grave likelihood of the activity being open to abusive practices. Including counselling courses first of a general nature and then for specific forms of counselling in existing social science and related syllabuses is being recommended here.

Given the meagre attention that is being paid to counselling, and accompanying that (inevitably) a total lack of realization that 'bad counselling is worse than no counselling', some steps need to be taken before any proposed long drawn-out attempts at including counselling in recognized courses are embarked upon. There are any number of locations (workplaces, offices, educational sites, etc.) where stress and tension of personnel are being addressed through 'counselling'. Often counsellors are young persons who have failed to get jobs elsewhere and have fitted a slot in the structure of the organization that is designed for 'counselling'. There are young do-gooders who have done courses in Social Work (a relatively new Masters course) and feel they are now well qualified to assist in interventions of a therapeutic nature: It could be in slums, in children's homes, in hospitals, in prisons and even in institutions for the mentally disturbed. They sit in secluded rooms, supposedly meeting the privacy/confidentiality requirement of counselling, and 'listen' to 'the client' with sombre looks on their faces and actually believe they are doing a service to the organization/company/institute. We found that they were often playing with people's emotional and mental lives.

Unfortunately no one can stop counselling as an activity. It is not illegal until it reveals visible damage. With an increasing awareness of the need for counselling (after all it is seen as vital all over the world for all those who are stressed, burnt out, in depressed states, etc.) counselling units are likely to mushroom at every street corner! How do we address the big challenge of having counselling and ensuring it is not the wrong kind? How do we stop the 'cowboy' approach to counselling?

We believe the answer for the time being lies in addressing two features of the problem: (*a*) the lack of adequate knowledge (including theoretical) about counselling and (*b*) the absence of training for engaging in so complex an activity that is passing off as being everyone's cup of tea. The first shortcoming has been tried to be addressed in this book—not wholly, perhaps not even adequately, but at least to a degree that makes for better understanding of the complexities surrounding counselling. As promoters of counselling as a therapeutic intervention for those who have never had opportunities for self-expression, we owed it to ourselves and others to take things in the direction suggested by experts the world over. What we did need to do was provide the needed modifications for the cultural and social context in question. That process is continuous.

There are two facets that relate to counselling and especially to counselling in the two locations that we have focused on that are critical:

1. Choosing the right persons as counsellors:

    (i) *For conflict resolution and mediation*
    (ii) *For custodial environments (prisons, police lockups, shelter and care homes, etc.)*

2. Training them suitably as counsellors:

    (i) *For conflict resolution and mediation*
    (ii) *For custodial institutions such as prisons etc.*

CHOOSING THE RIGHT PERSONS AS COUNSELLORS

There is a general feeling going around that anyone with the right intentions can get some kind of 'act' together and 'counsel'. The message throughout this book is that nothing is further from the truth. We have come across young girls in their 20s, waiting to get married, who thought they could pass away the intervening months in a setup that was counselling women who came to discuss their personal/family problems. The girls were 'educated' certainly, but whether they were 'counsellor material' had neither been investigated nor really put to the test. When we encountered them they were in the thick of a workload in counselling venues, a workload that they could neither cope with nor enjoyed. Our assessments of their work revealed that they were neither the right choice nor had training of even a meagre kind. In short, in evaluating their work, we were of the firm opinion that criteria for choosing counsellors in that set-up needed attention and development (PRAJA/PRI, 2002).

A brief word about our own competence as judges of their performance or indeed that of the Unit. Frankly we felt we fell short of what was really needed to judge what was a good job of counselling and what was not. Our proficiency, if we had any, came from some features of our academic backgrounds and our intense study of the subject of counselling as practised in other countries. We had rummaged through any amount of counselling books and participated in sessions conducted at sites in other parts of the world where the 'art' was at least developing, if not developed. Our team comprised social workers and psychologists who had conducted some counselling courses for students of the Masters course in Social Work (now a recognized degree in several Indian universities), social anthropologists and sociologists, social historians and lawyers, including those who had specialized in gender and the law. (This somewhat meets the requirements of the kind of interventionists or 'specialists' who would be capable of addressing the 'distress' end of the range of disorders. See Davar [1999] and Shankardass [2012] for further discussions.)

We have made repeated references to the fact that all the 'do-gooders' who believe they can just get up and decide to counsel are revealing their own ignorance both about themselves and about counselling. The fact is that the job is not a coveted one and those who decide to do it are either temporarily there biding time or permanently there because they are retired persons. Either way, the fault lies with the inadequate criterion used for choosing persons. In the absence of a set designed method of 'recruitment', clearly a selection mechanism is needed that fits the bill (which would mean the counselling site with its requirements and objectives). The prerequisites would be different for the locales that we have been discussing, although some features might well be similar. An important facet is that there has to be an element of seriousness attached to the whole activity, which means the activities of counselling *and* choosing the right counsellor. If these are treated lightly at any point there will always be a flaw in the way the Unit runs.

For Conflict Situations and/or Mediation-cum-Counselling

Here the criteria and method of selecting counsellors would need to meet the requirements of a problem-solving/mediation/counselling model. There are complaints, problems, conflicts, feared troubles, threats, coercive acts and/or intimidations; they may relate to family, neighbours, workplace, state institutions or any other agency. Each and all of these would have to be handled according to the rules and regulations that should have been set out by the Unit for the purpose. Clearly the choice of candidate would have to be done wisely so that the Unit's prestige and professionalism is enhanced.

Requirements and criteria for selecting counsellors: These requirements relate to the nature of the help that clients seek at such venues and to the knowledge and understandings that would be needed to handle the problems or disputes they bring. Some indication of the nature of complaints brought by women at these centres was suggested in the earlier chapters (dowry related, domestic violence, parents locking up their daughters to prevent them marrying men of their choice, young girls' problems with in-laws, sexual harassment at work, husbands committing adultery, etc.). Would-be counsellors would need to have some familiarity with the issues involved both socially and at the level of the law and its functioning.

Qualifications:

- *Academic*: A Bachelor's degree should be a minimum qualification with some further work in the form of a Masters degree in social work, sociology, psychology, anthropology and some qualification/knowledge of the law.
- *Work experience*: Working with women or on women's problems would be an asset.
- *Human rights awareness needs to be emphasized*: Knowledge of the literature on the subject of human rights in the area of women and the problems related to their lives should be tested.

There should be a *written test* with features that will test the following:

- The candidate's writing skills
- Problem-solving abilities (through life problems posed for solution)
- Concentration and application tests (see Annexures)
- Familiarity with some common phrases: fundamental rights, feminist movement, equality before the law, right to life and liberty, penal code, laws on dowry, domestic violence, rape, prostitution, etc.

Interview: An interview needs to be carried out to assess her knowledge and views on the following kinds of issues:

- What is counselling?
- Why does she want to be a counsellor?
- Why does she think she is fit for the work?
- Does she know who comes to the location to seek mediation/counselling?
- Does she have some idea of the kinds of problems women bring to such 'cells'?
- Does she have some views about the women who bring such problems?
- Does she have a view about the place of women in Indian society?
- Does she know about the Dowry Act?
- Does she know about the law on domestic violence in the country?
- What are her views about rape and how does she think rape victims can be helped?
- Is cinema affecting the lives of Indian women?
- What does she think of Indian films and film stars?
- What does she think of the concept of equality in Indian society?
- Should counsellors view women (clients) with different economic backgrounds differently?

The interview needs to assess her articulation, body language, language usage (including politeness and intonations), listening ability and knowledge of the subjects listed earlier. Quick posers such as 'what would you do if...' should be prepared to check the manner and kind of responses the candidate gives in the time given for an answer. Tests could be prepared to assess the candidate's presence of mind and ability to move from one line of questioning to another.

Tests would range from serious problem-solving exercises, questionnaires, knowledge and basic information tests to puzzles, 'games' or brain-teasers and perception testers. Each of these methods has its own place in the scheme of things and the trainer would be required to explain the importance of each to the would-be counsellor. Some of the formats or designs of these are given in the Annexures at the end. This is not a definitive list nor can it be duplicated without modification in other contexts, but the general direction for formulating and designing the training material would come out of the earlier sections and the queries and problematic that surface therein.

For Counselling in Custody

Choosing counsellors to work with women locked up either at police stations or in prisons is not to be taken lightly. The location, subject, atmosphere and routine all convey the same message of tension and apprehension and while all of these are adequate reasons for justifying the pressing need for counselling here, there is no easy way to set about doing it. The easy way *is* often followed and we have actually heard beginners comfort prisoners by saying unwittingly 'Do not worry everything will be alright!' Such pointless words of comfort and reassurance are not really of much use to those whose first anxiety and concern is that they are locked up and they want to be out! And over that state the counsellors (nor indeed the staff that manage the prison) have any control whatsoever. A similar simplistic approach is followed at police stations in India where senior officers from different states (police and prison are State subjects) inform us when questioned that their police stations have all been 'gender sensitized'.

Requirements for counsellors: We have already underlined the importance of *understanding the institution called 'prisons'* (called 'jails' in our part of the world). There is no other place that is comparable to the prison in modern society where so many strangers are compelled to live together and that too in a cage. Hospitals have strangers that are put together but there can be more difficult locations for patients and staff, and patients and staff are both there *voluntarily*. Prisoners have no choices in jails and cannot leave the four walls of the prison when they wish, not even for short spells, unless the machinery that sent them there deems it fit to allow them. Anyone from the outside world who wishes to do *anything* in a jail needs to understand these, the most basic features about this institution—its unnaturalness and its opaqueness. Those who wish to counsel prisoners (and here we are talking about the kind of counselling that is not necessarily always the problem-solving model) need to be quite familiar with some basic features about prisons. This does not just mean a *visit* to the prison, but a *journey* of another kind—a journey of acquaintance, information and facts leading to knowledge and understanding about the place; why it is there and who is there in it and why, leading perhaps to the question: Should they all really be there?

In a region like South Asia, diverse and divided by unyielding caste, class, religion, language, attire, gender and other boundaries, it is not an easy task for counsellors to step into 'alien' shoes on demand. Reservations based on all of the above divisions can be stumbling blocks in an activity that requires fluid movement to and fro into worlds that are foreign to the counsellors. 'Shed your prejudices' may sound easy as an instruction to give to would-be counsellors; in a highly stratified society it is as demanding as throwing non-swimmers in a pool and telling them to swim. Add to that the other deep divisions between the client and the counsellor—the former are prisoners allegedly locked up for having committed a transgression—something the counsellor would have great difficulty identifying with.

Qualifications: Some of the academic qualifications for counselling in prison would be the same as those suggested earlier for counsellors generally, given here again for reference. The rest would need to be uniquely suited for the context.

- *Academic*: A Bachelor's degree should be a minimum qualification with some further work either in the form of a Masters degree in social work, sociology, psychology, anthropology and some qualification/knowledge of the law.
- *Work experience*: Working with women or on women's problems in society would be an asset.
- *Human rights awareness needs to be emphasized*: Knowledge of the literature on the subject of human rights in the area of women and the problems related to their lives should be tested.

In addition:

- Some basic knowledge about the prison in general—its organizational structure, its rules and regulations and its place in the criminal justice system is necessary.
- Information about national and international minimum standards and rules for the management of prisons.
- A functioning knowledge of the kind of reforms that have been sought and agreed in the country (Mulla Committee, Krishna Iyer Committee, etc.).
- A familiarity with the manual that guides the staff in running prisons.
- Some information about the women who are in prison and their offences.
- An understanding of the basic health problems (including mental health) faced by women in custody.

A written test should be set to determine:

- The candidate's ability to take notes and prepare case studies (details of the latter would be taught in time).
- How a particular (hypothetical) case would be approached by the candidate.

- What the candidate understands by common phrases such as bail, surety, remand, etc.

  Interview: There is need for an interview to assess:

- Has the candidate ever been inside a prison/seen it from outside/never seen a prison?
- Does she know about the offences for which women are inside?
- Does she know about the Penal Code?
- Has she ever been to a police station?
- Does she think she could ever be an offender?
- What importance does she attach to counselling women in prison?
- Why does she wish to work in prison?
- What does she think of the prison as an institution?
- Does she think all these women need locking up?
- What kind of women does she think are inside?
- How would she handle an aggressive woman who wants to know why she is here?
- How would she handle a woman who is always silent?
- How does the candidate converse?
- What difference does she think counselling will make in a prison considering she can do little about getting a prisoner out?
- Does she think that for some women there should be alternatives to prison?

The interview would also give other helpful indications about the candidate's voice tenor, body language, facial expressions and eye movements (features we have mentioned as helpful in communication). If there is the slightest sign of an 'attitude' problem or a revelation of near ignorance, then the candidate should be reconsidered.

TRAINING THEM SUITABLY AS COUNSELLORS

The task that is most difficult is the training of counsellors. This applies both to the training to be imparted for counselling in conflict resolution and mediation, *and* even more so in training counsellors for prison work. The reality is that because of the lop-sided views and distorted ideas about the purposes and methods of counselling in regions like South Asia, training and ideas about it are even more skewed than one can imagine. The nascent stage at which counselling exists as an activity is revealed by the fact that no modules for training counsellors in separate counselling contexts have been developed. *General* training techniques usually used for good personnel management or for better administration of workplaces are used for training counsellors in the belief that as they are aimed at building up every manner of positive characteristics in the counsellor, they should be agreeable and 'can't go wrong'. While this may be partially true, the fact is unless the training is aimed at the specific purpose in view it is a waste of time and becomes the equivalent of telling every child 'be good, be honest, be truthful' and so on. Platitudes are of little use when the situation at hand is about depressed people, aggressive behaviour, people in denial, victimized persons or persons simply disillusioned with everything around them, and above all with the direction of their lives.

An equally important question is: Who would conduct the training? If the whole concept and purpose of counselling is somewhat corrupted and not quite agenda-free, to whom could the task of training counsellors be entrusted? And who would have trained the trainers?

Here we come up with a difficulty. The reasoning is circular: If counselling has not developed enough, clearly the trainers would be wanting and certainly not up to standard, and if the trainers are wanting then how do we get good counsellors! We hope that this book is a beginning in creating and then structuring counsellor training modes and building up a stock of material (in the form of data and information) that can be used and then supplemented with added strategies and guidelines that would get us nearer a manual for training. This would be different for different contexts, and the two contexts discussed in this book should in our view, and specifically for women, constitute areas of high priority.

As suggested at the beginning of this chapter, there are specific reasons for putting training at the end of the book. To highlight the centrality and essentialness of training counsellors appropriately, the discussion about training could either be at the beginning or the end of the treatise and not mixed up somewhere in the middle. It seems more fitting to place it at the end because while preparing a training module or even discussing the components of training all those features and factors and steps and paces that have been discussed in the earlier sections would need to be referred to.

In fact everything that has been set out, arranged, classified, categorized and analysed in the earlier sections would all be used in one way or another for preparing training modules for the specific contexts, circumstances or situations we are dealing with. This really means that there would be several methods, approaches and techniques that would be used and each would cover many aspects of the problems and issues that would be included in the sessions. The social context would demand some hard work as existing modules developed in other societies are adapted to the new situations.

For Conflict Resolution and/or Mediation-cum-Counselling

Training for this kind of counselling may seem relatively easy because it is about solving and resolving personal problems and disputes that most of us are acquainted with to some extent. If one woman comes with a dowry dispute and some kind of compromise is reached, it is assumed that when the next dowry case comes up repeat strategies could be used. Nothing could be further from the truth. The ability to address each case individually even if it falls within a broad category is what makes each counselling session meaningful for the client. The counsellor has to have a nose for being able to see differences and similarities and address both with equal vigour.

The most important aspect of training in this context is an emphasis on testing the (trainee) counsellor's responses to problem situations by posing the problems and asking her to be the client and express herself and indicate what she would expect of the counsellor. This would cover both the process that she would like the counsellor to follow as well as the skills and techniques that she (as client) would appreciate. A list should be drawn up at each training session, and this would contribute to the modules that would eventually develop for training.

All the steps of the process of counselling discussed in earlier chapters would feature in the training in order to impress on the trainee the significance of each step. Trainees often say that some parts of the process state the obvious. That would hold good for so many courses undertaken today in the interests of better personnel management and relations—now a vital ingredient of running private businesses and public organizations. This is a paragraph from the objectives of an online personnel skills course offered by the Open Study College in the UK that purports to provide an understanding of principles and practice of personnel skills:

- Gain an understanding of the importance of maintaining personnel records, identify the legal requirements of data protection and use of data, local sources of further information and keep abreast of legislation.
- Learn how to assist in conducting an effective recruitment and selection process.
- Contribute to an effective induction process, appreciate the concept of self-development and action-planning, state the difference between disciplinary capability and grievance procedures, and understand basic employment legislation including health and safety, equal opportunities and diversity.

We don't always have to read Plato and Aristotle to achieve the objectives of worthwhile pursuits in the quest for social harmony and/or change. Consolidating all the wisdom of tried and tested methods for enabling members of society to get a better deal than they do does not need to be pushed aside because it sounds 'obvious'. Doing it properly does make sense. Training is the process whereby a lot of scattered information, guidelines, approaches, courses of action, procedures, strategies, rules, plans of action and methodologies are coherently ordered and synchronized for the specific objectives and goals relating to a particular course of action. Counselling without this synchronization would be rudderless.

The training could be a one to one or it could be in a group. There could be one trainer or there could be more than one. Either way some things need to be worked out ahead of time before a training module is prepared:

- How long should the training period be (Two weeks? A month? More?)
- How long should the training last each day (Four hours? Six hours? More?)
- How long should each session be (Forty-five minutes? An hour? More?)
- How should sessions be divided in time? According to the problems that will come before counsellors? Or according to the steps that the counsellor will be taking in counselling?
- How should the counsellor be tested at the end of the training?

For Counselling in Institutions of Custody (Women's Prisons, Police Lockups)

This is an exceptional environment to work in and is unique in many ways. The training of counsellors at this venue is anything but straightforward; and the less simple it is made to sound, the more seriously the counsellor will take the training and the activity of counselling in a prison.

The first need in a training course designed for those wishing to counsel in a prison is to provide first and foremost *a point of reference for a proper understanding of where the trainee is and who she is dealing with.* Anyone who comes to work in a prison (and is not part of the prison establishment) knows little about the institution's inner workings and drives (the inner 'spirit of the prison'). Because the women in prisons are who they are (mostly uneducated, poor, ill-informed of rights and entitlements, cut off from the world and acutely demoralized and dispirited), it is assumed by any educated person who comes along to the prison that 'dealing with' prisoners should not be difficult given their near hopeless state.

1. An appropriate starting point for a trainer therefore is *to impart an orientation course* in the following:
   - A prison
   - The particular prison
   - The prisoners (this to be done in the most careful untainted agenda-free way)
   - The problems in a prison
   - The relationships in a prison
   - The standards that are needed and expected
   - The place of counselling (including what it cannot do)

2. The next step would be *to take the counsellor through each general point raised in this book* and question the counsellor on all of them. These would relate to what has been expressed about (*a*) women in general, (*b*) women in prison, (*c*) public attitudes towards the prison, (*d*) public attitudes to women in jails and (*e*) counselling for women.

3. It is only after the conceptual air has been 'cleared' that the counsellor should then be taken through the *'17 steps'* and each step meticulously debated and discussed so that uncertainties, misgivings and reservations are all aired and clarified.

Apart from these steps several other techniques—role-plays, puzzles, practical problems, case-study writing, 'if I were a millionaire' parleys—should all be used and as one goes along more modules prepared and added to for future references. Some exercises and questions to develop awareness of the many features of prison counselling that have been given in earlier sections. Samples of different tests to emphasize the qualities that enhance counselling are also set out in the Annexures. This is not a definitive list and can be added to after mutual consultation between those engaged in training and counselling.

Choosing and training of counsellors keeps developing as the whole idea of counselling develops. The context has much to do with the content, manner and direction of counselling for women. By context here we mean both the *general social context* of the cultural region and the *specific context* within which counselling is actually carried out at the appropriate venue. Both contexts also determine where counselling should be taken in the regional context. While it has been emphasized as an agenda-free activity within which no ideological features should be allowed to enter, the fact is that it does have potential as a site for providing the kind of untainted service that also contains within it an element of change and reform of the person and the institution. Being as unaware and ill-informed as the women who come for counselling are (this lack of awareness being not a small cause of their problems), the question that counsellors would be faced with and would need to be answered is whether a Counselling Unit may be utilized as a site for providing assistance to women on social, legal and other fronts to assist in the goal of making them better equipped for life.

The neutrality of counselling would not necessarily be compromised by attempts made alongside towards setting right some imbalances of society. It would almost be a shame to miss the opportunity of offering the women opportunities of better equipping themselves through greater awareness and learning and simply confining the help that is offered to these women to the particular problems at hand, or to the distresses triggered by specific situations in which women find themselves at that point in time. This would need careful working out but should not be dismissed as contrary to the objectives and principles of counselling given society's neglect of the women in question in the first place.

Chapter 8

Conclusion

This has been both a difficult and a (relatively) easy book to write—difficult not because of the complexities of the subject matter and the scant (serious) attention given to the subject in the region under focus, but (ironically) because of the apparent simplicity of what was required to be said. The likelihood of a reaction from readers that all this is surely common sense did make one wonder whether thought and activity that rest on common sense were beyond the pale of being considered laudatory. But then a man's common sense does tell him that wife battering is unacceptable; but he goes ahead anyway. Common sense can be as uncommon and rare as a shooting star if it is little used and even less imbibed. So all this needed to be said.

On the other hand, the book has also been relatively easy to write because of an innate confidence that what was being said came from (a) informed theoretical understandings and analyses elaborated in well-known tried and tested texts and sources in other parts of the world and (b) firsthand empirical perceptions imbibed after putting some of this analysis into practice while carrying out the activity of counselling in the particular contexts described in the book (i.e. forums of conflict resolution/mediation and custodial institutions/women's prisons).

Looking back at the beginning of the book, there seems to have been a hint of a need to justify both the writing of this book and counselling. Having gone through the process of putting it all together, and structuring it for further use, we now feel that neither the book nor professional counselling needs any defence. In the earlier chapters it was explained why when women suffered *serious* mental problems ('illnesses') that needed medical/psychiatric interventions no one thought twice about the need to get on with making the appropriate 'treatment' available—it was in society's interests not to have 'mentally abnormal' persons around, they might cause damage. However, *common* mental distress in all its manifestations was still not important enough: It did not need medical attention and we only had the subject's word for the fact that she was feeling depressed, stressed, anxious or even suicidal. Our responses so far had been that the condition would probably go away and no one bothered to investigate just how damaging it might really be for the person *and* for society. The approach was that if a problem cannot be medicalized it is not really a problem.

What brought the problems that were considered nonproblems into focus was the 'copability' factor that confronted women in different settings including the most commonplace setting of all—the home. Supposedly the safest place for a woman anywhere in the world, our encounters with women who came to Counselling Cells for help in resolving issues of domestic conflict made it amply clear that more than half of the problems in the women's anguished lives lay within the four walls of their home environs. Women's minds were getting imperceptibly damaged. Unfortunately while this was a reality that was becoming increasingly apparent to those who were beginning to address the causes of the assignment and acceptance of an 'inferior status' for women, the full-blown focus on women and their gendered roles was a while coming. While personality and behaviour issues related to people generally had come under the microscope much earlier in the twentieth-century Eurocentric circles, the particular focus on women came much later with the ripples caused by gender studies and feminist movements where the neglect and damage caused to women's bodies *and* minds became matters of grave concern. It was then (in the 1970s) that the lasting damage done to minds by acute or prolonged distress symptoms was realized and investigated, and the need for specific and special interventions that would address distress was recognized. Counselling was an obvious answer.

Where the distress emanated from and why it had become more accentuated with the rise of consumerism and so-called progress in society were matters that were of grave concern for women activists. Contradictory projections of women in the media (books, television and the cinema) have contributed to mixed-up images of real and ideal women. Preoccupation with physical beauty, aided by the cosmetic industry and the world of advertisement, has not helped the woman either in the private or the public domain. From domestic appliances to up-market motorcars, 'cosmeticized' women seem vital for advertisements. Is it really fair to send out these images to those men and women who are so remote from this razzmatazz world as to wonder what is the relationship of the car with the smart woman lolling all over it? When I discussed this with a school teacher from an Indian village, he said, *'Didi, to phir hamare gaon ke tractor ke advertisement me bhi aurat ko bonnet pe baitha diya jaye!'* (Perhaps tractors for the rural farmer should also be advertised with a woman lying on the bonnet!). Both of us knew such an advertisement would be incongruous and alien for the context but it was a point well taken. The same teacher is struggling hard to inculcate in the young men and women he teaches the values he believes will take them in directions of economic betterment and wise decision-making for all of their lives. 'I can do without this commercialization coming my way,' he says. His village school was one of the first where we advocated and set up a 'voluntary Counselling' Cell.

Hitherto confined to home and hearth where she is judged for performance and a (doubtful) confidence that goes with it, in her new incarnation brought on by the demands of the media projections of the 'new' woman, she is now struggling to work out which image she needs to be the ideal. TV serials and the cinema that had earlier created stereotypes of the ideal over-sacrificing self-effacing woman (the Nirupa Roys and Meena Kumaris of the old cinema) have created new stereotypes of the modern woman. Manipulative, aggressive, go-getting, unstoppable, bitchy and if need be even promiscuous, the 'new' woman of the media has unbound the old chains only to be bound by new destructive chains that, projected on the big and small screen, create a false sense of bravado that does nothing for the woman's real confidence and empowerment. *Looking* good rather than *feeling* good become the primary goals, opening the floodgates to new kinds of depressions as the gender-based oppressions and discriminations stay right where they are. Media reports and stories of individual examples of success and unparalleled courage give a false sense of hope to women whose focus shifts from the structural bases of oppressions to individual performance. The result is a feeling of swimming against the tide, causing further disenchantment and disillusionment leading in turn all manner of mental distress and a further incapacity to cope.

In the course of our work, in prisons we came across several upper class women (pre-trial prisoners) whose physical appearance and general demeanour baffled us. They were immaculately dressed, spoke good English, never forgot to manicure and paint their nails, pluck their eyebrows or apply makeup. They believed they were modern emancipated women and didn't belong in a prison. They were 'serviced' by the more humble prisoners from rural backgrounds who massaged their arms and legs and assisted them in dyeing their hair and washing their clothes. Partners in family businesses, these 'modern women' were in for fraudulent business activities (including drug trafficking) about which they knew little. It bothered them that they had landed themselves in a prison full of 'backward' women when they were the modern women of society. Their sense of frustration was different from that of their more humble lower class and rural counterparts. It was less about their children and the families they had left behind and more about their tarnished images and the frame up of which they were 'victims'. Would they like to come to our counselling units we asked some of them. *'Aap hamse yahin pe baat kar lijiye. Hum khushi se aapse baaten karenge'* ('You can talk to us here in our cell. We are more than happy to have a chat'). If ever there was a group that needed some counselling it was they.

Many of our ideas of counselling were shaped and reworked as a result of the clients we encountered 'outside' and 'inside'. In parts of the world where the experiences and circumstances of women's lives in 'normal' times were distress-causing enough (traditional, custom-ridden, developing societies), the need for counselling was even more urgent. Some women realized they needed it; some were in denial. We already expected that and took it in our stride. But the greatest need for effective therapeutic intervention was what we often referred to amongst ourselves as the 'deep end'—the motley crowd of women 'inside' who had layers and layers of hurts and wounds, big and small accumulated over the years in their homes and elsewhere and were often not even aware of the extent of the damage that had occurred to their psyche.

Having set out most of the important ideas on the role and need for counselling here with due corroboration from experts who have devoted more time than we have to this subject, as an author I do not now feel the need to justify either the book or the need for counselling. Simply put *help*, whether it is being asked for or given, never needs justification; and counselling it is being suggested is a special kind of help, different from other kinds and always contributing something even when there is no *apparent* outcome. This is because it is a two-way relationship and not a one-way act of kindness; it seeks to empower the 'helped' person(s) rather than dole out charity. In the three-dimensional context focused upon in the book—the region (South Asia), the subject (women) and the theme (counselling in conflict situations and in custodial institutions)—there is scarcely any doubt about the constructive effects of counselling.

The chapters above (especially Chapters 1 and 2) tried to explain why the three-dimensional emphasis was so vital particularly for women and why it had been neglected so far. Counselling, women and confinement (in home and custody)—all three are areas that have become sites of focus only recently, partly because of voluntary bodies that have brought about that focus and partly as suggested above because gender studies and feminist agendas have had an impact on many areas relating to women. Without them many a discussion in this book would be moribund.

What is unfortunate, however, is the flimsy kind of counselling that exists in these particular areas of engagement. There may be reasons why it is the buzzword of recent times in some locations—to get better performance from people, to build better personalities so that there are more self-confident young people around, to address problems in organizations (industry, commerce, professions). But the real significance of counselling—as the mode of intervention for those under stress and distress—is not really highlighted to the extent that it should be. And that is to help stressed and distressed persons lead wholesome lives for themselves. In any event, there is no professional counselling around; what passes off for counselling is advice giving and guidance. Some change is clearly in order.

Schools (and hospitals) are some of the locations where counsellors are available today. What are they meant for is the question. If it is to advise on careers and jobs, then they should be called just that—'career guidance units'. If they are for addressing children's personal and interpersonal problems, their stresses and anxieties, or their inability to cope with relationships (at school or at home), they would need to be professionally set up and run in keeping with most of the above principles and guidelines. In a hospital, patients would have different problems and anxieties depending on the nature of their ailments, their age, their support systems, their capacity to cope and other anxieties. There would be a need for the counsellor to be trained to do the task in both such situations strictly according to values and ethics that are an intrinsic part of the activity. Off the cuff advice, no matter how well meaning, is not the kind of counselling that would address the persons and problems at hand. The same would apply to police stations and family courts.

This book tries to offer some idea of how counselling as we see it has developed and what kinds of needs it has sought to address. After setting out what counselling is and what it is not, the book has provided a detailed plan, *a roadmap* if one likes, of what have been envisaged as the 'building blocks' of counselling. These are laid out in '17 steps' and it has been explained that *these are not sequential steps* but steps with a qualitative content that needs to be taken into account during counselling however and whenever it is carried out. The simplification of the process is not to suggest that a following of the 17 steps makes us all budding counsellors. Nothing could be further from the truth. It simply advocates that there are aspects of the relationship between counsellor and client that cannot be ignored if the counselling is to have its desired effect—that of addressing the known and unknown predicaments faced by a person.

The book would be severely flawed if it did not make some things clear, particularly at the conclusion stage when the concrete bits have been set out and an overview seems in order. Two Australian authors in their simple but effective book on counselling have at the beginning asked a question that is likely to arise in the minds of many who think they might have earned the title 'counsellor': 'If I use Counselling Skills will I be a Counsellor?' The short answer to this question, say the authors, is NO!

It is important to be clear about the difference between making use of some basic counselling skills in everyday life and counselling. They are not the same although they lie in the same continuum. (Geldard and Geldard, 2003: 6)

The authors also give a definition of counselling to clarify just what they are talking about in the contexts where they function and professional counselling is indeed a profession:

Counselling is practised according to a set of standards and guidelines drawn up by professional bodies that determine minimum accreditation standards and levels of competence. Counsellors are bound by codes of practice … and by ethical standards.

This is how a diagrammatic continuum of different kinds of counselling would appear:

Practical Help	*Paraprofessional Counselling*	*Volunteer Counselling*	*Professional Counselling*	*Counselling Psychologist/ Psychotherapist*

Source: Adapted from Geldard and Geldard (2003) and Kennedy and Charles (2001: 197).

There is no suggestion here that any one type of help is superior to another. But if the quest is to move from one end (left) of the continuum to the other (right) additional specific, precise and exact training and skills will be required. With basic guidelines and understandings of the theory and practice of counselling (set out in the book) in place and with a requisite amount of training to address the particular contextual issues and circumstances at hand the activity of counselling can begin.

Our book is a guide for effective counselling in specific contexts and tries to come as near to qualifying people to be *better* at counselling than they might otherwise be. But it is not a book that qualifies readers or users to begin to call themselves *professional* 'counsellors' (even if in the whole process we have referred to the two parties to the activity as client and counsellor). What the book is addressing could perhaps be placed roughly in the middle of the continuum, enabling people to be called *volunteer counsellors*. It was felt that a book such as this (that put down systematically the dos and don'ts of systematic counselling) be made available to prevent any gross misuse of the activity of 'counselling'. In the absence of 'minimum accreditation standards and levels of competence', formalized courses that provide the requisite qualifications for being a counsellor, or for that matter even of a simple collection of guidelines for counselling in the developing world, the need for a book that set out how to better understand what counselling is and is not becomes an imperative.

There is also a body of opinion that questions the fuss made about counselling in all walks of life in this day and age: 'Where was counselling all this time?' is probably another way of putting this scepticism. The answer is simple in the light of what we have placed before the reader: It was there all the time except it was there in the area that is at the left hand side of the above continuum ('Practical Help'); and some factors related to transformations in the demands of living life in a changing world probably shifted the need for the kind of counselling that is placed further down the continuum:

1. One of these factors is the augmentation of ordinary people living and working under greater (social, economic and mental) pressure than before.

2. Another factor is the increasing risks to life, family and property presented by newer fears and threats leading to greater insecurity and instability.

3. Yet another is the increasing awareness that in addition to physical hazards in life, there was also a risk to the mind that could have disastrous results for the individual and the collective of which he/she might be a vital part.

4. There are also greater concerns voiced about women and the need to drag out into the open the issues that surrounded women's lives and had hitherto been kept under wraps (such as domestic violence, rape, sexual abuse, etc.).

5. The emergence of conflicting views on how women should tackle the (hitherto accepted) oppression that defines their lives in the community (punitive measures for disobeying social mores, honour killings etc.).

All these are reasons that address 'difficulties' in life. They are not necessarily about specific 'problems'. This is something that this book has tried to highlight in suggesting that counselling is not always about specific 'problems' that require pointed solutions after which the problems can be said to be over. Counselling seems to be required, needed or asked for in the case of any kind of difficulty, suffering, anguish, distress, misfortune or danger, and this feature of counselling is crucial to our treatise about counselling for women. Some experts, albeit from the West, have tried to highlight this distinction to point out the limitations of the 'no problem–no counselling' approach. This approach shows shallowness in the understandings and vision of women's situations and predicaments and in turn determines the willingness or not of funding counselling/therapy of a long-term nature for women:

> Clearly funders who expect short-term solutions have failed to grasp the depth and extent of the effects of these on women. So once more women's experiences have been minimised and trivialised. There is moreover an expectation that counselling will only be offered if there is a problem. (Perry, 1993: 45)

We have singled out women and suggested that the kind of counselling they need is distinct, special and covers all of their lives; but we have also suggested that within this women-specific counselling a range of different types of counselling is required. It is not difficult to see why. At no point should there be an assumption that because women have some intense experiences that are characteristic of their being women, they would need the same kind of counselling as a collective group. It is true that the majority of women experience 'boundary problems' in a similar way. They have been conditioned into roles defined for them (by a male-dominated society everywhere) and they usually succumb to the social pressure that expects them to fit those roles (of carers and givers) in similar ways. There is usually no assertion of individual needs; several writers have alluded to the 'unclear boundaries' in women's lives and their constant description of themselves in one or other relationship with another or others (Eichenbaum and Orbach, in Perry, 1993). All of these similarities still do not justify a 'women only' model of counselling.

It is not enough to realize that the counselling process and techniques for counselling women are essentially different from that of men, and then proceed to develop a 'women only' model. Even as the differences relating to women are constantly alluded to in any intervention that relates to women, the theories on which most models of counselling have been based emerge out of images and experiences that are (*a*) *masculine* and (*b*) *Western*. When Freud and others built up personality development models, they were based on the development of the male (Perry, 1993: 41). In recent times (especially since the 1970s), models such as the Egan model (client's needs model), the Gestalt model ('taking a person as she is here and now'), or the Carl Rogers model ('entering the world of the client') have all been seen as valuable and interchangeable ways of using counselling skills. What has happened in all these models is that as individual and social features and factors are seen as constituents of the personality and its development, they are tacked on to older models of how a personality develops and theories are then based on these newer 'patchworks'. This works most of the time. But there are always newer needs and newer perceptions that cannot just be sewed on to the old patchwork.

Gender, race, religion and culture are some of the features that define the newer pictures that feed existing (counselling) theories. It is our view that even within these features (of gender, race, etc.) regions and communities further throw up their own variations that an experienced counsellor would have to take on board for purposes of being insightful and accurate in building a 'therapeutic alliance' (Dryden, 2008). It would be imprudent to minimize social divides and conflicts as constituents in a client's troubles and difficulties.

The question that arises out of this is how this may be amalgamated with existing theoretical positions. The whole idea behind writing a book on counselling placed in the South Asian (and specifically Indian) context is precisely to highlight these socio-cultural strands that need to be woven into the otherwise male and 'Euro-centric' models of the theoretical and practical aspects of counselling women in distress. It would have equal validity in the contexts of other developing countries (Africa, South America). This has to be done without disrupting or disturbing the principles of counselling that cannot be compromised in the manner that 'do-gooders' are trying to do in their home-baked counselling outfits. Agony aunts and 'comforters and healers' have all got on to the counselling bandwagon, and what we have tried to suggest here is that there are the unalterable (the principles) features of counselling and the alterable (the cultural circumstances) and each must be given serious consideration when making up models in each context.

On the subject of the 'alterable', the sheer volume of cases that come in areas that are characteristic of the region exemplify the need for in-depth scrutiny of the theoretical approach that would be adopted in the counselling process. Domestic violence or wife battering may be universal phenomena and therefore theoretically able to be addressed in universal language. The contextual dimensions, however, bring qualitative differences significant enough to require fundamental changes both in perceptual approaches and handling techniques in the theory and practice of counselling in the region in question. Regardless of how vocal the debate on such issues may be among informed circles in South Asia, the vast majority of battered wives consider it their beholden duty to 'suffer in silence'. A point comes in the interaction with them when there is a dead-end in the communication. A battered wife suddenly quotes the role models in our ancient texts that lay down the duties of a woman/wife and asks whether in our efforts to enable and empower her we are suggesting she defy the age-old beliefs of society.

Equally there are glimpses of the individual in women struggling to reveal themselves. In many counselling sessions, the struggle plays itself out and the counsellor is at pains to ensure that the rules of counselling are not flouted by staying neutral even as she facilitates the client in resolving the clashes within. Neutrality then has to be given an active and more vibrant (as opposed to passive and docile) meaning.

Dowry-related problems are another area where inner dilemmas continue and in fact multiply even as the rhetoric on dowry gets louder. Loud it may have become but the ambiguities remain, and even the passing of a law that clarifies where the dowry-seeker will land up if the law is violated has not upset or shaken the adherence to this age-old and supposedly 'fair' social practice of most of the region. In fact the law may have brought in its own bagful of problems on this subject, complicating the issue still further even as it does solve some of the problems. What kind of counselling does one undertake for a woman who ends up in prison because her daughter-in-law was 'killed' or 'cajoled into killing herself' for not bringing enough 'dowry' to the home she was married into? And yet it needs to be done regardless of who the woman is, what she did, and how the counsellor feels about it. And the counselling is not short-term or problem-specific; it is long-term and it is related to the relationship between the person and the society of which she is a part.

In the processes (*17 steps*) of counselling discussed both in the case of conflict or dispute resolution forums, and jails it has been clearly suggested that at various points there is a need for staying clear of being judgemental and almost jettisoning our own values in our interaction with clients. Whereas it may be vital to understand 'meanings' from the other's internal frame of reference, a fundamental question does arise (again with the contextual in view), that of figuring out just how much a counsellor should be avoiding by way of constructive reflection and observation about particular objectionable and unacceptable practices in our society that lead to some of the predicaments facing women in the first place. These are practices that we may otherwise be consciously trying to eradicate in the wider dimensions of the work we are engaged in. Should the counsellor keep 'mum' on practices like dowry (including 'dowry deaths'), child marriage, treatment of widows, prostitution, etc. because it may mean taking a value-based approach on these issues, and because there are appropriate forums for discussing them? Or would it be within the boundaries of impartial counselling if attempts were made to express some views on how practices that are detrimental to the development of women in society should be rethought in the client's scheme of things? Would it not be advisable to speak from a non-ideological position on practices that are contributory reasons for the client's failure to cope with or handle the reverses and setbacks in her life?

While we have not fitted this *question of counsellors as instruments of change* into the '17-steps process' set out earlier, it is worthwhile to take stock of this issue and discuss it within counsellors' deliberations so as not to dismiss it outright in a context that may well need an input on it. In tradition-bound societies, where most traditions go against women rather than men, and where the phrase 'hallowed traditions' is another name for perpetuating practices that are exploitative of women, there would surely be room for some comment from those who feel the urgent need to inculcate esteem-building qualities among the women they work with.

It has been suggested that the relationship between counsellor and client needs to be comfortable and amiable but that does not mean that nothing controversial or challenging should enter the picture. Once a minimum comfort zone has been established, the quality of counselling would be enhanced if challenges and differences of views were addressed. It is here that the knowledge and developed skills of the counsellor come into play and we have deemed it fit to insert the possibility of embarking on the debate that relates to this discourse in the *Conclusion* and leave it to the practitioners in question to address it in the manner they find most suitable; suggesting at the same time that address it they must!

On a more positive note, whereas there are enough negative features surrounding women's issues to warrant the emphasis on the need for positives suggested throughout our narrative, it would be grossly inaccurate to say that therapeutic intervention is a non-starter in this part of the world. Within the (South Asian) region there are examples in remote almost inaccessible places where volunteer mediation/counselling has been built into programmes of conflict and dispute resolution for women who find the formal justice machinery formidable and inaccessible. While we have instances of horrific punitive measures for women in some parts of the South Asian region (stoning to death or mutilation), constructive steps offer hope to many. Organizations in Bangladesh provide wholesome models of practices where the 'mountain goes to Mohammad' and achieves what would otherwise be impossible for thousands who live literally and figuratively too far away. The Madaripur experiment carried out by the Madaripur Legal Aid Association is one case in point. A replicable model (located in Madaripur, Shariatpur and Gopalganj) where training with a human rights and legal awareness component has been built into dispute resolution to alleviate the anguish and distress of those who needed hope-filled attention. The focus on women is significant. Adding professional counselling to the several methods used for addressing conflict-ridden situations that become unmanageable if left unattended would go a long way towards constructing more balances in such societies overpowered by patriarchy and traditional role structures.

Similarly, the urgent need to introduce some other forms of therapeutic interventions in prisons in India cannot be dismissed superficially. Apart from the quest for 'good practices' that seeks to address the experience of prison being a living hell, the goal of introducing programmes that teach meditation and positive thinking and living goes some distance towards alleviating (albeit minimally) the distress- and stress-causing symptoms that the prison environment intensifies. It still falls short of addressing what professional counselling is aimed at: The attempt at alleviation of distress that is accompanied by empowering individuals to have some control over their lives to enable liveable futures. A modicum of happiness is everyone's entitlement not just that of the rich and powerful. A person does not become a non-person because we have the right by law to lock her up for offending against State-made laws. She would still hopefully return to society. Do we build her or demolish her to enable her to return and get on with the rest of her life?

ANNEXURES

In addition to the training suggested in Chapter 7, the following are a few amongst the simple and basic test samples that have been used for the training of counsellors at locations where proficiency in English was limited and the trainees simply needed to be alert and fine-tuned to the environment. Tests with word skills were kept at a minimum and diagrams, figures and numbers were more commonly used.

There are tests of a higher level of sophistication than these but they were considered inappropriate for the contexts and situations at hand.

Annexure A

Analysis-related Test

Some tests were conducted to see how well the person could draw logical conclusions only from the information provided. Three examples of analysis tests are given below:

I. A forester needs to ferry a lion, a goat and a bundle of grass across a river. His boat will only take two (including himself) across at one time. His problem is ensuring that the lion does not eat the goat and the goat does not eat the grass when he is not around. How does he do it in the least ferry trips across?

He first takes the goat across and comes back. Next he takes the lion and returns with the goat. He then takes the grass and leaves it there with the lion. And in the final trip he takes the goat.

II. Mrs Ahmed has a problem feeding her four children as they all like and eat different foods. Sarah and Rubena eat rice and fish. Kamaal and Sarah are the only ones who have roti and daal. Kamaal and Salman both eat chicken and roti.

1. Which is the only food that Sarah does not eat?
   (a) roti   (b) chicken   (c) fish
   (d) rice   (e) daal
2. Who eats daal, chicken and roti?
   (a) Sarah   (b) Kamaal
   (c) Rubena   (d) Salman

3. Who does not eat daal but does eat fish and rice?
   (a) Sarah   (b) Kamaal
   (c) Rubena   (d) Salman
4. Which food will be acceptable to most of the children?
   (a) chicken (b) rice   (c) fish
   (d) roti   (e) pasta

III. On their way back from school five children stop at a sweet shop. Chameli and Trilok are the only ones who do not buy chocolate. Four of the children including Laila buy 'barfi'. Unlike the others, Shiela, Chameli and Samir do not buy any toffee. In fact, Chameli only buys fruit gums as she does not like other kinds of sweets.

1. Who only had a piece of toffee and a piece of barfi?
   (a) Shiela   (b) Chameli (c) Laila
   (d) Trilok   (e) Samir
2. Who had three sweets?
   (a) Shiela   (b) Chameli (c) Laila
   (d) Trilok   (e) Samir
3. Who are the two people who took the same number and type of sweets?
   (a) Shiela and Laila   (b) Samir and Laila
   (c) Laila and Trilok   (d) Trilok and Samir
   (e) Samir and Shiela
4. In total, how many sweets were taken by the group?
   (a) 7   (b) 8   (c) 9
   (d) 10   (e) 11

Annexure B

Personality-related Test

The 'big five' personality factors are:

- **Extraversion–Introversion**
- **Emotion–Stability**
- **Conscientious–Expedient**
- **Open to Experience–Closed to Experience**
- **Agreeableness–Challenging**

Personality Checklist: There is a list of personality traits given below. Provide your first instinctive response to the trait that fits you best:

Personality Traits	Disagree	Neutral	Agree
1. Carefree			
2. Sociable			
3. Realistic			
4. Courteous			
5. Neat			
6. Inferior			
7. Jolly			
8. Systematic			
9. Argumentative			
10. Structured			
11. Anxious			
12. Serious			
13. Artistic			
14. Self-centred			

15. Disorderly			
16. Happy			
17. Communicative			
18. Broad-minded			
19. Cooperative			
20. Conscientious			
21. Nervous			
22. Gregarious			
23. Cultured			
24. Sceptical			
25. Methodical			
26. Worthless			
27. Private			
28. Experimental			
29. Cynical			
30. Restless			
31. Confident			
32. Energetic			
33. Inquiring			
34. Popular			
35. Determined			
36. Angry			
37. Cheerful			
38. Traditional			
39. Calculating			
40. Committed			
41. Disheartened			
42. Pessimistic			
43. Imaginative			
44. Hard-headed			
45. Unreliable			
46. Optimistic			

47. Dynamic			
48. Pragmatic			
49. Considerate			
50. Productive			
51. Helpless			
52. Active			
53. Curious			
54. Forthright			
55. Disorganised			
56. Self-conscious			
57. Independent			
58. Theoretical			
59. Manipulative			
60. Perfectionist			

Annexure C

Creativity-related Test

This test is based on Gestalt and Jackson's Test of Divergent Ability, which requires that the subject name as many uses as possible for everyday objects such as a brick, a piece of string, or a bucket of clean water. Name up to 12 uses for a bucket of clean water in 10 minutes (precisely).

1. .... 2. ....

3. .... 4. ....

5. .... 6. ....

7. .... 8. ....

9. .... 10. ....

11. .... 12. ....

Now try the same for some more common household objects (e.g. a tooth brush, a comb, a rubber band or a brick).

Visual Attention and Spatial Relations

Shapes: The recognition of shapes is an aspect of attention and memory that is frequently used in daily life.

I. Take a careful look at the two figures below and count the number of squares each has:

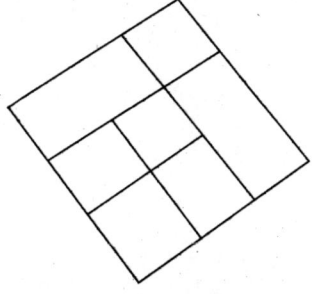

II.   Look at the figure below and count the number of triangles it has:

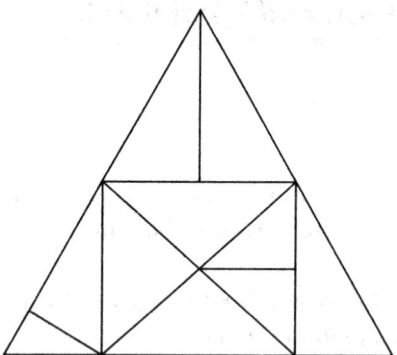

III. Look at the figure below and count the number of triangles it has:

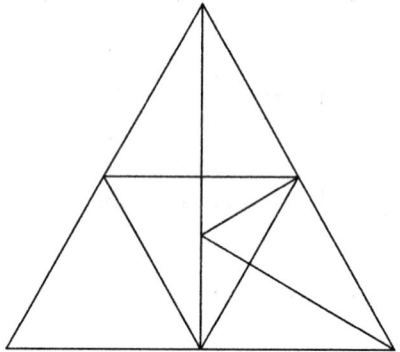

Annexure E

Spatial Capacities

Strong spatial capacities are crucial in helping a person evaluate distances, dimensions and shapes of objects in daily life.

I. Look at the figure below and count the number of triangles and squares it has:

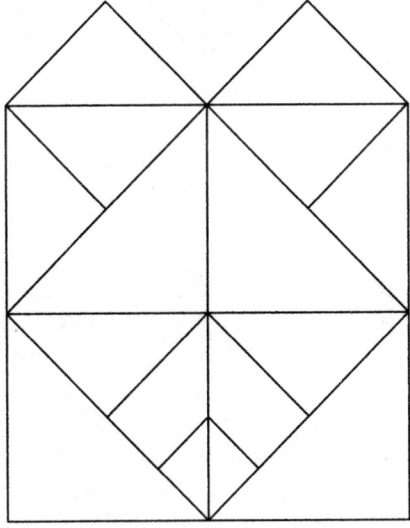

II. Look at the figure below and count the number of triangles and squares it has:

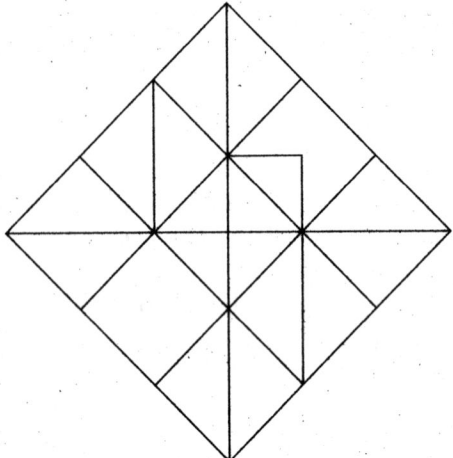

Annexure F

IQ Testing and Logical Reasoning

I. How many circles appear below?

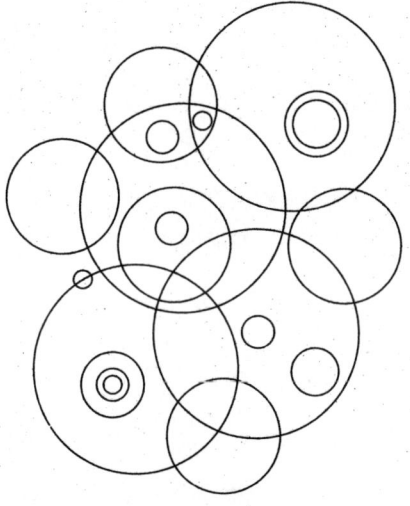

II. How many lines appear below?

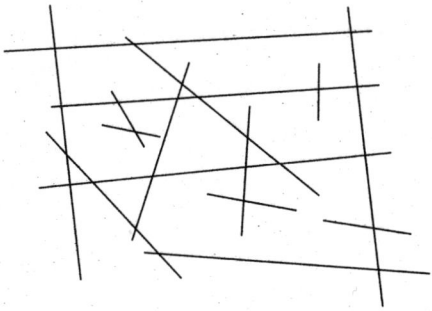

These are a few examples of simple tests used during training for alertness, creativity, perception, spatial capacities and simple Intelligence Quotient (IQ) testing and have been adapted from various sources (Michael Noir, Carter and Russel, Peter Rhodes, etc.).

References

Altekar, A. S. *The Position of Women in Hindu Civilization from Prehistoric Times to the Present Day* (Motilal Banarsidass, Delhi, 1959).

Avery, Brice. *Principles of Psychotherapy* (Thorson's, London, 1996).

de Board, Robert. *Counselling Skills* (Gower Publishing, Aldershot, 1987).

Burr, Vivien. *Gender and Social Psychology* (Routledge, London, 1998).

Butler, Sandra and Claire Wintram. *Feminist Groupwork* (SAGE Publications, London, 1991).

Cameron, Helen. *The Counselling Interview: Key Skills and Processes* (Palgrave Macmillan, New York, 2008).

Carter, Philip. *IQ and Personality Tests* (Kogan Page, London and Philadelphia, 2007).

Carter, Philip and Ken Russell. *IQ Testing* (Kogan Page, London and Philadelphia, 2009).

Casemore, Roger. *Person Centred Counselling in a Nutshell* (SAGE Publications, London, 2011).

Chaplin, Jocelyn. *Feminist Counselling in Action* (SAGE Publications, London, 1988).

Coomaraswamy, Radhika. 'Identity Within: Cultural Relativism, Minority Rights and the Empowerment of Women', in Indira Jaisingh (ed.), *Men's Laws, Women's Lives* (Women Unlimited, New Delhi, 2005).

Cooper, Mick and John Macleod. *Pluralistic Counselling and Psychotherapy* (SAGE Publications, London, 2011).

Dalton, Peggy. *Counselling People with Communication Problems* (SAGE Publications, London, 1994).

d'Ardenne, Patricia and Aruna Mehtani. *Transcultural Counselling in Action* (SAGE Publications, London, 1989).

Davar, Bhargavi. *Mental Health of Indian Women: A Feminist Agenda* (SAGE Publications, New Delhi, 1999).

————. *Mental Health from a Gender Perspective* (SAGE Publications, New Delhi, 2001).

Dryden, Windy (ed.). *The Stresses of Counselling in Action* (SAGE Publications, London, 1995).

————. *Overcoming Anxiety* (Sheldon Press, London, 2011).

Dryden, Windy and John C. Norcross (eds). *Eclecticism and Integration in Counselling and Psychotherapy* (Gale Centre Publications, Loughton, 1990).

Dryden, Windy and Brian Thorne (eds). *Training and Supervision for Counselling in Action* (SAGE Publications, London, 1991).

Dryden, Windy and Colin Feltham. *Developing the Practice of Counselling* (SAGE Publications, London, 1994).

———. *Counselling and Psychotherapy: A Consumer's Guide* (Sheldon Press, London, 1995).

———. *Brief Counselling: A Practical Guide for Beginning Practitioners* (Open University Press, Buckingham, 2006).

Dryden, Windy and Sarah Opic. *Overcoming Depression* (Sheldon Press, London, 2003).

Dryden, Windy and Andrew Reeves (ed.). *Key Issues for Counselling in Action* (SAGE Publications, London, 2008).

Dryden, Windy, Ian Horton and Dave Mearns. *Issues in Professional Counsellor Training* (Cassell, London, 1995).

Echebaum, Luise and Susie Orbach. *Understanding Women: A Feminist Psychoanalytic Approach* (Basic Books, New York, 1983).

Feltham, Colin. *Time-Limited Counselling* (SAGE Publications, London, 1997).

Foggo-Pays, Elizabeth. *An Introductory Guide to Counselling* (Ravenswood Publication, London, 1983).

Geldard, Kathryn and David Geldard. *Counselling Skills in Everyday Life* (Palgrave Macmillan, New York, 2003).

Guze, Samuel B. *Why Psychiatry Is a Branch of Medicine* (Oxford University Press, New York, 1992).

Hague, Gill and Ellen Malos. *Domestic Violence: Action for Change* (New Clarion Press, Cheltenham, 1998).

Hamel, John (ed.). *Intimate Partner Abuse: A Casebook of Gender Inclusive Therapy* (Springer, New York, 2008).

Hamel, John and Tonia Nicholls (ed.). *Family Intervention in Domestic Violence* (Springer, New York, 2007).

Heidensohn, Francis. *Women and Crime* (Macmillan and New York Press, New York, 1985).

Higdon, Juliet. *From Counselling Skills to Counsellor: A Psychodynamic Approach* (Palgrave Macmillan, New York, 2004).

Hough, Margaret. *Counselling Skills and Theory* (Hodder and Stoughton, London, 1998).

Howard, Susan. *Psychodynamic Counselling in a Nutshell* (SAGE Publications, London, 2011).

Humm, M. *Feminisms—A Reader* (Harvester Wheatsheaf, Hertford, 1992).

Jaisingh, Indira (ed.). *Men's Laws, Women's Lives* (Women Unlimited, New Delhi, 2005).

——— (ed.). *Handbook on Law of Domestic Violence* by Lawyer's Collective (Butterworths/Wadhwa, Nagpur, India, 2009).

Karasu, T. B. 'The Specificity Against Non-specificity Dilemma: Towards Identifying Therapeutic Change Agents', in *American Journal of Psychiatry*, Vol. 143, 1986, pp. 687–695.

Karasu, T. B. *Wisdom in the Practice of Psychotherapy* (Basic Books, New York, 1992).

Kennedy, Eugene and Sarah C. Charles. *On Becoming a Counsellor* (Gill and Macmillan, Dublin, 2001).

Lindon, Jenny and Lance Lindon. *Mastering Counselling Skills. Information, Help and Advice in the Caring Services* (Macmillan Press Ltd, Basingstoke and London, 2000).

Lockley, Paul. *Counselling Women in Violent Relationships* (Free Associated Books, New York, 1999).

Lombroso, C. and W. Ferrero. *The Female Offender* (T. Fisher Unwin, London, 1985).

Luft, J. and H. Ingham. 'The Johari Window: A Graphic Model of Interpersonal Awareness.' *Proceedings of the Western Training Laboratory in Group Development* (UCLA, Los Angeles, 1955).

Manthei, Robert. *Counselling: The Skills of Finding Solutions to Problems* (Routledge, London and New York, 1997).

Marcus-Mendoza, Susan. 'Feminist Therapy with Incarcerated Women: Practicing Subversion in Prison', in *Women and Therapy*, Vol. 34 (Issues 1 & 2), January 2011, pp. 77–92.

Mcleod, John. *The Counsellor's Workbook: Developing a Personal Approach* (Open University Press, Maidenhead, UK, 2004).

Mearns, Dave and Brian Thorne. *Person Centred Counselling in Action* (SAGE Publications, London, 1999).

Mearns, Dave and Windy Dryden (eds). *Experiences of Counselling in Action* (SAGE Publications, London, 1990).

Messer, Stanley B. and C. Seth Warren. *Models of Brief Psychodynamic Theory: A Comparative Approach* (Guilford Press, New York, 1998).

Murgatroyd, Stephen. *Counselling and Helping* (British Psychological Society and Routledge, London, 1985).

Noir, Michel. *Broccoli for the Brain* (McGraw Hill, New York, 2008).

O'Farrell, Ursula. *First Steps in Counselling* (Veritas Publications, Dublin, 1999).

Okun, Barbara F. *Effective Helping: Interviewing and Counselling Techniques* (Brooks-Cole Publishing Co./Wadsworth, Stamford, CT, 1992).

Palmer, Stephen, Sheila Dainow and Pat Milner (eds). *Counselling: The (BAC) British Association of Counselling Reader* (SAGE Publications, Los Angeles, CA, 1996).

Pedersen, Paul. 'The Multicultural Dilemma of White Cross-cultural Researchers', in *The Counseling Psychologist*, Vol. 21 (2), April 1993, pp. 229–232.

Perring, Christian. 'Mental Illness', in Edward N. Zalta (ed.), *The Stanford Encyclopedia of Philosophy*. (Stanford University, Stanford, CA, Spring 2010 Edition). First published 30 November 2001; substantive revision 20 February 2010.

Perry, Janet. *Counselling for Women* (Open University Press, Buckingham, 1993).

PRAJA. 'New Initiatives in Penal Reform and Access to Justice', Report of Conference organised by PRAJA and Prisons Department, Government of Andhra Pradesh, Hyderabad (PRAJA, New Delhi, 2001).

PRAJA/PRI. *Creating a Window to Redress Women's Grievances*, Report (Penal Reform and Justice Association, Gurgaon, India, and Penal Reform International, London, 2002).

Pollock, Joycelyn M. *Counselling Women in Prison* (SAGE Publications, Los Angeles, CA, 1998).

Porter, Roy. *Madness: A Brief History* (Oxford University Press, Oxford New York, 2002).

Rhodes, Peter S. *Practice Tests for Personality Testing* (Hodder Education, London, 2008).

Rogers, Carl. *Client-centered Therapy: Its Current Practice, Implications and Theory* (Constable, London, 1951).

———. *On Becoming a Person* (Houghton Mifflin, Boston, MA, 1961).

Sanders, Pete. *First Steps in Counselling* (PCCS Books, Ross-on-Wye, UK, 1996).

Seeley, Jon and Catherine Plunkett. *Women and Domestic Violence: Standards for Counselling Practice* (Salvation Army Crisis Service, Australia, 2002).

Shankardass, Rani D. *Punishment and the Prison: Indian and International Perspectives* (SAGE Publications, New Delhi, 2000).

———. *Of Women Inside: Prison Voices from India* (Routledge, New Delhi, 2012).

Stern, Vivien. *A Sin Against the Future* (Penguin, Harmondsworth, UK, 1998).

Strupp, H. H. *Psychotherapy and Behaviour Change* (Aldine Publishing, Chicago, IL, 1974).

Sutton, Jan and William Stewart. *Learning to Counsel* (How to Books, Oxford, 1997).

Swain, John. *The Use of Counselling Skills: A Guide for Therapists* (Butterworth-Heinemann, Oxford, 1995).

Tudor, Louise Embleton. *The Person-centred Approach: A Contemporary Introduction* (Palgrave Macmillan, New York, 2004).

Warrall, Anne. *Offending Women, Female Lawbreakers and the Criminal Justice System* (Routledge, London, 1990).

Worden, William J. *Grief Counselling and Grief Therapy* (Springer, New York, 1991).

OTHER REFERENCES

Lawyers Collective. *Ending Domestic Violence through Non-Violence: A Manual for PWDVA Protection Officers — Protection of Women from Domestic Violence Act 2005* (Lawyers Collective, New Delhi, 2009).

Penal Reform International. *Making Standards Work: An International Handbook on Good Prison Practice* (Penal Reform International, The Hague/London, 1995).

Report on Human Rights of Women in Custody, Amnesty International, Washington DC, March 1999.

Report of the All India Committee on Jail Reforms 1980–83, Vols. 1 & 2 (Mulla Committee Report), Ministry of Home Affairs, Government of India, New Delhi, 1983.

Report of the National Expert Committee on Women Prisoners, Vols. 1 & 2 (Krishna Iyer Committee Report), Government of India, Ministry of Home Affairs, Government of India, New Delhi, 1987.

Shankardass, Rani D. *Mental Health and Care of Women and Children in Prison in Andhra Pradesh*, Report (Penal Reform International, London, 2002).

Study on Women Prisoners of Bangladesh, Report Published by the Bangladesh National Women Lawyers Association (BNWLA), Dhaka, 1997.

United Nations Standard Minimum Rules for the Treatment of Prisoners (SMR), United Nations Congress, Geneva, 1955.

Index

About the Author

Rani Dhavan Shankardass is the Secretary General of Penal Reform and Justice Association (PRAJA), Gurgaon, India, and the President of Penal Reform International (PRI), London, UK.

Born in Allahabad, Dr Shankardass was educated in Nainital, Lucknow and Allahabad. She received her M.A. degrees from Allahabad University, India, and University of Pennsylvania, USA, and M.Sc., M.Litt. and Ph.D. degrees from the Cambridge University and the University of London, both in UK.

She has worked as a lecturer in Political Science at Kamla Nehru College, University of Delhi, India, and was a senior fellow at Centre for Contemporary Studies, Teen Murti House, New Delhi, India. She has been awarded the Nehru Memorial Museum and Library (NMML) Fellowship for her article 'Debt Bondage: The Survival of an Ancient Mechanism' and the Nehru Fellowship for 'Prison, Punishment and Criminal Justice'. Her published works include *The First Congress Raj: Provincial Autonomy in Bombay* (1982), *Vallabhbhai Patel: Power and Organization in Indian Politics* (1986) and *Of Women Inside: Their Yesterdays Todays and Tomorrows* (2011). She was also the editor and contributor to the book *Punishment and the Prison: Indian and International Perspectives* (2000) and the co-author of *Barred from Life and Scarred for Life: The Experiences of Women in the Criminal Justice System in India* (2004). She has been carrying out extensive research on penal reform in South Asia, as well as mental health and care of women in prisons and custodial justice.